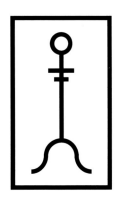

discovering
WINE

A Refreshingly Unfussy Beginner's Guide to Finding,
Tasting, Judging, Storing, Serving, Cellaring,
and, Most of All, *Discovering Wine*

JOANNA SIMON

A Fireside Book
Published by Simon & Schuster
New York   London   Toronto   Sydney   Singapore

For Robin

FIRESIDE
Rockefeller Center
1230 Avenue of the Americas
New York, NY 10020

For information regarding special discounts for
bulk purchases, please contact Simon & Schuster
Special Sales at 1-800-456-6798 or
business@simonandschuster.com

Manufactured in China

10 9 8 7 6 5 4 3 2 1
Library of Congress Cataloging-in-Publication
Simon, Joanna.
Discovering wine: A refreshingly unfussy
beginner's guide to finding, tasting, judging,
storing, serving, cellaring, and, most of all,
discovering wine / Joanna Simon. – Fireside ed.
p.cm.
1. Wine and wine making. I. Title.
TP548.S684_2003_.641.2'2–dc21_2003050603

Executive Editor: Anne Ryland; Hilary Lumsden
Art Director: Tim Foster; Viv Brar
Art Editor: Paul Tilby; Yasia Williams
Editors: Susan Keevil; Emma Rice
Editorial Assistant: Juanne Branquinho
Picture Research: Anna Smith
Indexer: Ann Barrett; Hilary Bird
Production: Michelle Thomas; Alexis Coogan

Photographers: James Johnson, Anita Corbin/
    John O'Grady, Simon Wheeler
Maps: Lovell Johns; Cosmographics
Illustrations: Conny Jude

Typeset in Swift and Meta

Contents

SECTION 3

WHERE THE BEST WINES ARE MADE

FOREWORD AND
INTRODUCTION

Foreword

What: another book on wine? Yes, but this I think neatly bridges various important aspects of a fascinating subject. It is sensible, logical, unpretentious, and, above all, helpful and informative. It is the sort of book you can read from start to finish and be very much the wiser, no matter how well you thought you knew your wine. Or you can dip into it by subject: practical tips on tasting, the wines of Alsace neatly summed up, common sense about that tricky question "when to drink".

As refreshing as a flute of Champagne, as deeply satisfying as a glass of the finest claret. Read on.

MICHAEL BROADBENT
CHRISTIE'S LONDON, 1994

Introduction

It really isn't that long since books about wine could confine themselves to the classic wines of Europe. There were so few other wines of more than local significance. The modern California wine industry was only just getting under way at the end of the 1960s. Australia was still predominantly a fortified wine producing country: its first commercial vintage of Chardonnay was as recent as 1973. South African wine exports were mostly fortified "sherry" types until the mid-eighties. New Zealand, another fortified wine producer, did not make enough table wines to export significantly until the 1980s. And the great progress in Chilean and Argentine wines is largely a phenomenon of the 1990s.

As for the traditional European wine-producing countries, they each had numerous regional wine styles of their own, but it was only the famous names of France and Germany, sherry and port, that really impinged on the mass of wine drinkers and producers in other countries. Most other wines were very basic (wicker-covered flasks of Chianti, Laski Rizling, anonymous *vins de table* etc) or they were household brands – often one and the same anyway.

Of course, there were *cognoscenti* – Italophiles and Hispanophiles who knew all about the wines of Barolo or Rioja and who knew how to distinguish the best from the dross (of which there was a great deal more two decades ago) – but wines such as these were not universally considered to be "classics". They did not dominate restaurant wine lists; they were not given pride of place by wine merchants; they were seldom laid down in private cellars; they did not change hands at high prices at auction; and – the crucial point so far as the modern international wine industry is concerned – they were not the wines and styles copied by the world's new producers in America, Australasia, and South Africa (which, for simplicity's sake, I refer to collectively in this book as the New World). It was this eruption of activity that marked the start of a completely new era in the history of wine – an era of more rapid and radical change than ever before.

To the wine drinker standing before ranks of bottles in a shop in the twenty-first century, probably the most obvious and enveloping change is the emphasis now placed on grape varieties. Thirty years ago few people had heard of Chardonnay – let alone Sauvignon Blanc and Pinot Grigio, Shiraz, and Malbec. Today, wines labelled Chardonnay come from every wine producing country, old and new. More excitingly, the interest in grape varieties has moved on a stage. Unusual, esoteric and even distinctly odd varieties, which not long ago looked as if they might sink under a tidal wave of Chardonnay and Cabernet, are quietly being revived and nurtured – Carmenère in Chile, Graciano, and Godello in Spain, Petit Manseng in France and California.

But the climb to prominence of grape varieties is not by any means the only change to penetrate the entire winemaking world – nor is it even the most dramatic. More fundamental is the improvement in quality and reliability of wine – at all levels, but especially at the bottom. The word "plonk", which used to signify something undrinkable (and if you drank it the consequences could be dire), is now more likely to be applied to something cheap but cheerful. It might be bland or lacking in any regional character (the loss of regional differences *is* a concern today), but it is unlikely to be truly awful. If it is, there is a high chance that it has been spoiled by a tainted cork or poor storage conditions. There are still undeniably badly made wines, but they find it ever harder to gain an *entrée* into markets outside their immediate locality.

The improvements came about through technical advances in cellars and wineries – and these came via the New World. Unencumbered by preconceptions and dyed-in-the-wool older generations, the new producers studied, questioned, travelled, and applied their new knowledge back home using the latest equipment. In no time at all their wines were competing with

some of the best of the Old World. The tables were turned; it was time for the Old World to take something from the New. Gradually (and often grudgingly) winemakers in the traditional areas of Europe began to absorb and apply lessons learned from visiting Californian, Australian, and New Zealand winemakers – winemakers who had originally come to Europe to learn from the old order.

It is not just that wine today is better, it is different. Few New World wines need to be laid down to improve for years before they are ready to be drunk and many of the European classics are deliberately being made in such a way that they can be enjoyed sooner – so that they can compete, in fact, with the new. Moreover, wine is drunk by more people and in more varied circumstances than ever before. Enjoyment of, and interest in, wine is open to anyone today; the aim of this book is to show the way. And take note, whenever you find yourself agonising over the matching of wine and food, be reassured that, though there are some foods that need rigorous attention, there are few truly unpalatable combinations.

HOW TO GET THE MOST OUT OF
EVERY GLASS

1 Wine is for drinking, not for worshipping, but there is a world of difference between drinking without thinking and making the most of every mouthful. Knowing how to taste wine to appreciate all its flavours and nuances, knowing about serving temperatures, wine-friendly glasses and the purpose of decanting, being confident about matching food and wine and confident about which wines to lay down and which to drink tomorrow are the keys to a lifetime's fun and appreciation.

WHY AND HOW
TO TASTE

UNLESS YOU HAVE ASPIRATIONS TO BECOME A WINE-TASTER BY TRADE, YOU WILL KNOW THAT YOU WOULDN'T WANT TO BE SEEN DEAD GOING THROUGH THAT EXTRAORDINARY CONTORTIONIST TASTING RITUAL OF SIPPING (OR SLURPING), SUCKING IN AIR (FAR FROM SOUNDLESSLY), CHEWING AS IF BATTLING WITH A PIECE OF TOUGH STEAK, THEN SPITTING.

And you wouldn't want to get into that habit of writing reports of every wine (usually littered with references to fruit and vegetables) and grandly calling them your tasting notes, would you? It all seems so pretentious, doesn't it?

In fact, it is pretentious to do all that outside the environs of a wine tasting. It is not only that you don't spit out wine when you are drinking it for pleasure. It is simply that you don't need to make a noisy spectacle of yourself to get a lot more pleasure out of every sip than you would if you simply knocked it back without thinking. And that's the point. You can treat wine simply as the unobtrusive stage set for the important action – whether food, conversation, or a good book – or you can let the wine play the title role. Give it your attention, concentrate on it – and you will be duly rewarded.

The middle route, between drinking without taking any interest and the painstaking (and painful-looking) ritual of the professional in the tasting room, is simply the one which delivers most pleasure. (The aim of the professional, after all, is not personal enjoyment, but assessment of whether wines will give enjoyment at the right time and right price to those who are destined to drink them.)

To get more out of every sip, glass, and bottle, you simply need to consider the wine in three stages: look, smell, then taste. Then, if you want a record for the future, you write down what you sensed in the same order, giving an overall impression at the end. (It is, I'm afraid, a mistake to rely on memory alone, especially if you are tasting or drinking more than one wine.) Lavishly bound cellar books look the part – provided you fill them in – but I've never managed more than a few entries in one of these before I've returned to my infinitely less glamorous, but always accessible, common-or-garden notebooks. I start each entry by writing the date, the place, details on the wine label (of which more in a moment), where I bought it, the price and size of bottle. On the whole labels are getting easier to understand, but it can still be difficult to work out which are the pertinent details. Label-reading is explained in the last section of the book under each relevant country or region, but, as a guide, look for the name of the wine and/or grape variety; the name of the property and/or producer; the name of a region or appellation; a vintage; and any indication of style (for example *blanc de blancs* or *moelleux*) or age-related quality designation (such as Reserva) or classification (such as *cru bourgeois*). You are now ready for the fun.

LOOK

Begin by looking at the wine, in a reasonably good, but not fluorescent light, and against a plain, pale background (a sheet of white paper is ideal). If you are doing the pouring, don't fill the glass too full: it makes the tasting process far easier if you don't. Hold the glass by the base or the stem and tip it away from you at an angle of about forty-five degrees (if the glass was too full, there will now be wine everywhere). Look down on it and you should be able to see how clear the wine is – whether it has any minute bubbles or foreign bodies, how deep the colour is, its hue, and how much the colour graduates from the centre to the rim. (With white wines it isn't actually so necessary to tilt the wine – you can hold the glass up and look at it at eye level – but it's a good habit to get into.)

(Top left) **Your first move is to check that the wine looks clean and bright:** with white wine you can usually do this at eye level.

(Left) **To see what the colour – particularly of red wine – tells you, tilt the glass away from you** against a plain, pale background, such as a piece of white paper or a table-cloth, and look at the surface of the wine.

(Above) **Hold the glass either by the stem** (above left) **or, if you have a steady hand, by the base** (above right). **This not only gives you an unimpeded view of the wine, but also stops your hand from warming it.** (Cupping your hands around the bowl is a useful trick for quickly raising the temperature of a wine, if it's too cold.)

Wine should always be clear and bright, never cloudy or hazy. At best the latter is caused by sediment that has been shaken up. At worst it suggests some kind of contamination. Sediment is far less common in white wine than red, but if it is present, apart from indicating that the wine is quite mature, it shows that it has not been over-filtered – which is a point in its favour. Of course, as with red wine (where a deposit may begin to appear within months of bottling), the sediment should remain in the bottle and not be tipped carelessly into the glass, because it muddies both the taste (it is often bitter) and texture, as well as the appearance. Small colourless crystals at the bottom of a glass or bottle of white wine are harmless tartrate deposits and are a sign that the wine has not been over-treated.

Bubbles in still wines can be a danger sign, indicating an unwanted re-fermentation, but a few tiny bubbles in a white wine – especially a pale, young, light one for drinking young – might be deliberate: such wines are bottled with a little carbon dioxide to give a bit more zip to the palate (which you experience as a slight, refreshing prickle on the tongue). Bad – secondary fermentation – bubbles, on the other hand, give a vinegary sharpness to both smell and flavour.

Although colour is less indicative for white wine than red, it still varies from almost colourless, with perhaps a hint of green in a Mosel or a Chablis, to

(Left) **Most of the world's greatest sweet wines are made from grapes affected by botrytis (aka noble rot), a mould which attacks the grapes on the vine and dehydrates them. This concentrates both flavour and colour, giving the typically deep yellow to this Sauternes.**

(Left) **Warm climates give deeper coloured wines – both red and white – than cool climates. On colour alone, it would be hard to confuse this sunny-hued Australian Chardonnay with a Chardonnay from Chablis.**

(Left) **Age and production methods affect colour in several ways: this** *vin de pays* **from the south of France owes its paleness to youth, to cold fermentation and to early bottling.**

deep yellow. Once you see brownish tinges, however, it means that things are not looking good: white wines go darker with age (the reverse of reds) and by the browning stage they are usually heavily oxidised, or maderised, which gives them an increasingly sherry-like, or "*rancio*", off-taste. Broadly speaking, paler wines come from cooler climates and deeper yellow ones come from warmer, especially southern hemisphere, regions, but sweet botrytis-affected wines (*see* page 92), including northern German ones, and oak-aged whites have more colour too.

The colour in red wine gives more away – in terms of age, quality, and provenance. Red wines gradually shed their colour (eventually as sediment), which means they become paler with age,

changing from a deep purple-red, through to ruby, to brick-red, and finally to an over-the-hill tawny. The place to look to get a feel for a wine's age is the rim: the paler and browner it is (and the greater the gradation of colour from the centre of the glass), the more mature the wine. And generally speaking a red wine of some quality that is intended to be aged, rather than drunk within a couple of years, needs to have considerable colour to start with – because colour is closely linked to tannin content, and tannin is a major life-giver in red wines.

Inevitably, though, some grape varieties and climates produce more colour than others. As with white wines, warmer regions produce deeper colours, but Cabernet Sauvignon grapes, for

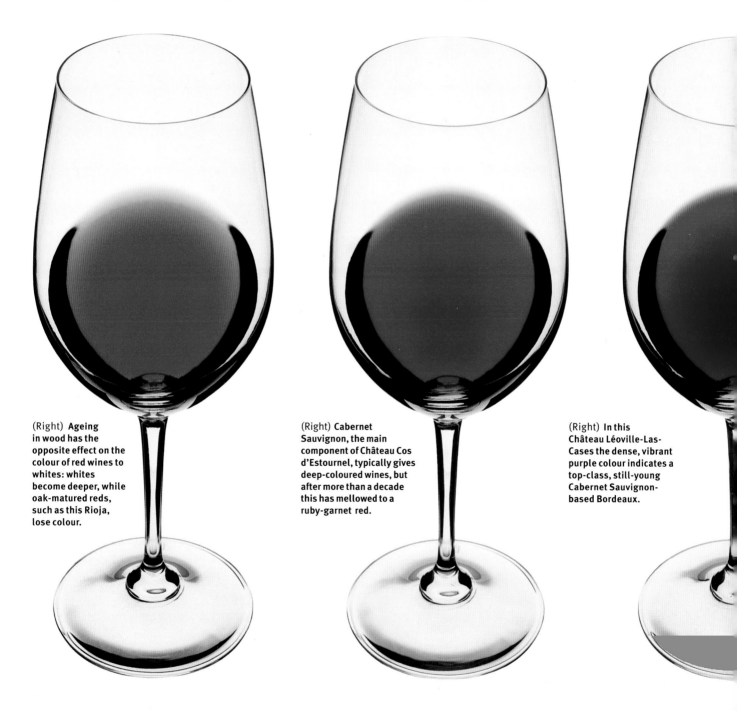

(Right) **Ageing in wood has the opposite effect on the colour of red wines to whites: whites become deeper, while oak-matured reds, such as this Rioja, lose colour.**

(Right) **Cabernet Sauvignon, the main component of Château Cos d'Estournel, typically gives deep-coloured wines, but after more than a decade this has mellowed to a ruby-garnet red.**

(Right) **In this Château Léoville-Las-Cases the dense, vibrant purple colour indicates a top-class, still-young Cabernet Sauvignon-based Bordeaux.**

example, should produce a good strong-coloured wine everywhere. The same, only more so, goes for Syrah (or Shiraz) and Petit Verdot, although Syrah is basically only grown in reasonably warm climates anyway. The Nebbiolo of Piedmont is another dark variety, but its wine turns browner more quickly than most, as does Grenache. Pinot Noir, on the other hand, is naturally paler than wines such as Cabernet Sauvignon and Syrah.

The way red wine is fermented and aged also affects colour. Wines matured in wood lose more colour than those matured predominantly in the bottle: wood-aged tawny port versus bottle-aged vintage port is the archetypal example. Rioja is another: although Tempranillo grapes produce well-coloured wines, Gran Reservas and Reservas can be relatively pale because of their long oak maturation. But the fashion almost everywhere is to produce deeper coloured reds, often by leaving the skins with the newly fermented wine for a longer period.

(Below) **After swirling, look to see if there are "legs" or "tears" of wine down the inside of the glass: these can be a clue to the wine's alcohol and sugar content.**

(Right) **Watching as you do it, gently twirl the glass round so that wine and air interact to bring out the aromas.**

SWIRL

Now for the first swirl. Either put the glass on the table, or continue to hold it by the stem or base (the base is more difficult), then twirl it round to get the wine moving – and do practice at home with water first, rather than drench your neighbouring taster. The main point of doing this is to aerate the wine so that it releases its volatile compounds – that's to say its smells, or aromas – but, before you plunge your nose into the glass, take a look.

The way the wine clings to the glass and then trickles down may tell you something. A wine that trickles back only slowly and in distinct streams, or "legs", is fairly viscous, which means that it is high in alcohol, sugar, or both. A wine with an edge that breaks quickly and raggedly may be old, very light, and dry, or you may have a not very well-rinsed glass! (Detergent and cloth residues interfere with the surface tension of the wine.)

NOSE

Put your nose down to the glass and sniff. Then give your glass its second twirl, put your nose further into it and sniff more deeply. Most people find one deep sniff more rewarding than several short sharp ones, but the important thing is to do what is most effective for you.

The first thing you learn is that wine, with the exception of wine made from the Muscat grape, doesn't smell of grapes. In fact it smells of wine. And wine smells of... if you weren't afraid of sounding like one of those wine writers who have what you had always assumed was chronic Purple Prose syndrome, you would say it reminded you of blackcurrants, gooseberries, grass, vanilla, petrol, linoleum, sweat – and you would be right. You would be right because your brain's interpretation of any aroma is what counts. It is useless to pretend that a wine smells of pineapple, butter, and vanilla, because that is what you think it is supposed to smell of, when it actually reminds you of nothing so much as stale stair carpet, cardboard, and cabbage. You won't kid yourself or anyone else.

The other reason you are right to trust your own senses is that, however outlandish your identification of a smell seems, you might well have hit the scientific bull's-eye. Wines smell of strawberries, bananas, blackcurrants, peaches, green peppers, and an extraordinary number of other familiar non-wine substances, precisely because they share the same volatile chemical compounds. Some 500 aromatic compounds have been identified in wine to date (*see* next page for further details), variously derived from the grapes themselves, the fermentation process and the maturation process (although some wines are drunk before they have had a chance to develop any real aromas at this third stage, either because they are so delicious or because they are simple wines with no development potential).

The most obvious and fruity aromas (the so-called primary aromas) come from the grapes – especially from the skin and flesh just beneath. The fermentation process yields more complex aromas, which at their most easily identifiable include yeast, butter, freshly sawn oak, and other oak-derived aromas such as vanilla, spice, and toast. The complicated and still partly mysterious chemical and physical changes that take place as wine matures produce the so-called tertiary

aromas – the most subtle and difficult to describe and identify, but ultimately perhaps the most rewarding. In white wines, both sweet and dry, the most obvious is usually honey, with toast or brioche in Champagne (but not, incidentally, derived from oak) and petrol in Riesling. Red wine maturation aromas are even harder to pinpoint, except that the fruit character becomes mellower and the good wines simply become richer (sometimes it is a gamey richness) and more profound. Together, the secondary and tertiary aromas are called the "bouquet", although the word tends to be loosely used – often for the smell as a whole. The less euphonious but succinct "nose" is also used for the overall smell.

So, that's the science, but how does it shape up in practice? Assuming that the wine is in prime condition (without specific faults and not getting too old), it should smell clean and fresh rather than stale or baked – although, with a wine of some age, it isn't the invigorating freshness of youth. It should also smell in some way fruity, although not all grape varieties have the strong, fruity identity of, say, Cabernet Sauvignon (blackcurrants) or Gewurztraminer

Wines and grapes mentioned in this chapter are described in more detail in the final part of the book (pages 94–157) and in "The Importance of Grapes" (pages 50–59).

(Below) **Having swirled your glass to release the aromas, don't be afraid to sniff deeply and decisively.**

(lychees), and in older wines the vivid, youthful fruit is replaced by mellower, more complex, less clearly defined fruit aromas – sometimes with more of the character of dried fruit and autumnal fruit compotes.

On the whole you should feel that the aromas are attractive, but there are some honourable exceptions, especially among old wines. Mature burgundy, for example, can smack of farmyards and well-patronised stables, while other old reds, especially claret, can be oddly mushroomy. Red wines from the Syrah (Shiraz) grape can be quite leathery, or tarry, and in the Hunter Valley in Australia, Shiraz commonly used to have a pungent pong of sweaty saddles; nowadays, though, this is considered to come from a fault occurring in the winemaking process. Among white wines, the strong petrol or kerosene smell acquired by the Riesling grape can come as a shock to the uninitiated and both young Sauvignon Blanc and Müller-Thurgau are sometimes enthusiastically described as having a smell of cat's pee.

The flavour connection

Around 500 chemical compounds have so far been identified in wine, many of them shared with fruits, vegetables, and some rather more surprising common substances. To give you just a few examples: pyrazines give the green pepper aroma to Cabernet Sauvignon and Cabernet Franc; ethyl caprylate gives Chardonnay a pineapple aroma; both piperonal and one of the deltalactones can give a peach aroma; another deltalactone is responsible for coconut smells; terpenes give Muscat its unmistakeable grapey scent; ionones give flowery aromas; cyanohydrin benzaldehyde is responsible for cherry aromas; isoamyl acetate gives Pinotage, for example, a smell of bananas; and the oxidation of certain fatty acids results in grassy, herbaceous smells. The chemical compounds that give aromas – pong would be more apt in some cases – of garlic, goat, camphor, carnations, mouse, butter, honey, horse sweat, and numerous others have all been found in wine. I could go on, but I'm sure you've got the picture – and the point, which is to have confidence in your own interpretations, by all means using prompts. My aromas and flavours crib (see pages 20–21) helps link common and distinctive aromas with wines in which they are often found.

If you do encounter an off-putting smell, but one which is not positively bad, and if you sense that there is more to the wine than this one particular pong, think of it as a kindred spirit to one of those awe-inspiringly smelly, but wonderfully tasty cheeses.

So far as positively bad smells are concerned, all you will really need to know about are the few easily recognised ones. A musty, dank, mouldy smell indicates a "corked" wine, one irredeemably tainted by contaminated cork (frustratingly the problem appeared to increase during the 1990s, but may now be decreasing). The corked smell always gets worse rather than better when the wine is in the glass and exposed to air.

A wine that smells of vinegar is almost certain to be beyond hope. The same goes for a wine smelling of cheap, tired sherry; but oxidation or maderization – the problem in this case – takes a while to reach such a stage. On its way it may give a flat, stale, cardboardy smell to white wines, or a stewed, sharp, tomato purée aroma to reds, but it isn't always the most obvious of off-smells. A whiff of bad eggs, struck matches, blocked drains, old over-cooked cabbage, or burnt rubber is. These are all caused by sulphur-related problems. If they are not too bad, they can sometimes be overcome with a spot of rough handling – pouring the wine into a jug and swirling it around for example or dropping a copper coin into the wine – but this is only potentially a solution at home. In a restaurant, the rule is reject it.

There is one final scenario: you put your nose down, inhale deeply, and get more or less nothing from the glass. It could be because your nose is begging for a few moments' rest after a period of concentrated sniffing. If you think that's the case, then do oblige. But if you are sure your faculties are in full working order you may have a wine in your glass that is going through a "dumb" phase. This is as mysterious as it sounds. The scientists don't know why, but many good wines that need maturing suddenly seem to batten down the hatches after their first flush of exuberant youth. The fruit goes into retreat and not much else seems to be there. (On the palate they are equally withdrawn: red wines display rather pugnacious tannins, whites show acidity, both hide behind oak.) This moody adolescent phase often starts after about two to four years and goes on for as long as a piece of string. Maybe two years, maybe five. If the wine is yours and you have several more bottles of it, you just have to sit it out patiently and bravely until the time seem right to try another bottle. Perhaps in a year's time, perhaps in three.

TASTE

Take a sip – a generous sip, but not a mouth so full that the reflex is to swallow immediately. Savour the flavours, rolling the wine gently around your mouth so that it reaches every tastebud. Then, if you're on your own, or feeling brave in sympathetic company, open your lips and draw in some air. (Yes, the slurping sound is you.) This aerates the wine, just as the earlier twirl of the glass did, and helps send the volatile compounds up from the back of your mouth to your olfactory bulb, the all-important organ at the top and back of your nose. Swallow (or spit) only when you have really got a sense of the flavours and feel of the wine. Then pay attention to the taste that is left – known as the finish or aftertaste. It should be pleasant and it should linger (try counting the seconds).

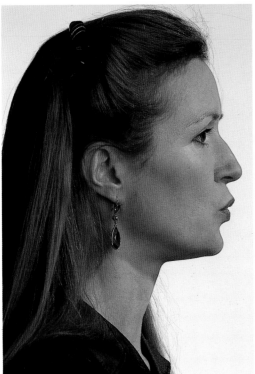

(Above) **Now taste the wine – take enough to be able to roll the wine all around your mouth, so that it reaches all the tastebuds. Think about texture as well as flavour.**

(Left) **Nose and mouth work in tandem – so, if you're feeling brave, open your mouth slightly and draw in some air to help aerate the wine and send aromas from the back of your mouth up to your olfactory bulb (a very perceptive organ).**

The first thing you usually learn is that your nose was right. You smelt blackcurrants, cedar wood, and tobacco, or melon, vanilla, and honey, and those are the flavours you taste. The mouth, by sending these volatile compounds up to the olfactory bulb, largely confirms what bulb and brain have already told you about the aromas. But the emphasis may be different: you may find their relative intensity has changed now you are experiencing them with other flavours and sensations. And taste reveals other facets of a wine's make-up, quality, and constitution.

Although tastebuds on their own only pick up a few basic, non-volatile flavours, they play a crucial role in that they "feel" the wine, with certain groups of tastebuds having particular strengths. Those at the tip of the tongue are especially sensitive to sugar. Those at the sides are more alert to acid sharpness, and those at the back are often acutely aware of bitterness (a feature of tannin, the dry, mouth-coating substance of cold tea fame). The tastebuds also register astringency (from tannin or acid), roughness or harshness (from tannin), smoothness (glycerol), and three other very important aspects of any wine – its "weight", its balance of flavours, and its length or aftertaste.

Weight (light-, medium-, or full-bodied) is perceived through alcohol, glycerol, tannin, sugar, and all the other non-water elements that together are called "extract". It is basically a matter of style. The question of balance (harmony of sugar, acid, tannin, and alcohol levels) and the length of time the flavours last (which is usually allied to their concentration) are aspects more related to quality. The greater the wine, the more harmonious all the elements appear to be and the longer and more intensely the taste lingers.

But balance can be difficult to assess, particularly in young wines that need cellaring for some years before they are drinkably mature. Red wines for laying down will have a certain amount of acidity and rather more tannin. Tannin is the inherent red wine preservative that gradually softens as the wine matures, but it is not in itself very pleasant, either in flavour or feel. What the expert looks for in a young red wine is sufficient (i.e. a balance of) ripe fruit flavour behind the tannin – *see* page 90 for more details on how winemakers manipulate tannins. Then, by the time the wine is fully mature, the tannin should be mellow and seamlessly blended with the other flavours and textures.

It is much less prominent in white wines (although certainly not absent), but it is the acid levels in whites intended to age that need to be high – sometimes raspingly so. The effect of age is to soften acidity to the taste (although it doesn't actually reduce it). Again, the key is to have sufficient fruit at the outset, so that it does not "dry out", or fade, before the acidity has softened. The acid balance is also very important, and particularly precarious, in sweet wines. If lacking, as it tends to be in cheaper wines, they simply become cloying.

The taste of new oak offers another area of potential imbalance. It gives dimension and complexity of texture to a wine, as well as contributing its own seductive flavours, but it shouldn't be intrusive – and certainly it should not be so assertive that you feel you might as well be chewing toothpicks. You will have no trouble spotting an old wine with too much oak: it will be dry, sawdusty, and fruitless. But in a young wine you may have to delve behind the oaky exterior to a fruity core: the fruit must be there if the wine is to develop well.

Finally, when you have swallowed or spat out the wine, you should be left with a taste that is undeniably clean and pleasant. It shouldn't, for example, be predominantly tart or bitter. And this pleasant "aftertaste" should linger. If it disappears in an instant, you have a very ordinary, simple wine (so I should go on to the next), but if it lasts more than about thirty seconds you probably have something rather good. So take another sip.

All this might have read as if tasting a wine takes an inordinately long time. It really doesn't – a minute or two, and I can assure you they will be minutes well and pleasurably spent.

P.S. Spitting

The other thing you need to get to grips with, if you are going to taste a lot of wines in earnest, is spitting. I know it goes against the grain to spit out good wine and against what you always thought was good manners, but spitting is the done thing. Fortunately it isn't difficult and you don't have to be aim-perfect from a great distance, but, if you take the time to have a few private practise runs, you are less likely to spatter fellow tasters and less likely to be embarrassed by your spitting image.

Take a little time to practise when you are cleaning your teeth, spit in the bath, or practise with water and a bucket in the kitchen. And so that you don't learn the hard way, can I point out that, as you spit, the following need to be held, pinned, or tucked out of the way: ties, long hair (I learnt the hard way years ago), strings of beads, pendants, and dangling scarves.

You would also be well advised to eschew pale colours and hard-to-clean silks, cashmeres, kid shoes and so on. And please note that, even if you can't see a sign, you shouldn't smoke. You may argue that you are so used to tobacco fumes they don't interfere with your tasting, but other people are unlikely to have developed a similar inbuilt filtration system.

(Above) **Spitting is not a pretty sight, but at least the Spittoo, a nifty portable spittoon designed by Hugh Johnson, looks attractive.**

(Below) **Spitting is essential at a large tasting, if you are to keep a clear head, but rest assured there is no great virtue in being able to spit from great distances. Practise first if you feel hesitant.**

TASTING TERMS

The following terms are in common usage and are mostly fairly self-explanatory:

Aggressive (said of young wine or older wine that hasn't mellowed as it should have done)
Aromatic (plenty of aromas and flavours – often the spicy or flowery grape varieties)
Astringent (mouth-puckering tannin or acid – acceptable in a young wine, but not in one supposedly ready to drink)
Austere (rather tough and ungiving – maybe because the wine is too young)
Closed (young wine needing time to open out and develop its full aromas and flavours)
Complex (lots of interesting aromas, flavours, and textures – a sign of quality)
Concentrated (plenty of everything)
Creamy (wines of quality, especially Champagne, can develop a creamy richness, which is half flavour and half texture)
Crisp (fresh and positively refreshing – especially whites)
Dense (solid colour and/or densely packed with flavour – usually positive)
Dilute (watery and lacking in flavour – the opposite of concentrated)
Dried-out (a wine that is over-the-hill because the fruit flavours have faded away)
Earthy (an earthy, gravelly, minerally smell that seems to come straight from the soil, eg. in fine Graves, as well as some more rustic wines)
Elegant (self-explanatory – and much used)
Extracted (usually in the sense of of over-extracted, meaning too much tannin and possibly acidity)
Fat (full-bodied with high glycerol – maybe sweet)
Finesse (high quality – self-explanatory)
Firm (good tannin and/or acid)
Flabby (lacking acidity)
Flat (lacking freshness and acid)
Fleshy (generously flavoured, round with no edges)
Forward (more mature than you would expect)
Fragrant (attractive, usually flowery)
Green (young and raw – may develop or the grapes may simply have been unripe)
Grip (a young wine with grip has the tannin and/or acid potential to develop)
Hard (too much tannin or acid – but can be a question of youth and the need for more time)
Heavy (full-bodied and alcoholic – usually used to indicate imperfect balance, although not in the case of fortified wines)
Hollow (wine that has an initial taste and an end-taste, but a disappointing lack of flavours in between)
Hot (high, out-of-balance alcohol – usually in wines from warm climates)
Jammy (jam rather than fresh fruit flavours – from hot climates)
Juicy (lively and fruity)
Lean (lacking breadth of flavours)
Long (wine the taste of which lasts – a very positive feature)

Meaty (richly flavoured, full-bodied wine – sometimes literally savoury meat flavours)
Mouth-filling (wine with a satisfying richness of texture and flavours that fill the whole mouth)
Neutral (short on aroma and flavour – very common among inexpensive dry whites)
Oily (some grapes have an oily character in the mouth – Gewurztraminer is one, Viognier another; Sauternes and other botrytis-affected sweet wines can also have a rich, slightly oily texture, but otherwise not usually a quality sign)
Penetrating (intense aromas and flavours)
Perfumed (fragrant, scented, often flowery)
Rich (having depth and breadth of flavour)
Robust (full-bodied, sturdy wine, usually red)
Round (no hard edges – ready to drink)
Sharp (a sharp, acid flavour that may simply need time to soften – mostly whites)
Short (no aftertaste – can't be a high quality wine)
Silky (smooth texture – high quality)
Simple (sound, drinkable wine of no great distinction and unlikely to improve with keeping)
Soft (sometimes interchangeable with smooth, but often refers to soft, mellow flavours rather than just texture)
Solid (plenty of substance, usually full-bodied)
Spritz (prickle on the tongue of carbon dioxide in young, light-bodied whites)
Stalky (bitter aroma and taste of stalks and stems)
Steely (hard to describe: firm, sinewy character, usually allied to quite high acid, found in Chablis and some other good quality young French whites)
Stewed (coarse, cooked flavours from overripe grapes and/or over-hot fermentation)
Stringy (thin, mean wine)
Structure (as in good, firm structure or poor, weak structure – the balance and strength of the basic components, i.e. acid, tannin, fruit, alcohol, and maybe sugar)
Supple (round and smooth)
Tangy (a lively aftertaste, in white wines, sherry and madeira)
Thin (lacking flavour and body)
Tough (too much tannin)
Velvety (similar to silky, but richer)
Woody (smell of old, probably dirty casks instead of clean, young ones, although occasionally used favourably for long-aged wines such as tawny port)
Zesty (fresh, crisp, and lively – usually young white wine)

(Right) **A silver tastevin – still used as a tasting tool by a few producers, especially in Burgundy. It is specially dimpled to catch the light and show the colour.**

AROMAS AND FLAVOURS CRIB

Almond – usually Italian, especially Soave and Valpolicella

Apple – many dry white wines, sweet Loires, and, when particularly aromatic, German Riesling

Apricot – Condrieu, Viognier, and good sweet Loires eg. Coteaux du Layon and Vouvray

Asparagus – Sauvignon Blanc, especially New World

Banana – young, inexpensive whites, Beaujolais and Pinotage

Biscuit – Champagne

Blackcurrant – Cabernet Sauvignon, including claret, and less pronounced in Merlot and Cabernet Franc

Blackberries – Argentine Malbec, Tannat (Uruguay), Cahors, Madiran, Shiraz

Bread (fresh baked, yeasty) – Champagne

Brioche – Champagne

Bubblegum – Beaujolais Nouveau

Butter – Chardonnay, including white burgundy

Cat's pee – Sauvignon Blanc from France and Müller-Thurgau

Cedar or cigar box – claret, above all, also other Cabernet Sauvignons

Cherry – burgundy, Beaujolais, and a lot of Italian reds

Chocolate – many medium- and full-bodied reds (New World and Old), claret and burgundy

Coffee (fresh ground) – various reds, usually good quality, oak-aged, fairly young

Currant leaf – Sauvignon Blanc

Earth (earthy smells) – reds made from Cabernet Franc in the Loire

Eucalyptus – New World Cabernet, some claret, some Shiraz

Flint and wet stones – Pouilly-Fumé, Chablis

Floral – German Riesling

Game – northern Rhône (Hermitage), Shiraz, mature red burgundy

Gooseberry – Sauvignon Blanc, especially Loire and New Zealand

Grape – Muscat, Irsai Oliver

Grapefruit – Scheurebe

Grass – Sauvignon Blanc

Green pepper – Cabernet Sauvignon and Cabernet Franc, eg. Chinon and Bourgueil, Carmenère from Chile

Herbs (herbaceous smells) – Sauvignon Blanc and other young, fresh, unoaked whites

Honey – lots of sweet wines, especially botrytis affected ones; also mature dry whites including burgundy

Lanolin – Sauternes

Leather – Mourvèdre, Syrah/Shiraz

Lemon – many young whites
Lime – Australian Riesling and Verdelho
Liquorice – many reds, especially young, tannic, full-bodied ones
Lychee – Gewurztraminer
Marzipan – sweet white Loires, eg. Coteaux du Layon, Quarts de Chaume, Bonnezeaux
Melon – New World Chardonnay
Mineral – Chablis, Pouilly-Fumé, German Riesling, reds from southwest France, eg. Cahors and Marcillac
Mint – Cabernet Sauvignon (New World) and Coonawarra Shiraz
Nivea or Pond's Cold Cream – Gewurztraminer
Nut (hazelnut or walnut) – white burgundy, Champagne, and other Chardonnays
Oak – any wine, red or white, that has been fermented and/or aged in oak (or has been aged with oak chips)
Olive – Cabernet Sauvignon and Cabernet Franc
Orange – many sweet whites, including fortified
Peach – many whites, including New World Chardonnay and sweet
Pepper (fresh ground) – red southern Rhônes, eg. Châteauneuf-du-Pape and Côtes du Rhône, Grenache, Shiraz, Austrian Grüner Veltliner
Petrol or kerosene – a good sign in mature Riesling, especially German and some Australian

Plum – a less pronounced fruit smell in many red wines
Raisins – sweet fortified wines, some southern Italian reds
Raspberry – many reds, including Rhônes and Grenache, red burgundy and New World Pinot Noir, Beaujolais, red Loires, Zinfandel, and Malbec
Rose – dry Alsace Muscat, Gewurztraminer; some red burgundy
Salt – manzanilla sherry
Smoke – full-bodied reds, especially Syrah, Pouilly-Fumé, and Alsace Tokay-Pinot Gris
Soot – South African reds, Cahors
Spice – many reds, especially Rhônes; Alsace whites, and any wine that has been oak-aged, especially in American oak
Strawberry – Beaujolais, red burgundy, and Rioja
Tar – Barolo especially, but also northern Rhônes
Toast – any wine that has been in new oak barrels, but especially Chardonnay; also mature, unoaked Champagne (especially blanc de blancs), Hunter Valley Semillon, and aged Australian Riesling
Tobacco – many reds, but especially claret and Sangiovese (eg. Chianti)
Vanilla – wine that's been in new French or American oak, eg. Rioja
Violets – Nebbiolo (eg. Barolo), Petit Verdot
Wool (wet) – white burgundy

A PERSPECTIVE
ON SERVING

SO MUCH DAUNTINGLY DOGMATIC AND POMPOUS STUFF HAS BEEN WRITTEN AND PREACHED ABOUT THE CORRECT WAY OF SERVING WINE, IT'S A WONDER THAT PEOPLE DON'T GIVE UP AND TURN TO BEER, OR AT LEAST GIVE UP TRYING TO GET IT RIGHT AND STOCK UP ON TUMBLERS OR PARIS GOBLETS.

The point is to get things in perspective. Some aspects of serving wine are more important than others. I put temperature at the top of my list. That doesn't mean I carry a wine thermometer or have worked out supposedly ideal and immutable serving temperatures for different wines, but I hope it means that I never serve a red wine lukewarm. Attending to other details, such as glasses, can undoubtedly enhance your enjoyment of wine by bringing out the best in it, but doing the the right thing for the wine should not end up being a stultifying exercise in making everyone else's life a misery, or making everyone else feel inadequate because they don't know the rules. The rules are there to be adapted and broken, as the situation and enjoyment of the wine demand.

Gadgets not gimmicks

I'm not a great fan of gadgets, least of all of the kind that supposedly aerate wine (what's wrong with swirling it in the glass?), speed up the maturation process (isn't anticipation part of the fun?), and catch drips (I'm sure you can run to a spare napkin). But there are a few items, apart from an effortless corkscrew (opposite), to which I happily devote drawer space. One, or several, that I wouldn't be without are chiller sleeves that are kept in the ice compartment or freezer and taken out when needed to chill a bottle in six or seven minutes. Not essential, but handy, is a foil cutter (opposite). In the same category I put the Champagne Star, a four-pronged clamp for uncorking sparkling wine, and Champagne stoppers for keeping the fizz in for a day or two.

The best corkscrews are those which ease the cork out vertically – not at a potentially cork-breaking angle – and have a rounded, rather than a chisel-edged, "worm" or screw. The brush (on the corkscrew below) is for dusting down the capsule of an old, cellar-encrusted bottle. The champagne pliers (bottom left) are for easing out champagne corks.

(Above) **The enormous size and out-turned lip of this glass are designed to show top red burgundy at its best.**

Glass

Like many wine producers, I am a fan of a range of glasses, each one designed for specific grape varieties, types, or ages of wine (although I only have a few of the many different shapes and sizes). I am also very attached to a pair of portable plastic Champagne flutes that come in two parts – the stem screwing into the flute – that are perfect for a bumpy ride in a cramped picnic basket or holdall.

You see the point I am making. Fine glasses, expertly designed, do enhance fine wine, but glasses, like wines, may have to be adapted to the occasion. Anything is better than nothing – and, since much of the pleasure of wine is related to the occasion, I have found Champagne none the worse for an occasional plastic flute and other wine none the worse for an imperfectly shaped and proportioned glass.

But at home you can afford to be more of a perfectionist, choosing glasses that will show off the wine's colour, smell, and flavours. For still wines you should aim to have fine, plain, colourless glass – not chunky, cut, or coloured, which won't allow you to see the wine properly. Wine glasses should also be generously sized to give plenty of room for aeration (I have a pair of glasses for red burgundy that can hold a bottle and a half each – as seen to the left – but I can't say I use them very often, and not only because I am not a regular consumer of elevated Grand Cru burgundy). Very roughly, a sixth to a quarter of a bottle should fill a third to half the glass. Slightly smaller glasses are traditional for white wine, but not necessary. As for shape, the bowl should be round, and slightly elongated and tapering towards the top, so that when the wine is swirled to release the volatile aromas they are caught in the top of the glass, rather than wafting into the distance. The International Standards Organization (ISO) glass is an effective and attractive tasting glass, but rather small for drinking wine – although it is certainly good for port.

For Champagne, the traditional flutes or slender tulip shapes are ideal: they preserve the bubbles and the subtle bouquet. The sprawling Champagne saucer, or *coupe*, is hopeless as both bubbles and bouquet are lost almost immediately. Sherry's best interests are served by a traditional *copita* (never a schooner), that can also double-up as a slightly small port glass (or a malt whisky glass).

(Below) **The shape and size of glass can dramatically affect your perceptions of a wine and so it is worth taking time and trouble when choosing.**

A word on washing

The finest glasses in the world are no use if you don't keep them in peak condition – which means detergent-, dust- and smell-free. And the best way of doing this is not to spend hours washing and drying them by hand but to put them in the dishwasher – ideally on their own, and certainly not with anything very grimy. If the glasses aren't greasy, wash them on the shortest cycle without detergent. If they need detergent, be very sparing and avoid rinsing agent. As soon as the cycle ends, open the door so that the glasses don't sit in a heavily humid atmosphere, and, if they need drying at all, use a clean linen cloth; wrap it around the handle of a wooden spoon to reach the bottom of Champagne flutes. If hand-washing, follow similar principles – hot water, a minimum of detergent, thorough rinsing and thorough drying with a linen cloth. Store glasses upright so that they don't trap stale air, but in a closed cupboard to keep dust at bay. And remember that if you haven't used a glass for a while, you will need to wash it. The wine deserves it, after all.

(Below) **Most of us can't run to a different glass for every wine, but it is worth looking at the sizes of these hand-blown glasses by the Austrian firm of Riedel.**

(From left to right) **For red burgundy (Pinot Noir); young Bordeaux (Cabernet Sauvignon); vintage Champagne; white burgundy (Chardonnay); Riesling; vintage port.**

Breathing and decanting
(air or hot air?)

A great deal of energy and hot air – complete with variedly inclusive and contradictory results from assorted experiments – has been expended on the subject of whether wine benefits from being allowed to "breathe" before it is served; and, if so, whether it should be decanted for the purpose or simply left in the bottle with the cork removed. Advocates of breathing (which simply means allowing the wine to come into contact with air) maintain that it helps develop the bouquet and softens the taste – a logical enough mini-maturation process. Those against say that aromas, and consequently bouquet and flavour, are lost, and that all desirable development can take place in the period when the wine is in the glass and the drinker can enjoy every stage of it. There are others who think breathing is wildly overrated as a subject of debate, because it doesn't make much difference to the wine.

Certainly, merely removing the cork from the bottle commits you to drinking it, but promotes very little air contact, so it is hard to see how it can have much effect. That said, with a very old and potentially fragile wine, I draw the cork no more than half an hour or so before serving – time enough to dispel any stale air trapped between wine and cork, but not long enough for bouquet and flavour to fade and die. Equally, if, as is often the case with old wine, I am going to decant it because of the sediment, I do not do so until the last half hour before serving.

With young, vigorous, medium- to full-bodied reds, I often pull the cork two or three hours before pouring, simply because that is convenient, but it could be less, it could be more. I usually decant fine reds of medium maturity, an hour or ninety minutes before serving. And occasionally, if, after leaving open a bottle of good young red for an hour, I taste it and find it rather tannic – Languedoc, northern Rhône, Barolo, Chianti, or California Cabernet, as it might be – I decant the wine to see if aeration will soften the tannins. I can't say that it is invariably effective, but then the mystery and unpredictability of wine is all part of its fascination.

Sediment

Aeration is really only a by-product of decanting. The real purpose of decanting is to remove the sediment (deposited colouring matter and tannin) from the wine so that it doesn't end up in anyone's glass. Any good-quality red wine of several years' age and even some relatively young, full-bodied reds need to be checked for sediment. Mass-market brands are unlikely to produce any, but that is about as hard and fast as the rules come nowadays.

(Above) **Elegant contemporary decanters based on traditional designs. My favourite is the "classic" (bottom).**

Wines and grapes mentioned in this chapter are described in more detail in the final part of the book (pages 94–157) and in "The Importance of Grapes" (pages 50–59).

Some grape varieties typically throw a heavy deposit (Cabernet Sauvignon and Syrah) and some throw little (Pinot Noir), but the way the wine has been made can have a considerable impact. A wine that has not been filtered, or only lightly so, will produce a sediment. On the whole this means high quality, relatively small-scale, hand-crafted wines are the most likely to throw a deposit, but there has been a global trend away from heavy filtering in the past decade. Some producers now point out the likelihood of sediment on their labels (as in "unfiltered" or "*non-filtré*"). This may be part marketing gimmick, but dispensing with the filtration equipment is something to be proud rather than ashamed of: it means that none of the wine's precious flavour has been inadvertently filtered out.

How to decant

Even when you know there is sediment in the bottle, you still need to look carefully to see where it is, because ensuring that all the sediment is gathered in one place is one of the essentials of successful decanting. For this, all you need is a bright light (a spot light, bare bulb, powerful torch, cycle lamp, or a candle) along with a steady hand for the decanting itself.

Whether you use a decanting basket (one of those baskets with handles that holds a bottle at an angle of about twenty degrees and which some pretentious restaurants use for serving the wine), or do without, the sediment-manoeuvring stage should start at least twenty-four hours, and preferably two or three days, before the wine is to be served (vintage port with its very heavy and quickly moved sediment is the exception). Either put the

bottle in a decanting basket or stand it upright. Then, when you are ready to decant, either draw the cork and pour the wine slowly into the decanter without taking the bottle from the basket, or, if the bottle has been standing, tilt it gently and try to pour all in one go.

The advantage of a basket is that the sediment is even less likely to be dislodged when the wine is poured, but the disadvantage is that you cannot see the wine nearly as well as you can if you are holding the bottle directly in front of a light. Whatever you do, watch carefully as you approach the end of the bottle. You may well have to sacrifice an inch, perhaps more, but it is far better to be over-cautious than spoil a good bottle with sludge.

(Right) **The keys to decanting are getting the sediment in one place in the bottle in advance – and a good light source.**

Temperatures

Everybody knows that warm white wine is an abomination – but so is warm red and it seems to be far more common nowadays than tepid white. The problem is central heating. "Room temperature", the traditional axiom for red wine, simply doesn't mean today's centrally heated room temperatures of about 21˚C (70˚F). It means 18˚C (65˚F) at most – and that for full-bodied and tannic red wines, particularly from the New World. Most clarets are best served a degree cooler, Pinot Noirs (including burgundies) a little cooler again, and an increasing number of modern reds, made in a relatively tannin-free, soft, fruity style for drinking young are delicious served at anything from a fairly cool 12˚C (54˚F), like Beaujolais, to a moderate 16˚C (61˚F).

Having said all that, I don't go around dunking a wine thermometer into every glass of wine that comes my way. In fact, I have rarely used one. The average body, or hand clasping a bottle, seems to me a sufficiently good judge of temperature – perhaps a better one in that it takes into account both atmospheric temperature and ambience. While 17˚C (63˚F) might be theoretically ideal for claret, the wine is unlikely to be spoiled at 16˚C (61˚F) or even at 18˚C (65˚F) – and certainly a wine that is slightly too cool can quickly be warmed by cupping your hands around the glass. If, however, you are lucky enough to be bringing a red wine from a proper cellar temperature of, say, 11–12˚C (52–54˚F) to 18˚C (65˚F), you will need to leave it at room temperature for about three hours, or put it in a bucket of tepid water for about twenty minutes. If you only have twenty seconds to spare, you can use a microwave, but remember to take the foil capsule off first.

If you need to cool a red wine, you can simply put the bottle in the fridge – for twenty to thirty minutes, but this depends on the temperature of the wine when it goes in, the temperature you want to serve it at, and the temperature of the fridge. You can also make use of more rapid methods – a bucket of ice and water, the deep-freeze, or the back garden in winter, but be wary of bringing these to bear on an old and fragile wine.

White wines should be served between about 6˚C (43˚F) and 11˚C (52˚F), but, as with red, err on the low side (chilled wines

(Below) **Sparkling wines and sweet wines, light-bodied and cheap white wines are best served a little cooler than full-bodied, not very acid whites.**

(Below) **Wine warms up quickly at room temperature, so err slightly on the cool side, but don't chill a fine wine, such as white burgundy, to death.**

(Right) **The quickest way to cool wine is to plunge it into a container of iced water. (Similarly, a bucket of tepid water will quickly warm a cellar-temperature red).**

warm up quickly in the glass). As a guide, but not a gospel, full-bodied, not notably acid whites – especially good-quality Chardonnays and burgundy – are the ones to serve at the higher end of the spectrum. Wines with higher acidity, such as Sauvignon Blanc, Riesling, and Albariño should be served cooler, as should sweet wines, Champagne, light-bodied and aromatic wines, such as dry Muscat. Another useful rule of thumb is that the cheaper the wine, whether still, sparkling, dry, or sweet, the cooler it should be.

If you are in a hurry, the quickest way to chill a bottle of wine is to use a chiller sleeve (*see* Gadgets page 23). Without one of these, the most effective method is to plunge the bottle into a bucket of ice and water. In under twenty minutes, a bottle at 21˚C (70˚F) will be down to about 10˚C

(50˚F). A freezer will take about forty-five minutes to do the same job and you should allow up to two hours in an ordinary fridge.

Serving order

Naturally, you need to take into account the food being served when deciding which wines you will be serving when, and I go into the intriguing and mouth-watering business of food and wine

(Left) **A wine thermometer will allow you to be precise about temperature, but remember that there is no single "correct" temperature for a wine. It may depend on the weather.**

(Below) **Pour the wine gently and with the bottle close to the glass – the idea is to disturb the wine as little as possible, especially if it is old.**

(Above) **Stoppers for helping preserve part-finished bottles for a few days. Put the bottles in the fridge or somewhere cool.**

matching in the next chapter (pages 30–39), but these are the basic guidelines: dry white before red, light before heavy, young before old, dry before sweet. That doesn't mean that you shouldn't drink sherry with soup, simply because it is more alcoholic than the wine that follows, or that you have to continue drinking sweet wines if you have started with foie gras and Sauternes, or that a red wine must always be older than a white that preceded it. They are simply pointers – flexible ones – rather than rules.

Preservation

Once a bottle is opened, the air immediately begins to work on it. At first the effects are likely to be beneficial (*q.v.* Breathing, page 25), but exposure to air is, ultimately, the road to vinegar. Devising ways to preserve unfinished bottles of wine was one of the growth industries of the late twentieth century. Before that, wine drinkers who wanted to save the remains of an unfinished bottle simply had to jam the cork back in, put the wine in the fridge or cellar and just hope for the best.

Unsophisticated as it is, this is still a useful way of doing the job in the short term. You can't expect old wines to survive, but most young whites, rosés, and reds will last a couple of days if the bottle is at least half-full, if it was not relentlessly tipped up and down to be poured and if it was only open for two or three hours.

With the same provisos, fuller reds in their prime may well last three or four days. The wines will almost certainly lose a little freshness and taste a little flatter – so it would be a pity to treat a grand or treasured bottle in this way – but they will seldom become unpleasantly oxidized. With red wine you will, of course, have to remember to take the bottle out of the fridge before you want to drink it (probably a couple of hours, depending on room and fridge temperature). You can put it in a bucket of nearly tepid water, but bear in mind that you have already put the wine through one endurance test and changing the temperature too rapidly could be the straw that breaks the camel's back.

If you know that only half a bottle is going to be consumed, as soon as you open it, decant half the wine into a half-bottle, then recork it and put it in the fridge or cellar. I have had wines keep for weeks like this, but it's not a fail-safe method and it is far better to plan to drink the other half the following day.

Wine conserving gadgets work on two basic principles: removing the air in the bottle to leave a vacuum; and putting an inert gas (usually nitrogen with a little carbon dioxide) that is heavier than air on to the surface of the wine. You don't need to refrigerate wines thus protected (although it makes sense to keep them cool) and the manufacturers would like us to think that they will keep fresh for a week, if not a fortnight. In practice, results seem to me to be erratic.

I don't find the vacuum method sufficiently effective, although some people swear by the Vacuvin – an inexpensive vacuum pump with reusable stoppers. I sometimes use canisters of gas that you simply squirt into the neck of the bottle, although some wines stored this way seem quickly to acquire a slightly stale, sweaty smell without actually becoming oxidized.

So what is the solution? It's really very simple: drink, or rather share, any grand bottles in one sitting. And, for fun, try blending the remains of some less grand bottles together – Cabernet with your Chianti perhaps, a little Sauvignon with your Chardonnay. There's no law against it.

As for Champagne and other sparkling wines, if kept in the fridge they will keep their sparkle, but you will need a stopper to keep oxidation and food taints at bay.

(Left) **It is one of the enduring myths that a teaspoon in the neck of a bottle of Champagne will preserve its fizz in the fridge. Providing the opened bottle hasn't already been left to go flat, the pressure in the fridge will preserve much of its fizz, but only a Champagne stopper will prevent it from picking up unwanted flavours from other foods.**

MATCHING
FOOD AND WINE

WHENEVER YOU FIND YOURSELF AGONIZING OVER THE MATCHING OF WINE AND FOOD, BE REASSURED THAT, THOUGH THERE ARE SOME FOODS THAT NEED RIGOROUS ATTENTION, THERE ARE FEW TRULY UNPALATABLE COMBINATIONS.

Chocolate and bone dry Chablis, rare steak and Muscat de Beaumes-de-Venise, mackerel and tannic Barolo all sound horrendous to me (not even in the interests of this book could I bring myself to test them), but even so, if anyone has tried them and found them pleasing, that person can't be "wrong".

A problem obviously arises if a devotee of, say, the steak and sticky combination decides to serve it to other people. It would be better if he or she had a few self-doubts and played safe, or certainly infinitely safer, with the traditional colour formula – red wine with red meat, dry white wine with fish and white meat, sweet white with puddings. These and other more specific classic marriages have stood the test of time (and sometimes more recently the test of scientific enquiry). So, too, have most of the traditional regional combinations. Drinking the local wine with the food of Bologna, Tuscany, Piedmont, Provence, Burgundy, or Alsace is almost always satisfying – although, personally, I draw the line, which many Champenois apparently do not, at drinking dry Champagne with puddings.

The difficulty with the natural regional pairings is that gastronomy has become much more complicated in recent decades. Although there has been a welcome revival of traditional local dishes – British as well as French, Italian, and others – there has also been a great deal of cross-dressing in cosmopolitan cities around the globe. How do you decide what to drink with a dish of seared venison

loin with pomegranate seeds, goat's cheese fondue infused with lemongrass, and artichoke spring roll? The smart answers, I suppose, are don't order that dish, or drink water, but it makes the point, somewhat extremely, that nowadays you need more than
the basic age-old maxims – unless you are permanently ensconced in a small, off-the-beaten-track, European wine village, or, equally, in one of London's smart gentlemen's clubs where plain (aka nursery) food is still the order of every day and wine lists only cautiously stray from the perceived security of the European classics.

The other point you should reassure yourself on is that while there are some food and wine marriages apparently made in heaven (such as Sauternes with Roquefort) and some foods that are peculiarly treacherous, these are more the exception than the rule. This means, in effect, that most foods can be accompanied happily by several different wine types.

You should be aiming, then, for food and wine that complement each other – in part, simply by their mutual presence – rather than for some magical mutual enhancement. The fashion for panels of tasters setting to and palate-testing myriad

Wines and grapes mentioned in this chapter are described in more detail in the final part of the book (pages 94–157) and in 'The Importance of Grapes' (pages 50–59).

wines with specific foods and dishes to divine some definitive perfect partnership may produce interesting and sometimes quirky results, but it seldom sets many useful new guidelines, not only because the results from one panel to another are often endearingly contradictory, but because they are usually too specific. They relate to one recipe, one set of ingredients, one chef, and one set of tasters or feeders in one set of surroundings. So it's no wonder conclusions vary from one occasion to another.

They are also apt to come up with supposedly definitive pairings that have limitations in practice. I don't deny that dry sherry is surprisingly versatile with food, but most people don't want to go on drinking it beyond the first course – if indeed that far. The "discovery" that Muscadet's very neutrality makes it a largely non-combative partner doesn't actually mean it makes any thrilling combinations (other than with seafood perhaps). Similarly, goat's cheese and Sancerre or Pouilly-Fumé make a delicious combination when the cheese, with salad, is a starter, but, if it is the cheese after the main course, are you going to want to go back to Sancerre or Pouilly Fumé, after California Cabernet, Chianti Classico, Barossa Chardonnay, or, if you are eating pudding before cheese, after Sauternes? And drinking Sancerre or Fumé all the way through to the cheese doesn't strike me as much fun either.

Weight for weight

So where do you start? Whether or not you have already decided what colour of wine you want to be drinking, matching the weight, or body, of the wine to the food is usually the key. It should certainly be allowed to take precedence over the colour formula. A delicately poached chicken breast can be rendered almost as lifeless by a heavy, high-alcohol, extravagantly fruity, buttery, oaky Chardonnay as it can by a powerful red Hermitage. Equally, a richly flavoured Coq au Vin would knock a light or dry white for six – a Mosel *Kabinett*, a Vin de Pays des Côtes de Gascogne, or a Chablis, for example. In fact a logical answer when cooking something in a significant quantity of wine, whether Coq au Vin or risotto, is to drink the same, or a similar type of wine, but even here you need to be wary of the power of heavily reduced stocks, fumets, and sauces – that is intensity of flavour – particularly if using a wine of light to medium body.

Flavour intensity

Intensity of flavour – which may be allied to weight, but not invariably so – can be decisive in either food or wine. Fine German Rieslings can be intensely flavoured but are traditionally light-bodied and low in alcohol; Sauvignon Blanc is another variety with a powerful flavour which, although it is not as light as German Riesling, is seldom a real heavyweight. Wines such as these can sometimes be used as a contrast, to cut through food with some richness, or they may complement intensity of flavour – a ripe New Zealand Sauvignon Blanc with the vivid flavour of red peppers in Peperonata, for example.

Acid, sugar, and salt

When it comes to the food, take account of its acidity, its sweetness (not least in savoury dishes), and its saltiness. A dish with a definite element of acid – a citrus sauce, or a squeeze of lemon – will usually need a wine with acidity to match, otherwise the wine will taste flat.

It is harder to generalize about savoury dishes with some sweetness, simply because the degree of sweetness can vary so much. It may be an integral part of the dish – as in rabbit or pork with prunes – or it may only be an entirely dispensable garnish. I would put redcurrant jelly and mint sauce in the latter category (although I know that their fans would not agree). But with an integral fruit sauce I might veer towards wine with a slight sweetness, such as a Pfalz *Spätlese Halbtrocken* or a red wine made from Pinot Noir, from New Zealand for example.

Salty dishes may benefit from a touch of apparent sweetness in the wine. In a white wine it may mean actual sweetness, (Sauternes with Roquefort and port with Stilton are obvious examples). But more often salty foods, such as

(Left) **Traditional regional combinations have stood the test of time: charcuterie with Beaujolais; proscuitto and salami with north Italian whites.**

anchovies, olives, and shellfish, cry out for a white wine with refreshing acidity: with a white wine this is easy to find; with reds the solution is often to go for the sort of fresh, crisp, low-tannin style that takes well to a light chill (red Loires or Beaujolais, for example). Salt, used with care, can also help to moderate tannin in red wine.

Texture

After weight, intensity, and specific flavours, there is the texture of some foods to consider. When this is linked to weight, it is straightforward enough – you are unlikely to choose a delicate white wine to sip between chewing hunks of steak – but there are some foods that have a mouth-coating effect that naturally affects your perception of any wine. Certain cheeses are undoubted offenders (*see* Cheese, page 38), but egg and chocolate are potentially worse and are often dismissed outright as inimical to wine. I put them instead into a category of "would-be food outcasts" – those that need special care – and it is an area that vegetarians should look at and I hope take comfort from, because several of their staples – eggs, vegetables, salad dressings – are often dismissed too readily as unkind to wine.

Would-be outcasts

Soft-yolked egg undoubtedly coats the mouth, effectively blocking the tastebuds and therefore the wine, so I wouldn't waste a great cellar treasure

on, for example, baked eggs. That said, eggs' coating quality has not stood in the way of Oeufs en Meurette, the classic starter of poached eggs in a rich red burgundy sauce, which is eaten with red burgundy (I would choose a lesser village wine or a Passe-Touts-Grains, rather than something grand). Egg-based sauces and soufflés seem to me to be without hazards: with mayonnaise and hollandaise, Sauvignon Blanc and young Chardonnay are good; while cheese soufflés, in particular, show off all sorts of wines rather well. Quail's eggs, with their finer texture, are a treat with Champagne or crisp, dry, elegant, and not too assertive still whites.

Vinegar doesn't go with wine, but salads with vinaigrette need not be a problem – provided good vinegar is used (not the fish and chip sort) and used with a healthy proportion of oil (the quantity depends on the individual oil and vinegar, as well as taste, but start perhaps with five parts oil to one of vinegar). An alternative, a trick favoured in the salad bowls of some top wine producers, is to use vinegar's precursor – wine itself – with less oil (again, proportions depend on oil, wine, and personal preference, but three to one would be a start). Another tip is to use walnut or hazelnut oil and serve a Chardonnay, because Chardonnay's nutty character has an affinity with nut oils.

I find mint sauce much more vicious than most vinaigrettes, and I skip it rather than try to accommodate it, but its fans say that it blends seamlessly with a mouthful of lamb and therefore does no damage to wine. If you do find yourself with the lingering flavours of an aggressive mint sauce or vinaigrette – or indeed any other clashing food – a painless sip of water or a chunk of bread will usually dampen them down.

Globe artichokes, spinach, asparagus, and even **fennel** have all come in for the wine connoisseur's axe, but only artichokes really deserve it and even they can be knocked into shape. The culprit in artichokes is a substance called cynarin which, for most people, makes wine taste sweet, but squeezing lemon quite generously over the artichoke seems to moderate the effect and give a chance to young, crisp whites such as Sauvignon, Greek and Italian whites. Reds are difficult: try fairly basic, peppery, southern French reds (eg. Côtes du Rhône and *vin de pays*).

As spinach tends to be a side dish or an ingredient, rather than a centre-piece (even in vegetarian dishes), it seldom determines the choice of wine, but if you do find that it makes wine taste unpleasantly bitter/metallic it is worth trying the lemon juice trick. Alternatively, enriching spinach

(Left) **Soft-yolked egg undoubtedly coats the mouth, effectively blocking the tastebuds and therefore the wine, so I wouldn't waste a great cellar treasure.**

with butter, cream, or Parmesan, and nutmeg usually prevents clashes – so vegetarian dishes based on spinach seldom cause problems.

The distinctive flavour of asparagus is hard on most wines, but a well-concentrated, fruity New Zealand Sauvignon Blanc or a rounded but young, unoaked Chardonnay (even burgundy such as Mâcon or Chablis) is usually successful. Lighter whites tend to get lost, but red Loire wines (Chinon, Bourgueil, Saumur-Champigny) made from Cabernet Franc (which shares a currant-leaf flavour with Sauvignon) can be a surprising hit. Similar recommendations apply to fennel, which doesn't actually clash with most wines, but can sometimes have a rather bullying presence on the palate.

Oily fish, above all mackerel, both smoked and unsmoked, can do terrible things to wine, so it is probably best to aim for cheap, fairly neutral, dry, crisp whites like Muscadet, Touraine Sauvignon, Aligoté (admittedly only cheap by Burgundian standards), Greek whites, or Italian whites such as Soave which are slightly softer. Beaujolais Blanc and Fino sherry are possibilities too.

Hot-and-spicy foods. Hot chillis will kill any wine by numbing and burning your palate, so it's pointless to try to match wine to a ferociously hot curry, but there are plenty of dishes from India and the Far East which can be partnered. The choice of wines that will go with any one dish is more limited than with less spicy food, but at least that makes life simpler.

Indian, Thai, Chinese, and Japanese food are completely different, but, as a quick guide, the kind of wines that are most accomodating are fresh, crisp, moderately aromatic, and fruity whites. Steer clear of whites that are very oaky or fat and buttery or neutral and dry. Red wines are more difficult with spicy food and tannic and oaky wines are especially to be avoided.

Indian. Even when Indian food is not particularly hot, it is often very complex and may have bitter, sour and astringent elements. White wines cope with these more readily and modern, New World-type wines are more successful than the European classics. Young, unoaked Semillon, Riesling, and Verdelho from Australia and well-chilled Australian and New Zealand sparkling wines are good starting points. Chardonnay/Sauvignon blends can work, as can subtle, barely oaked Chardonnay from a cool region, especially with mild coconut-infused curries, but, generally, Chardonnay and Sauvignon are a bit of a mismatch. If you want a European wine, dry Muscat works for light, but spicy dishes and Alsace Pinot Blanc is also worth trying. Alsace Gewürztraminer is a useful fallback for tricky, highly spiced dishes. Red wines are more difficult. Think in terms of Zinfandel, Shiraz, modern Rioja Crianza, and the full, soft reds of Chile and Argentina; remember that you are trying to avoid heavy tannins, oak, and alcohol – and try chilling them lightly.

(Above) **The choice of wines that will go with any one dish is more limited than with less spicy food, but at least that makes life simpler.**

Thai. The hot, sour, and sometimes salty, sweet flavours of Thai food are expressive at the very least, but they are not as hard on wine as you might expect. Assertive, dry, but fruity whites are the key – above all, punchy Sauvignons (Sancerre, New Zealand, and South African among them), closely followed by Australian Riesling and the more grassy style of Semillon (from Western Australia, for example). Chardonnay comes into its own with the coconuty peanut sauce accompanying satays. Most reds struggle, but lightly chilled, everyday new world reds and Beaujolais-Villages are options.

Chinese. The trick with partnering Chinese food is not to let the wine overwhelm it. Hot, spicy Sichuan excepted, most Chinese food is delicate and slightly sweet. The most flattering grape is Riesling, ideally German in *Kabinett* or *Spätlese Halbtrocken* form. Failing Germany, try New Zealand or Australian Riesling. Champagne, *demi-sec* or *brut*, can work well, as can New World Pinot Noirs and German Spätburgunder. If you need something stronger with spare ribs or Peking duck, try a Gewürztraminer.

Japanese. Thanks to the hot, pungent wasabi, pickles, and dipping sauces, finding wines to go with Japanese food isn't easy. German and New World Rieslings, dry Champagne, and New Zealand sparkling wines are the safest bets; Chablis and other firm, dry whites usually cope quite well. Although the Japanese have a soft spot for Pomerol, most reds make for rather uneasy alliances. I would opt for a good Beaujolais, a Côte de Beaune or New Zealand Pinot Noir.

Chocolate smothers the tastebuds even more effectively than eggs, but, as with most wine killers, remedial treatment can work. Unrehabilitated neat chocolate and the densest of dark rum truffles are probably best left for coffee, liqueurs, or water, but mousses, marquises, puddings, and gateaux can be tackled with the sweetest wines, especially those made from the Muscat (Moscato or Moscatel) grape. The richest and darkest may need the strength of flavour and alcohol of old, raisiny fortified wines – such as Australian Liqueur Muscats and the red Grenache-based Maury and Banyuls – but marginally lighter chocolate mousses and puddings often take to Muscat de Beaumes-de-Venise, Rivesaltes, California, and Australian Orange Muscats, and old (*i.e.* twenty-year-old) tawny port. With positively light frothy mousses, try Sauternes, or Asti or Moscato d'Asti. And if you are still drinking your red wine when it comes to the (chocolate) pudding, make sure it is a lush, ripe, not too tannic California Cabernet or Merlot. It may just work.

Starters

Lumping all the world's starters together may seem cavalier, but they are linked by the fact that at this stage in the meal you are usually aiming at a relatively light and/or a white wine to precede fuller-bodied wines.

With **soup** you will find that most people don't drink much, but, if you don't want to do without, try sherry (fino, manzanilla, or dry amontillado according to the weight of the soup), try matching the principal ingredient (dry rosés can be very good with fish soup), or simply pour a little of the next course's wine.

Fino and manzanilla also score well with olives and anchovies, and where there are several contrasting elements to deal with – mixed hors d'oeuvres or antipasti, crudités with dips, or *salades composées*. You could also consider medium weight, moderately fruity, or aromatic whites and

(Above) **It is not so common to drink wine with soup, but, if you do want to, try sherry or try matching the principal ingredient.**

the mood for Champagne or top Chablis, but a respectable Muscadet or Sancerre would be fine. It doesn't have to be French of course, but beware anything too assertively fruity or oaky, or short on refreshing acidity. With lobster, too, it is worth going for gold: Champagne, great white burgundy, or a top Chardonnay from elsewhere, a good white Rhône, dry Bordeaux, or Arneis from Piedmont. Prawns can take the same treatment, or more modest wines, and mussels, too, are very accommodating. Crab is trickier, but Chablis is classic and Viognier and German Rieslings with some sweetness (especially *Spätlese*) work well. Scallops also often appreciate a little sweetness – and/or richness.

With smoked fish such as salmon and trout, Champagne, the best dry sparkling wines from elsewhere, aromatic Alsace whites and Riesling *Spätlese* from the Rhine (Mosels tend to be too light) are good.

Pasta

Pasta goes with anything – it is the sauce that is of concern. Youngish fruity reds, quite assertive but not necessarily full-bodied, and dry but not astringently so, are the best all-rounders in that they go with meaty and tomato sauces – and tomato, because of its sharpness, can be difficult. The Italians naturally have plenty of answers in Dolcetto, Barbera, Montepulciano d'Abruzzo, Valpolicella, Negroamaro, Teroldego Rotaliano, Rosso del Montalcino *et al*, but most other countries have something possible – Chilean Carmenère, Navarra reds, Côtes du Rhône, *vin de pays*, Australian Petit Verdot, lighter California Zinfandels.

With **Carbonara** and **creamy sauces,** go for medium- to full-bodied whites with some flavour – like Lugana or Gavi from Italy, Pinot Blanc, or Chardonnay from anywhere as long as it is not too exuberantly fruity and oaky.

Dry white also goes better than red with **Pesto,** but it needs to be crisp and firm – Gavi, Soave, or good Pinot Grigio, a Sardinian or Sicilian white, a Rueda from Spain, or, at a pinch, a light Sauvignon Blanc from Hungary or an unoaked Chardonnay.

Risotto is fairly accommodating across the spectrum from off-dry to dry white wines and light reds, but you need to take account of any added ingredients or flavourings such as porcini and beware of overpowering what should usually be quite a delicate dish.

rosés (eg. Austrian Grüner Veltliner, Verdicchio, Pinot Grigio, Hungarian whites, Alsace Sylvaner, or Pinot Blanc, properly dry Vinho Verde, unoaked white Rioja, *Halbtrocken* German Rieslings, dry southern French, or Spanish rosés). Light- to medium-bodied fruity reds – Beaujolais and other Gamays, young Merlot, Dolcetto, Montepulciano d'Abruzzo, simple southern French reds – come into their own if meat is involved (eg. salami, bacon, chicken livers, or duck in antipasti and salads).

Pâtés vary enormously. The most unctuous liver pâtés (above all, that of foie gras) can take unctuous sweet wine – notably Sauternes. If you find that a bit heavy, try a late-harvest (*Vendange Tardive*) Alsace Tokay-Pinot Gris. Meaty, but less rich pâtés go well with assertive but dry Alsace whites and fruity, spicy reds from all over.

Shellfish go with all sorts of dry whites, so choice probably depends a lot on your pocket. If you've splashed out on oysters, you will presumably be in

(Above) **Pasta goes with anything – it is the sauce that is of concern. Youngish fruity reds, quite assertive but not necessarily full-bodied, and dry but not astringently so, are the best all-rounders.**

Fish

Though you certainly shouldn't regard red wines as a problem if you only eat fish, it is worth knowing what is behind the white wine with fish instruction. The main reason is that fish – especially white and shellfish – can make red wines, particularly those with discernible tannin, taste metallic or tinny. The other two reasons are that fish dishes, very broadly, tend to be lighter than meat dishes (and there are more light white wines than light reds); and secondly that fish is often dressed with lemon, an acidity that is easier to match with a white wine. For all these reasons a plainly cooked, fairly delicate white fish (such as sole, plaice, hake, or cod), deserves a dry white wine that is not too heavy or too aromatic. That cuts out, for example, Alsace Gewurztraminer and Tokay-Pinot Gris and ebullient New Zealand Sauvignons and Australian Chardonnays, but otherwise leaves a huge choice from Chablis to Pinot Blanc to Albariño to Verdicchio.

Fish in rich sauces can take richer, fuller wines: white burgundies from the best downwards, other Chardonnays in the Meursault mould (eg. California or New Zealand), Hunter Valley Semillon, Condrieu, Alsace Riesling, and Tokay-Pinot Gris, or, if you want to be adventurous, a *demi-sec* Loire wine (Vouvray or Montlouis) from a good vintage.

As far as red wines are concerned, any fish that has been cooked in red wine – as salmon and red mullet often are – calls out to be served with one, but any other fairly full-flavoured or substantial fish (such as turbot, salmon, or tuna) will go with the right kind of red wine or a good dry rosé. Aim for light, low-tannin, young reds that you would tend to serve cool: Loire reds (both the Cabernet Franc-based ones such as Chinon and the Pinot Noir-based Sancerre), other Pinot Noirs, Beaujolais, and other Gamays, German Dornfelder, and light Italian reds such as Bardolino.

Poultry, meat, and game

Clashes of flavour are encouragingly few with meat (although the sweetness of calf's liver and the fatty richness of goose are not without the potential). As far as the red wine with red meat and white wine with white meat rule goes, it only goes so far; it doesn't begin to touch on the weight or intensity of flavour of the sauces, gravies, stuffings, and marinades that may dominate or dictate the finished dish.

That said, I don't know of any white wine that goes better than red with beef, whether roast or grilled, or turned into a rich, pungent stew. And I can't recommend a white wine to go with lamb, unless the lamb is leftover cold roast, in which case German Riesling (preferably *Kabinett* or *Spätlese Halbtrocken*) and Mâcon are surprising successes. They cut through the close-textured density of the cold meat – and work with pork and turkey, too.

Plain roast beef shows off any medium- to full-bodied fine red wine: burgundy, California Pinot Noir, northern Rhône, Chianti Classico Riserva, Barbaresco, Rioja Reserva, Cahors, Madiran, good Cabernet from anywhere, and, perhaps surprisingly, the softer, rounder clarets of St-Emilion, Pomerol, and Fronsac in preference to top Médocs. Richly flavoured beef casseroles can take big wines – California Zinfandels and Cabernets,

(Below) **Though you certainly shouldn't regard red wines as a problem if you only eat fish, it is worth knowing what is behind the white wine with fish instruction.**

Shiraz, Châteauneuf-du-Pape, and northern Rhônes, Ribera del Duero and Priorat Brunello, and other top Tuscans, Barolo, Bandol, and reds from Languedoc. Impressive heavyweight wines also suit powerful game such as hare, venison, grouse, and casseroled birds, although the depth and complexity of a top Côte de Nuits burgundy can be just as successful, so long as the birds have not been too well hung. Some people swear by the contrasting sweetness of a German *Spätlese* or an Alsace Tokay-Pinot Gris *Vendange Tardive* with venison, but I prefer Pinot Noir or Syrah-based wines. Good burgundy is also ideal for young, plainly roasted game birds; so, too, are mature Bordeaux, Douro reds, Rioja, and Crozes-Hermitage.

Simple roast lamb or **grilled chops** are perfect for showing off your best mature clarets from the Médoc and Graves, Gran Reserva Riojas, mature Coonawarra Cabernets, and Napa Cabernets. If you are going for a more pungent effect with the lamb, with masses of garlic and rosemary, juniper, or even anchovy, choose a younger more vigorous claret or a fruity, fairly full-bodied Cabernet or Merlot from elsewhere, eg. Chile, a Portuguese red from Bairrada, Dão, or the Douro, or a soft, minty Australian Cabernet/Shiraz.

Pork is marvellously easygoing (although apple sauce can be a bit of a killer). Plain roast or chops go with off-dry and dry whites, from neutral to aromatic or spicy, to full-bodied and complex – which means anything from South African Chenin Blanc via Alsace to Premier Cru burgundy. With red wines, all but the heaviest and most drily tannic are possible.

Chicken, turkey, and **guinea fowl** are the poultry equivalents of pork – extremely adaptable. Roast plainly they are kind to red, white, and rosé, from humble to high quality, but are better with reds if there is a herby, oniony, or meaty stuffing to support them. Red wines, such as spicy, peppery southern French reds or Shiraz, are also the obvious answer with rich red-wine-based casseroles, while medium- to quite full-bodied whites go with cream sauces.

With **duck** and **goose,** you can either go for a white with some sweetness – an Alsace *Vendange Tardive*, a German *Spätlese,* or a Vouvray *moelleux* – or a classic high quality red from Burgundy, Bordeaux, Australia, or Spain. With Bordeaux, lean towards the softer, riper wines of St-Emilion or Pomerol.

Both **liver** and **kidneys** are a good foil for a variety of reds, young and old – so go for anything from

Barbera and Valpolicella to South African Pinotage, Australian Shiraz, and Corbières. The key with pan-fried or grilled calf's liver is to resist the temptation to try to match its sweetness: a supple Pomerol, St-Emilion, or Torgiano is a better option. Sweetbreads need something subtle but mellow – an elegant Volnay or Margaux, or, if in a creamy sauce, a Rhine *Spätlese*.

Sausages vary so much in herb, spice, meat type, and fat content that it is difficult to generalize, but full-bodied fruity, spicy reds are usually a strong suit – more or less rustic or grand according to sausage and occasion, so anything from Alentejo to Châteauneuf-du-Pape to Argentine Malbec and beyond.

(Above) **I don't know of any white that goes well with beef, whether plainly roast or grilled, or turned into a rich, pungent stew.**

Cheese

How we ever came to regard cheese and red wine as natural partners I cannot imagine. Perhaps the success of port and Stilton blinded everyone to the fact that cheese and wine, especially dry red wine, often clash – or at least do nothing for each other. However much I like red wine and cheese individually and however much I am in the mood for red wine at the cheese course stage, I have to admit that, overall, white wines go with more cheeses than do red wines and that sweet whites are often more successful than dry whites.

All that said, I have not given up dry red wine with cheese and nor need you. You will want to choose both wine and cheese carefully and you may not find yourself serving up your grandest bottles of red wine with cheese, but it can be successful, particularly if it is during a meal that naturally progresses from dry white with the starter to red with both the main course and the cheese to sweet wine with the pudding. (While sweet wine might be better with cheese in theory, where there is pudding as well it can be too much of a good thing.)

On the whole, if you want to serve red wine, you should avoid strong, pungent cheese – which rules out most traditional blue cheeses, mature Cheddars and very ripe Camemberts. You should also aim for fairly hard cheeses, or at least be aware that the mouth-coating texture of soft cheeses, such as Brie and Camembert, is hard work for red wine. The sort of cheeses, then, that do go with red wine – and even quite fine red wine – are fairly young, hard English cheeses such as Cheddar and Double Gloucester, Cantal (Doux or Entre-Deux), mature Gouda, Manchego, French ewe's milk hard cheeses such as Etorki and Ossau Iraty (but some of them simply labelled *pur brebis*), Parmesan, and Grana Padano.

Blue cheeses almost always go better with sweet wines, whether Sauternes, port (vintage character and tawny when true vintage is out of reach), Recioto della Valpolicella, Bual madeira, or even Hungarian Tokaji Aszú (five putts – *see* page 155 for explanation). Except for some hard goat's milk cheeses, such as Tomme de Chèvre, most goat's cheeses are happier with dry white wine, especially Sauvignon Blanc, although the Cabécou of south west France is always drunk with the local red (Cahors, Marcillac, or whatever). Brie and Camembert won't do favours for any fine wine,

(Above) **White wines – dry and sweet – go better overall with cheeses than do red wines, but that doesn't mean you have to forgo red wine with cheese.**

so stick with whatever you are drinking and hope that wine and cheese will at least accommodate, if not complement, each other.

One final point: I have put this section before Puddings, because that is my own preferred order, but if you eat pudding before cheese you will find it easier to continue drinking the sweet pudding wine with the cheese or move on to something sweet and fortified, such as port, as it is hard to go back to dry wines.

(Below) **Sweet wines need to be at least as sweet as the pudding: Austrian *Beerenauslese* and *Trockenbeerenauslese* could cope with this fruit and cream combination.**

Puddings

Apart from the difficulties of chocolate (*q.v.*), and ice-cream – which really isn't worth trying to match (Asti, Australian Liqueur Muscat, or PX

sherry, if you must) – the one "rule" to observe when matching sweet wines to puddings is to err on the side of sweetness with the wine, otherwise the wine will taste thin and tart. It is easy to be caught out in this way by German *Auslesen* which simply don't have the opulence to stand up to most puddings; *Beerenauslesen* and *Trockenbeerenauslesen* are better, but heavier wines are often easier to match.

Sauternes and its cousins (including Monbazillac, Loupiac, and Ste-Croix-du-Mont) and botrytized wines from Australia and New Zealand, together with Muscat de Beaumes-de-Venise and Austrian *Beerenauslese* and *Trockenbeerenauslese* are very obliging with everything from fruit salads, pies, and tarts to rich, creamy puddings such as crème brûlée, fools, mousses, and custards, to more solid ones such as bread-and-butter pudding, cheesecake, and other cakes.

The best of the sweet Chenin-based Loires (Coteaux du Layon, Bonnezeaux, Vouvray *et al*) are also fairly adaptable, although they don't have the easygoing, luscious opulence of Sauternes-type wines and their more prominent acidity needs to be accommodated. They are particularly good at cutting through the richness of pastry and also go well with fruits such as strawberries, raspberries, apples, peaches, and apricots (and puddings based on them). German *Auslesen* will also go with these fruits if they are not too heavily doused in sugar and cream.

It is also worth bearing in mind Malmsey and Bual madeira, Vin Santo, Moscato di Pantelleria, Spanish Moscatels, and Tokaji Aszú (five or six putts) for cakes and almond biscuits; and, at the other extreme, fresh, bubbly Asti to complement light, frothy mousses or to contrast completely with the richness of Christmas pudding. Australian Liqueur Muscat is another plum pudding possibility, while all sorts of traditional fortified wines, together with local specialities like Vin Santo, Recioto della Valpolicella and Hungarian Tokáji are perfect companions for nuts.

Three flavours that can, if dominant, pose probelms are coffee, rum, and ginger. Fortunately, the versatile Muscat grape is good at handling them, so think in terms of Asti, California Orange Muscat, Muscat de Beaumes-de-Venise, or Australian liqueur Muscats, depending on the weight and richness of the puding.

If you really don't like sweet wines and puddings, you could be kind to summer guests by giving them strawberries over which to pour their red wine (straight from glass or bottle). It's done with the best clarets in Bordeaux.

WAYS TO
STORE YOUR WINE

IF IT'S ANY CONSOLATION, FEW PEOPLE HAVE PURPOSE-BUILT, CAVERNOUS, SUBTERRANEAN CELLARS AND MOST WINE DRINKERS HAVE IMPERFECT STORAGE ARRANGEMENTS, BUT THAT'S NOT TO UNDERESTIMATE THE IMPORTANCE OF PROTECTING WINE FROM DAMAGING CONDITIONS. THERE IS NO GETTING ROUND THE FACT THAT GOOD CONDITIONS – AND BY THAT I DON'T NECESSARILY MEAN ABSOLUTELY PERFECT ONES – ARE ESSENTIAL IF YOU ARE KEEPING WINE FOR ANY LENGTH OF TIME, AND THE MORE SO THE FINER THE WINE AND THE LONGER YOU HOPE TO STORE IT.

Like humans, some wines turn out to be remarkably robust and capable of surviving intact a surprising amount of apparent ill-treatment, but others really are fragile. On the whole, white wines – sweet wines and Champagne above all – are more frail than reds, but some reds which have been given the minimum of stabilization treatment (for example, red burgundies which have not been filtered, in an effort to preserve every scrap of their flavour) are more likely, more quickly, to suffer from adverse conditions.

Grape variety also makes a difference – Cabernet Sauvignon and Syrah wines are generally more resilient than Pinot Noirs – but it is far more sensible to try to minimize the risks than cross your fingers and hope that your wines are some of the more long-suffering ones.

Ideal conditions

Temperature

The public enemies of wine are heat, light, lack of humidity, and constant movement – but the first two are the ones that cause the most problems.

An ideal cellar temperature is 7–13°C (45–55°F), but you can safely store wine within a degree or two of freezing (although obviously it will expand and pop its cork if it actually freezes) or up to 20°C (68°F) – providing you take account of the fact that wine matures much more rapidly at the higher temperatures (and more slowly at lower temperatures) and providing also that you don't allow the temperature to swing from one extreme to another. Constant temperature, or as near to it as possible, is the key; chronic fluctuations are undoubtedly bad for wine.If a steady temperature coincides with otherwise good conditions, you will probably get away with storage at the average household temperature of 21˚C (70˚F), albeit with faster-maturing wines as a result, but I certainly wouldn't recommend it, and it is worth bearing in mind that a few hot summer days will catapult many rooms well into the thirties (80˚F plus). One long hot summer, my London kitchen and I sweltered at 32˚C (90˚F) for days on end and the cupboard-under-the-stairs, once refuge to several wine racks, wasn't much better at 28˚C (82˚F).

Similarly, it is no good priding yourself on maintaining a wine-friendly, cold spare bedroom if it is periodically blasted up to 21˚C (70˚F) and down again with the arrival and departure of guests. Garages and attics also give a false sense of security by seeming cool: in fact few are sufficiently insulated to prevent dramatic temperature variations.

If this all sounds rather limiting, don't be put off. It is often possible to store wine at an acceptable temperature in an ordinary house or flat, so long as you choose your spot carefully. North-facing walls and nooks and crannies are places to investigate, as are defunct fireplaces and under-stairs cupboards (though not mine). And you may be lucky enough to have a well-insulated garage, coal-hole, or loft.

Wherever you choose, keep a resident thermometer under close surveillance and keep an eye out for traces of wine seeping from the cork and out from under the capsule. This is likely to be a sign that the wine has got too hot (and that it has expanded as its temperature has risen).

Light

Sunlight and ultra-violet light are as bad for wine as excessive heat, but are problems usually much easier to overcome. Most wines are partially protected by coloured glass bottles (occasionally coloured cellophane), but you can do your bit by covering wines exposed to light with something such as a blanket. If your storehouse is under the stairs, you won't need to worry.

(Left) **Cool, dark, dank, dungeon-like underground cellars are the perfect place to store wine. Some of the miles of cellars tunnelled into the hills in the Tokáji region have been used since the thirteenth century.**

Humidity

The role of humidity is slightly more controversial, although it is obviously significant that most producers try to keep a relatively high level of humidity in their cellars (in Europe they specialize in quite extraordinarily dank, mouldy, cold ones). Very low humidity appears to cause oxidation (by

(Below) **It does nothing for labels, of course, but wine producers are always immensely proud of their mould-encrusted bottles: it shows that their cellars are nicely humid.**

(Left) **Coloured glass, or coloured cellophane, gives wine inside the bottle useful protection against potentially damaging light.**

allowing water in the wine to evaporate through the cork – because of lower vapour pressure outside the bottle – leaving space for air to move in). That said, most of the notable problems have been with rarefied old wines in the excessively dry atmosphere produced by air-conditioning in the USA. Ideally, relative humidity should be at least fifty-five per cent and ideally seventy to seventy-five. Above that the only real problem usually is that you begin to lose labels – making choosing a bottle for supper something of a lucky dip ever after.

Movement

Wine does not take well to constant movement and vibration, so, if your wine is shaken all day long by high-speed trains or juggernauts outside the door, I would advise you to find somewhere else to mature it. But I have to add the rider that, traditionally, many London wine merchants had their cellars under railway arches – and some still do – apparently with no ill-effect. Normal household movement (even teenagers thundering up and down the stairs all day and night) is unlikely to damage your wine, whatever it does to your nerves. Car journeys are not

(Right) **These modern versions of the traditional cellar "bins" are most useful for people who buy bottles by the dozen or half-dozen.**

Wines and grapes mentioned in this chapter are described in more detail in the final part of the book (pages 94–157) and in "The Importance of Grapes" (pages 50–59).

walls lined with a honeycomb of concrete wine bins and a spiral staircase at its centre, is sunk into the ground to a depth of between two and three metres (6.56 to 9.84 feet), (you choose the size). This can be a good option, but, again, it is an expensive one. (When I had both the cabinet and Spiral Cellar-types, I decided that I would never again buy a house without a traditional underground cellar; so that's what I now have.)

kind to wine. So long as they are not too hot and too long (beware drives from the south of France and Spain), the wine should recover, but it is only fair to give it time – a few days – to do so. And certainly, if there is sediment in it, it will really need it.

Keep it horizontal

Except for Champagne and similarly stoppered sparkling wines, which can be stored upright, wine should be stored on its side to keep the liquid in contact with the cork and so stop the cork drying out and letting air in. The simplest way of storing wine horizontally is in common-or-garden wine racks. Several firms make these to measure, should you wish to fit out a curiously shaped cranny. Insulated pigeon-hole-type systems (made from polystyrene or something more substantial) can be good, but take up more room.

Buying a cellar

If you want to splash out, you can actually buy a cellar. Temperature- and humidity-controlled cabinets, rather like fridges, come in various sizes, holding from about fifty to 500 bottles. They are effective, but space-consuming and expensive. The Spiral Cellar is an ingenious French creation in which a two-metre diameter cylindrical cellar, its

(Above) **The simple wood and metal rack is as functional as it ever was – and nowadays you can have them made to measure.**

(Above right) **Purpose-designed temperature- and humidity-controlled wine cabinets are an efficient, if expensive, option.**

Renting cellar space

If you are buying wine by the case for laying down and you don't have a cellar, the best place to buy it is from a reputable wine merchant who has proper facilities to store it for you. It's costly, but it will be money well spent. Alternatively there are self-storage systems in some countries (based on a USA practice), where you rent a vault and come and go with your wine as you please during the day, but you need to ensure proper temperature-control.

(Left) **The most ambitious solution to a cellarless house is to install an underground Spiral Cellar, an ingenious French invention.**

THE HARDEST QUESTION:
WHEN TO DRINK

THE HARDEST QUESTION TO ANSWER, BUT ONE OF THE MOST FREQUENTLY ASKED IS "WHEN WILL THIS WINE BE READY TO DRINK?". IT IS DIFFICULT FOR THE MOST STRAIGHTFORWARD OF REASONS: THERE IS NO SINGLE CORRECT ANSWER FOR ANY INDIVIDUAL WINE. CAREFULLY SEALED IN ITS BOTTLE, WINE CONTINUES TO CHANGE — AND ALTHOUGH IT FOLLOWS A CERTAIN SCIENTIFIC PATH, NO ONE HAS BEEN ABLE TO DEVISE A FORMULA THAT PREDICTS PRECISELY THE RATE AND DEGREE OF PROGRESS OF ANY GIVEN WINE ALONG THE PATH. I HAVE TO SAY THIS PLEASES ME IMMENSELY, FOR THIS ASPECT OF THE MYSTIQUE OF WINE IS SURELY ONE THAT GIVES A GREAT DEAL OF THE THRILL AND ENJOYMENT.

That mystery still remains is not to suggest we are completely in the dark about what happens behind closed bottles. With past experience of a particular region, vintage, or château, or knowledge of the grape variety (or blend), climate, and winemaking techniques, it is possible to estimate broadly how the wine will evolve. We know that the most obviously fruity aromas and flavours are gradually replaced by softer, more complex ones (*see* Why and how to taste, page 15) and we know that eventually wine begins to "dry out" – the fruit fades altogether leaving a rather acerbic, dry, or flat wine. We even know that these changes are the result of the small amount of undissolved oxygen in all young wine reacting with the tannins, anthocyanins (pigments), acids, and alcohol in the processes of polymerization (the one which results finally in sediment) and esterification (which gives the more

complex aromas). But that's by the by: being familiar with the scientific nitty-gritty of ageing wine is not a direct aid to getting more enjoyment from it and, to date, it has not yielded a magic formula to tell us when a wine is at its peak.

So how do you know when a wine is ready to drink? Perhaps the first point to derive comfort from is that talking about a wine's peak is misleading. It implies that the wine matures to a single perfect peak and then immediately begins to go downhill – miss the day and you've missed the wine at its party best. Fortunately, this just isn't the case. Between the improving and the declining phases there is not a peak but a plateau, during which the wine will continue to change (even if almost imperceptibly), but will be neither improving nor deteriorating. This is the time to drink your wine. But of course you still need to know when the plateau is likely to be reached and how long it will last.

Assuming that storage conditions are favourable (*see* Ways to store your wine, pages 40–43), and bearing in mind that some types of wine age longer than others (*see* below), it is a fair, if very broad, generalization that the finer the wine the longer it will take to reach its plateau, the longer it will stay there and the slower its eventual descent will be. Conversely, the lesser the wine, the shorter each phase will be in a consequently shorter lifespan. Put another way, modest wines – that is modestly priced wines, no matter how grand sounding the château name and illustration on the label and no matter where you bought them – seldom improve with keeping. Some may improve encouragingly in the short term, losing the angles and edges of youth, but they simply won't have the degree of concentration and the right balance of tannins, acids, and so on to allow them to evolve and gain with age. And the fact is that the vast majority of wines today are made to be drunk as soon as they are released. They are not intended to age. Please do remember that.

Even fine wines are being made with earlier consumption in mind – which means they have riper fruit, softer tannins, and lower acidity from inception. The finest clarets and Barolos now have much more velvety tannins than in the past and should therefore reach their peak – or rather their plateau of maturity – sooner. Most classed growth clarets of even the top vintages will probably be at the start of the plateau after ten years, whereas in top vintages of the 1970s and before, they would have needed fifteen or more years. Whether the wines will last as long is arguable. The producers say they will (because the rise is shorter but the plateau longer) but we still need a few more years before we can be sure – and by then, tantalizingly, we shall know which New World areas are consistently capable of producing wines of great ageing potential.

So far, despite the huge expansion of the wine world, the wines suitable for laying down have not changed dramatically. They are still predominantly red and the same classic European styles – red Bordeaux and Sauternes, northern Rhônes, red and white burgundy, sweet Loires such as Quarts de Chaume, Barolo and Barbaresco, the best Tuscan reds, vintage port, German Rieslings (from *Spätlese* to *Trockenbeerenauslese*), Ribera del Duero and Priorato, and Hungarian Tokáji. From the New World, the wines to consider include top Australian Shiraz-based wines (especially old-vine Shiraz), traditional Hunter Valley Semillon,

Eden and Clare Valley Riesling, and the top California Cabernet Sauvignon and Cabernet blends, especially from Napa Valley.

As far as grape varieties are concerned, among the longest-lived reds are Cabernet Sauvignon, Syrah, Mourvèdre, and Nebbiolo; the longest-lived whites are Riesling and Chenin Blanc. Bear in mind also that bottle size makes a difference: the larger the bottle, the slower the maturation. Many feel that the magnum is the perfect size for ageing wine.

Vintage charts –
guides not gospels

Whatever type of wine you choose, there is one cardinal rule if you are laying it down: you must choose a good vintage (unless you know that a particular property's wine was unusually successful). "Off" years may be cheaper – indeed, they certainly should be – but they are "off" because they lack one or both of the essentials for graceful development: concentration and balance. Of course there will always be exceptions (surprisingly impressive wines from slated years, as well as disappointing wines from universally highly rated ones), but, unless you know for sure, it is not worth taking the risk.

Use the vintage charts in the regional chapters of this book and elsewhere to build up a picture of different vintages (always remembering that the charts are based on leading wines in their class, not modest names). Part of the fun of wine is that opinions vary among the "experts" – because tastes vary. Different nations, particularly Britain, France, and America, have a habit of forming decidedly different opinions of vintages, especially when it comes to saying which is the superior of two or three good to great years. Even within nations there are party lines. Red Bordeaux drinkers in Britain tend to divide into those who like the power and fruit of the more voluptuous, riper claret vintages and those who favour the leaner, more austere years on the grounds that they are more elegant and will ultimately prove to be better balanced. They draw up their vintage charts accordingly. There may be a consensus in the end, but while the wines are still some way from maturity the battle lines are basically drawn stylistically. Experts also change their opinions and charts when wines evolve differently from the way they anticipated: better that than not admitting that they got it wrong.

Personal taste also has an influence on deciding when a wine is at its best. The British generally drink vintages long after French and American wine drinkers have progressed on to

Wines and grapes mentioned in this chapter are described in more detail in the final part of the book (pages 94–157) and in "The Importance of Grapes" (pages 50–59).

more recent ones. Personally I am no great fan of wines that seem to me to be on the edge of decay – just beginning to fade and tire, although undoubtedly complex. I hear the accusations of vinous infanticide, but I would rather drink a wine when it is slightly too young than too old – when it still has plenty of fruit, but probably needs the tannin or acid to soften further. There is no wrong or right about it. It's a matter of taste – and working out your own preference is the fun of the chase.

Nil desperandum –
the low-down on what to lay down

It may seem banal to reduce it all down to price, but if in doubt it can be a useful indicator. The cheapest wines, as we've seen already, are not made to improve: whites often need drinking within a year of the vintage and reds within two years (don't forget that the southern hemisphere harvest takes place early in the year, making the wines roughly six months older than European and California wines of the same vintage). Another useful pointer is that any wine with a synthetic ("plastic") cork is intended to be drunk within a year. (Screw caps, in contrast, are now being used in some wine regions for wines that can be aged – Clare Valley Riesling, for example.)

Even slightly more expensive wines have seldom been made to mature, although, as long as they have not been kept in wood too long before bottling, they will tend to last longer – keeping their youthful attractiveness and probably softening and filling out slightly, but developing little in the way of complexity. Among whites at this level, Chardonnays and German Rieslings are a better bet for keeping than Sauvignon Blanc and Viognier, and medium- to full-bodied reds from the fairly tannic grape varieties Cabernet Sauvignon and Syrah may gently improve over a period of three to five years. (Note that most inexpensive red Bordeaux is made largely from Merlot which, except in very rare instances, does not have Cabernet's stamina and potential longevity.)

Once you get into higher price brackets, you should be able to find wines worth saving for several years – five, ten, or even more – from styles such as late-harvest Alsace, top white Graves, Rhônes, classed growth clarets, New World Cabernets and Shiraz, and, with great care, burgundy. But don't forget the good vintage rule and only choose producers or properties with a proven track record.

Nil desperandum –
in restaurants

■ *Don't go for the house wine unless you know that it is good. Sadly, most aren't.*

■ *Anything very familiar and easy-to-pronounce – Sancerre, Chablis, Cloudy Bay – will be less good value than something from an obscure region or grape variety that is torture to pronounce.*

■ *If you are trying to choose one wine for a variety of dishes (fish, meat, vegetarian), consider Pinot Noir, a Beaujolais* cru *(such as Brouilly) or a red Loire such as Saumur-Champigny.*

■ *Australian Chardonnay may be reliable, but Australian dry Riesling is liable to be better value and is more versatile with food. It also ages well, unlike most Australian Chardonnay and other whites, so you needn't worry if it is a few years old. Australian Verdelhos are few and far between, but are well worth trying.*

■ *With all other New World whites, especially Sauvignon Blanc, choose the youngest available vintage.*

■ *Alsace whites are often good value in restaurants, especially Pinot Blanc which is an adaptable wine with starters, salads, and fish.*

■ *Avoid the cheap, common Italian wines (Frascati, Soave, Valpolicella* et al*), but do take a chance with unknowns from Italy, both red and white and*

The life spans of four top white wines

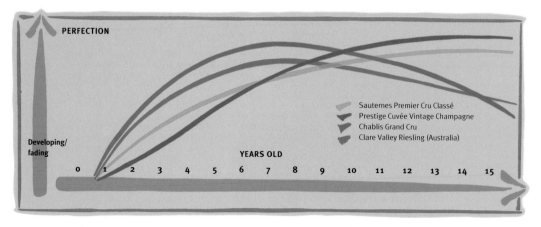

PERFECTION

Developing/ fading

YEARS OLD

0 1 2 3 4 5 6 7 8 9 10 11 12 13 14 15

Sauternes Premier Cru Classé
Prestige Cuvée Vintage Champagne
Chablis Grand Cru
Clare Valley Riesling (Australia)

(Left) **Different wines have different life spans. Most whites evolve more quickly and last less long than reds, but the top sweet wines (like Château d'Yquem) and Vintage Champagnes (eg. Roederer Cristal) are long-lived. New World whites usually have a shorter life span, but some of Australia's Rieslings, especially from the Clare and Eden Valleys are made for the long-haul.**

especially from the south (as long as any white is of a recent vintage).

■ *Except on their home territory, California wines are usually expensive compared to the same quality from the southern hemisphere, but the best are very good – and full-bodied red Zinfandel is a uniquely Californian style.*

■ *Chilean and Argentine reds can be a good inexpensive choice in a restaurant. Choose Argentine Malbec and Chilean Carmenère to make a change from Merlot and Cabernet Sauvignon.*

■ *Bordeaux is seldom a good buy in a restaurant, with high mark-ups and too many of the less good vintages.*

■ *Burgundy also tends to be very expensive, but relative bargains (some red, some white) can be found among the less known or less fashionable villages such as St-Aubin and St-Romain, Rully, Mercurey, and Givry and, increasingly, among domaine-bottled white Mâcons.*

■ *Crozes-Hermitage and St-Joseph can be a wallet-friendly alternative to expensive Hermitage and Côte-Rôtie. From the southern Rhône, look for red Côtes du Rhône from specified villages, such as Cairanne, Séguret, and Valréas. Lirac, Vacqueyras, and Gigondas are good alternatives to Châteauneuf-du-Pape.*

■ *Look out for the new breed of serious, single-estate wines from Languedoc-Roussillon (especially from sub-appellations such as Minervois-La Livinière and Coteaux du Languedoc Pic St-Loup).*

Alcohol content

The alcohol content of wine is measured as a percentage of its volume and stated on all labels. Table or light wines (as opposed to heavy or fortified wines such as port and sherry) range from 5.5 per cent (fizzy Italian Moscatos) to 15.5 per cent (Recioto della Valpolicella), with a very rough average for quality wines of 12.5 per cent – a figure that has been rising with the trends to fuller, riper wine and to red wines.

Generally, warmer climates produce higher alcohol, but things get complicated by cooler regions often being allowed to chaptalize (increase alcohol by adding sugar at fermentation). Equally, in warmer climates, if you pick the grapes less ripe (perhaps to retain acidity), they will contain less sugar to turn into alcohol and so make lighter, less alcoholic wines. In addition, heavy yields reduce sugar concentration.

■ *White wines tend to be a little lower in alcohol than reds, but Chardonnay is almost always at least twelve per cent and often 13.5 per cent or more.*

■ *Champagne and burgundy, despite their cool climate origins, are usually thirteen per cent (because they are chaptalized), as is, to most drinkers' surprise, Beaujolais – for the same reason. Red Bordeaux (usually chaptalized) is mostly 12.5 per cent. Sauternes in a good year is often fourteen (and of course very sweet too).*

■ *Although a few Australian Rieslings, Hunter Semillons and cheap wines don't reach twelve per cent, most Australian wines are now thirteen to 13.5 per cent and fourteen is not uncommon. The same applies in California, South America, and South Africa. Even in New Zealand, with its cooler climate, most Sauvignons and Chardonnays hit thirteen or 13.5 per cent.*

■ *Sherry ranges from about fifteen to eighteen per cent – the lower figure for finos and manzanillas, the higher one for darker, heavier styles such as oloroso. Most port is nineteen to twenty per cent. Vins doux naturels, such as Muscat de Beaumes de Venise, are usually fifteen to sixteen per cent.*

■ *To keep your alcohol intake low, most traditional German wines are at the low end of the spectrum (eight to nine per cent, sometimes less), but the new drier styles (Trocken and Halbtrocken) are ten to twelve per cent.*

The life spans of four top red wines

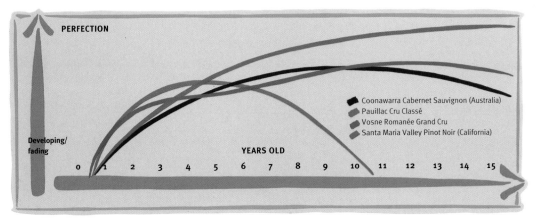

(Left) **Generally, the finer the wine, the longer it takes to reach its peak (or plateau) of perfection, and the more gradual its decline. Overall, Old World wines last longer than New World wines and Cabernet Sauvignon-based wines live longer than Pinot Noirs. The graph showing the projected evolution of four top red wines in a good vintage bears this out.**

THE MAKING OF
FIRST-CLASS
WINE

2

Wine is simply the fermented juice of the grape, but there are thousands of different varieties of wine grape, each one with its own characteristics. A mere handful are responsible for the main classic wine styles, but when transported to other soils and climates, or when subjected to different winemaking traditions and techniques, they may turn out quite different wines – or they may sometimes produce textbook copies.

THE IMPORTANCE OF
GRAPES

ALTHOUGH WINE RARELY SMELLS AND TASTES OF GRAPES, THE VARIETY OF GRAPE, OR GRAPES, IN ANY WINE IS THE PRINCIPAL INFLUENCE ON ITS STYLE AND CHARACTER. SOIL, CLIMATE, AND HUMAN INTERVENTION PLAY THEIR PARTS, BUT GRAPES ARE THE ESSENTIAL INGREDIENT AND PRIME SOURCE OF FLAVOUR. THERE ARE THOUSANDS OF VARIETIES OF *VITIS VINIFERA* (THE SPECIES OF THE VINE FAMILY ALMOST ENTIRELY RESPONSIBLE FOR WINE GRAPES), BUT MANY ARE VERY SIMILAR AND MANY OTHERS ARE OF NO SIGNIFICANCE, EITHER BECAUSE THE WINE THEY PRODUCE IS POOR OR VERY DULL, OR BECAUSE THEY ARE SO TEMPERAMENTAL THAT FEW GROWERS BOTHER WITH THEM.

Classic white grapes

Chardonnay

Flavours: apple, pear, citrus fruits, melon, pineapple, peach, butter, wax, honey, toffee, butterscotch, vanilla, mixed spice, wet wool (burgundy), minerals, and flint (Chablis).

The world's most famous white grape variety and its most popular white, Chardonnay is grown in every wine-producing country from France to Australia, India to Peru. Growers like it because it is easy to cultivate – vigorous, resistant, and generously productive in most climates and soils (which is why it has appeared in some outlandish-seeming places). Winemakers like it because it is so malleable: it can be fashioned in a whole range of styles, and in Burgundy and Champagne it has long since shown that it is capable of producing some of the world's greatest wines and most long-lived of whites. Drinkers like it, because, with few exceptions, it gives

immediate satisfaction. Full, supple, buttery, and fruity, with or without the seductive vanilla-oak flavours of oak barrels, it has no hard edges or aggressive acidity. Whether you are the grower, winemaker, or consumer, you seldom have to work at Chardonnay. It even emerges as a star in regions so cool that it barely ripens. In Champagne, above all, but also in chilly places such as Tasmania, Marlborough, and Sussex, it produces the sort of thin, high-acid wines that are perfect for making top-quality sparkling wines.

(Left) **Everyone likes Chardonnay: growers because it is easy to cultivate and a generous cropper; winemakers because it can be moulded to order in the winery; and consumers because of its instantly appealing, no-hard-edges style.**

Sauvignon Blanc

Sauvignon is the grape variety wine drinkers often turn to when they want a change from the full-bodied and often oaky white wines made from varieties such as Chardonnay and Viognier. Sauvignon is crisper and firmer with refreshing acidity and more verdant flavours – gooseberries, cut grass, currant leaves, and elderflowers. It rarely has any discernible oak, simply because it doesn't take well to oak, unless it is blended with Sémillon, as in the classic white Graves blend of Bordeaux. Many countries are trying their hand with Sauvignon, but it is a much less adaptable variety than Chardonnay and the best manifestations still come from the vineyards of the upper Loire (Sancerre and Pouilly Fumé) and the Marlborough region of New Zealand.

Flavours: freshly cut grass, gooseberries, flowering currant leaves, cat's pee (not necessarily a fault), tinned asparagus or green beans (generally undesirable), and occasionally stony or flinty (upper Loire).

Sémillon

Sémillon is the mainstay of white Bordeaux, both dry (especially Graves) and sweet (Sauternes), and it also scales the heights as an unusual dry white in Australia's Hunter Valley (where Semillon loses its "é"). In Bordeaux it is appreciated for its round, lanoliney quality, and to a lesser extent, in the young dry wines only, for herbaceous flavours (similar to those of the Sauvignon Blanc with which it is paired). In the Hunter Valley it is renowned as a long-lived dry white that, although unoaked, becomes increasingly honeyed and toasty with age. Elsewhere, it produces rich, lemony, often oak-aged whites in the Barossa Valley of Australia and more intensely fruity, fresh wines in Western Australia, Washington State in the USA, and New Zealand.

Flavours: grass, lemon, lanolin, honey, and toast.

Riesling

The true Riesling of German origin (aka Johannis-berg, White, Rhine, or Renano Riesling) is one of the world's great grapes. In common with Sauvignon Blanc it has both a strong personality – one that is better off without any oak influence – and high acidity, but it is far more adaptable than Sauvignon. It thrives in the cool climates of Europe (Germany and Alsace) and equally in the much warmer climes of Australia, and is susceptible to noble rot (the fungus which attacks certain ripe grapes and dehydrates them so that they give wines of immense richness and sweetness). The result is a spectrum of styles that ranges from dry to intensely sweet and that doesn't need a great weight of alcohol – with as little as 6.5 per cent in Germany (although levels often reach thirteen per cent in Alsace and Australia). In addition, like fine Chardonnay, Riesling has the potential to age for many years. Wherever it is grown, young or old, and whether sweet or dry, Riesling should have a vivid fruitiness and lively balancing acidity. Beware Welschriesling, Riesling Italico, and Rizling: they are not the real thing.

(Left) **Riesling thrives in cool climates such as Germany's and warm ones such as Australia's, giving a spectrum of wines from light and very sweet to bone dry and quite alcoholic.**

Flavours: crunchy green apples, spiced baked apples, quince, orange, lime (Australia), passion-fruit (Australia), honey (sweet wines), mineral notes (especially Mosel), petrol, and toast (mature wines).

Chenin Blanc

A grape of very high acidity and, potentially, great longevity, but also a grape of nastier than average wines when there is insufficient sun: unripe Chenin has a cheesy and – sorry – vomit-like flavour. But, in the sort of favourable conditions that don't happen every year in the middle Loire (Coteaux du Layon, Vouvray *et al*), there are glorious honeyed sweet wines with bracing but harmonious acidity. In lesser years, they are lighter, less concentrated, and more likely to be medium-dry or dry, and their high acid is nearly always useful for the dry sparkling wines of Saumur, Vouvray, and Montlouis. In the New World, Chenin Blanc is mainly used for simple, soft, crisp, fruity wines, but in South Africa in particular, a few producers are making serious, oak-fermented Chenin.

Flavours: apples, apricots, nuts, honey, and marzipan.

Classic red grapes

Cabernet Sauvignon

In terms of status and popularity, Cabernet Sauvignon can still be regarded as Chardonnay's red wine counterpart, although it is increasingly challenged by Syrah/Shiraz. Cabernet Sauvignon is a deep-coloured, thick-skinned grape that produces dark, flavoursome wine, particularly noted for its blackcurrant and, in Bordeaux, cedary, cigar box, or lead pencils character. The wines have the potential (largely because of the tannins which come from the skins) to age a long time and they gain in stature if aged in oak. In fact, the fashion among many of the world's most ambitious producers, including some of those in Bordeaux, is to transfer their Cabernet wines to new oak barrels part-way through the fermentation process in an effort to produce wines with softer, richer textures. From the grower's point of view the variety is nearly as accommodating of its environment as Chardonnay, although, if the climate is too warm, the wines will have jammy flavours and will lack structure, and, if denied sufficient sun, will be thin, stalky, and herbaceous. Cabernet Sauvignon is now so well travelled and entrenched that the only significant wine-producing country that doesn't cultivate it on a commercial scale is Germany (because it is too cold), but Cabernet's heartland is, of course, Bordeaux – claret country. Here it is always part of a blend, a tradition that grew up because the climate is too unreliable for growers to be able to rely on just this one variety.

(Left) **Whether producing some of the greatest wines in the world or simple, fruity, purple *vin de pays*, the wines of the well-travelled Cabernet Sauvignon vine are among the most easily recognisable reds.**

Flavours: blackcurrant, cedar, cigar boxes, lead pencils, green pepper, mint, dark chocolate, tobacco, and olives.

Merlot

Merlot is similar to Cabernet Sauvignon, which it partners in red Bordeaux, but is less incisively blackcurranty, less tannic, and earlier-maturing. Its wines taste softer, plumper, and seemingly sweeter. It is very widely planted around the world and has a large following as an inexpensive varietal wine (unblended with other varieties) among people who like its easy style. Chile has been particularly successful, although much of its so-called Merlot is now known to be Carmenère (*see* page 58). There are some cult Merlots in California, but, other than those, the most sought-after Merlot-dominated wines are the clarets of the Pomerol and St-Emilion regions in Bordeaux: the names Pétrus and Le Pin should ring bells.

Flavours: often similar to Cabernet Sauvignon, but sometimes more plums and roses than blackcurrants, more spice and rich fruit-cake, less mint and lead pencils.

Pinot Noir

Chardonnay's red wine compatriot in Burgundy is as ill at ease in the world outside as Chardonnay is comfortable. Pinot Noir is both extremely pernickety about its climate and a much less generous producer than Chardonnay. In Burgundy, achieving sufficient ripeness is always the critical factor (or one of them). It is a variety of relatively low tannin and acidity, medium rather than deep colour, and a medium rather than long life span: a shortage of warmth simply yields pale, anaemic, thin wines, with none of the heady red-fruits character, the silky textures, the gamey complexity of great red burgundy. In the New World's mostly warmer climates, producers suffer the opposite problem: overripe grapes giving cooked, coarse, jammy flavours. But things are changing and some extremely good Pinot Noirs are now being made in cooler spots, particularly in California, Oregon, and New Zealand and quality is being helped along everywhere by the use of better clones and a greater variety of them (variety gives complexity).

(Left) In contrast to the easily pleased Cabernet Sauvignon, Pinot Noir is sensitive to climate and to the way it is handled in the winery.

Flavours: raspberries, strawberries, cherries, cranberries, violets, roses, game, incense, and truffles.

Syrah

Whether it is called Syrah or Shiraz, this is the hot new variety of the twenty-first century. Classic Syrah from France's Rhône Valley, epitomized by Hermitage, and classic Shiraz from Australia are dark, full-bodied, powerful wines with great ageing potential. It is a variety that flourishes in warmer climates than Pinot Noir, but is altogether more adaptable. In cooler conditions, it simply produces slightly lighter, more peppery wines with less ripe berry fruit and less meaty or chocolaty richness. From the drinker's point of view, one of the interesting things is that, despite the tannin and staying power, the wines often reach a drinkably mature stage quite soon (Hermitage excepted). Another is that, as Australia has demonstrated, Shiraz can be used to make very good, full-bodied red sparkling wines. Other regions and countries that have been planting a lot of Syrah/Shiraz include California, Washington State, South Africa, Chile, and Argentina.

Flavours: blackberries, blackcurrants, raspberries, freshly ground pepper, smoke, spice, leather, game, and tar.

Important white grapes

Gewurztraminer

The highly aromatic Gewurztraminer – at its best in Alsace, where it may be dry or sweet, and in the German Pfalz region – is the most distinctive-smelling of all wine grapes. The wine has an exotic, spicy perfume with a taste of lychees and tends to be full-bodied, sometimes slightly oily-textured, quite alcoholic, and with lowish acidity. It's worth looking out for New World examples especially from New Zealand, Chile, and Oregon.

Flavours: lychees, spice (often ginger and cinnamon), Nivea cream, Turkish Delight, and roses.

Pinot Gris / Grigio

Pinot Gris has fewer faces than the extended Muscat family, but it is a versatile grape. In Alsace, it can be dry, medium sweet (*Vendange Tardive*), or very sweet (*Sélection de Grains Nobles*), but always with a rich, spicy, honeyed perfume. In Italy, as Pinot Grigio, it is often little more than a crisp, light, fairly neutral, dry white. As Ruländer, in Germany, it falls between the two, with some of the honey and perfume of Alsace, but less richness and intensity. Pinot Gris is also attracting attention in the New World, with Oregon, Canada, New Zealand, and more recently Australia all bringing out the Alsace characteristics of the grape, although often with a little more fruit and a little less nuttiness.

Flavours: honey, nougat, nuts, apple, pear, apricot, spring blossom, spice, and musk.

Important red grapes

Grenache / Garnacha

This productive, high-alcohol grape is the most planted red, extensively grown in Spain (Garnacha), the South of France, the Central Valley of California, Australia, and, as Cannonau, in Sardinia. Much is used for fairly cheap wines – *rosado* (rosé) in Spain, in blends in Languedoc-Roussillon, in Côtes du Rhône, and California jug wines – but, if its yields are kept in check, as they are naturally when the vines are old, it can produce concentrated wines with ageing potential and the hallmark flavours of raspberries and freshly ground pepper. Among the best are Priorat from Spain, Châteauneuf-du-Pape, and Gigondas (in both of which it is the main constituent), and old-vine Grenache from Australia.

Viognier

Viognier used to be one of the great rarities. Its claim to fame was Condrieu, the head-spinningly perfumed, opulent, dry wine from a tiny patch of the northern Rhône. Condrieu is still rare, but Viognier is less so. Growers in the southern Rhône, in Languedoc, California, and Australia have been planting this variety and learning to manage it in the winery as well as in the vineyard. Some examples, especially inexpensive ones from Languedoc, manage little more than a confected peach flavour, but the best from California and Australia are exotically scented, powerful wines.

Flavours: jasmine, honeysuckle or freesia, apricots, peaches, musk, and ginger.

Muscat / Moscatel

If a wine smells of grapes, it is almost certain to be made from one of the Muscat family. It may be dry, as in Alsace; light-bodied, sweet, and fizzy as in Asti, Moscato d'Asti, and Clairette de Die; very sweet as in Moscatel de Valencia (Spain); or very sweet and fortified, as in the heavy, super-sweet, amber-brown Australian Liqueur Muscats ("stickies"), and the *Vins Doux Naturels* of the Rhône and South of France (among them Muscat de Beaumes-de-Venise, Muscat de Rivesaltes, Muscat de Frontignan, and Muscat de Lunel).

Flavours: grapes, oranges, roses (Alsace), bergamot (Alsace), raisins and maramalade (fortified wines), barley sugar, and demerara sugar.

(Left) **The peppery, alcoholic Grenache grape thrives in warm climates and a variety of – sometimes very inhospitable-looking – soils.**

Flavours: raspberry, freshly ground pepper, herbs (in France), and linseed oil (Châteauneuf-du-Pape).

Nebbiolo

The small, thick-skinned Nebbiolo grape is famous for just two wines, Barolo and Barbaresco from Piedmont. It is grown elsewhere – a little in neighbouring Lombardy and in California, Mexico, Chile, and Australia, but so far it hasn't shown any inclination to reproduce the quality and character of its Piedmont wines. Typically, these are high in tannin and acid and austerely dry when young, but most producers aim for a style that is more approachable – one which shows off the tantalizing perfumed fruit and savoury depths earlier. The trick is to achieve this, while retaining Nebbiolo's unique flavours and its ageing potential.

Flavours: liquorice, roses, damsons, prunes, truffles, tar, violets, and chocolate.

Sangiovese

Sangiovese dominates central Italy, but aspires to greatness only really in Tuscany, most notably in Chianti, Brunello di Montalcino, and Vino Nobile di Montepulciano. Even in Tuscany, it can be light and astringent if over-cropped and badly made and there are wines that fit that description, but there have been huge improvements in overall quality in recent years, especially in Chianti. A lot of vineyards have simply been replanted with better quality clones and with the vines planted closer together. This may not sound very significant, but it has had a dramatic effect on the quality and flavour concentration of the grapes. Sangiovese has a natural austerity born of high acid and tannin, but when these are allied to proper ripeness and concentration, you get black cherry and spiced-plum fruit, edged with herbs and, with age, a gamey mellowness. The wines of Morellino di Scansano (southwest Tuscany) tend to be suppler, but if you want softer, rounder, less distinctive Sangiovese, head for California, Australia, or Argentina.

Flavours: black cherry, spiced plum, tobacco-leaf, and herbs.

Tempranillo

Tempranillo is grown throughout Spain under numerous pseudonyms, but is best known as the mainstay of Rioja and, under the name Tinto Fino, of Ribera del Duero. In the past, much of the taste associated with it was the spicy, vanilla, and buttered-toffee flavour of the oak barrels it had been matured in. The trend in recent years has been to reduce yields to give more flavour to the grapes and hence the wines. The young wines (Joven, rather than oak-aged Crianza or Reserva) tend to be soft and juicy with strawberry and mulberry fruit. The oak-matured wines are fuller and firmer with the fruit supported (but not overwhelmed) by oak flavours. Under various names, including Tinta Roriz in port and the Douro Valley's table wines, Tempranillo is an important grape in Portugal. It is being planted with serious intent in Australia and California and is used to produce simple everyday reds in Argentina.

Flavours: mulberry, strawberry, tobacco, and the spice, vanilla, and coffee flavours that come from oak-ageing.

Zinfandel/Primitivo

While Zinfandel is always regarded as California's very own grape, DNA fingerprinting has now proved beyond doubt that it is the same variety as the Primitivo of southern Italy and an old Croatian variety called Crljenak. The red wines made from Zinfandel and Primitivo don't taste the same, because they are different clones (of the original Crljenak) grown in different places, but they share key characteristics – high alcohol and heady sweet, ripe, spicy fruit. In California, this can veer towards porty, bramble-jelly flavours, while in Primitivo it may be a bit more savoury and earthy. Pale pink Blush or White Zinfandel is an exclusively American style. As for Crljenak Kastelanski, the cutting taken from Croatia to California for DNA testing in late 2001 came from a forty-year-old vineyard with just nine vines of Crljenak; so, until more vines are found or propagated, we shan't know how wine made from Crljenak differs from in flavour and constitution from that made from Zinfandel in California and Primitivo in Italy.

Flavours: raspberries, blackberries, bramble jelly, black pepper, and spice in Zinfandel; plum, black cherry, spice in Primitivo.

Other white grapes often seen

Albariño

The high-fashion Albariño has given Spain a white wine to shout about. It is grown mainly in Rías Baixas in the northwest and is appetizingly aromatic with full, peachy fruit – a bit like Viognier, except that it has high, steely acidity. Over the border, it appears as Alvarinho in the lighter, greener-tasting Portuguese Vinho Verde.

Aligoté

Burgundy's other white grape and the original wine for Kir, but very much second fiddle to Chardonnay. Bourgogne Aligoté is a simpler wine with higher acidity and a crème fraîche flavour. The best, with its own appellation, is from Bouzeron. Also widespread in Eastern Europe and used extensively for workaday whites.

Bacchus

An aromatic German crossing that is coming into its own in England as a dry, herby white. Britain's answer to Sancerre?

Chasselas

Widely planted variety that produces modest, lightweight whites and table grapes, except in Switzerland where, under various names, including Fendant and Perlant, the wines have more character – some floral, some honeyed, some mineral, depending on the soil.

Colombard

Not a variety of any great distinction, but widely grown to make fresh, fruity whites in southwest France, California's Central Valley, South Africa, and Australia. Vin de Pays des Côtes de Gascogne has been a particular success, providing an outlet for the grapes no longer needed for Armagnac.

Furmint

Top quality, lime-scented, spicy Hungarian grape, famous as the principal component of Hungary's sweet Tokaji wines, but also used for tangy, flavoursome dry whites.

Grüner Veltliner

Austria's most widely planted grape variety is also grown in the Czech Republic and Hungary, but nowhere else. In Austria, it produces everything from simple, everyday dry whites to more serious wines capable of ageing like Riesling. It has good acidity and sometimes mineral notes (like Riesling), but also a distinctive white pepper flavour with notes of white peach, dill, and sometimes smoke.

Irsai Oliver

A useful East European crossing which produces fresh, young light- to medium-bodied dry wines with a distinctive, grapey, Muscat-like aroma. Hungary and Slovakia (where is is spelt Irsay) are the main sources.

Malvasia

Except in sweet Malmsey madeira, it is hard to say what Malvasia tastes like because it comes in so many forms, especially in Italy, where there is a black (red) variant, as well as sweet and fortified wines. It is also an element of many blends: it is an improving agent in Frascati, for example, and in Spain it crops up in traditional, oaky white Rioja.

Müller-Thurgau

One of the least fashionable varieties, Müller Thurgau is still widespread in Germany, where it is the base for wines such as Liebfraumilch, but it is declining there as everywhere. It can give quite refreshing off-dry whites – in England, New Zealand, Luxembourg, and the Alto Adige – but it's not a variety with a future.

Muscadet

Correctly speaking, this is the Melon de Bourgogne grape, but, since it has long since disappeared from Burgundy, it is now usually known by the name of the single dry white wine it does produce.

Pinot Blanc

At its most characterful, as grown in Alsace and Itlay's Alto Adige, Pinot Blanc is like a light, unoaked Chardonnay – fresh and leafy, with appley, buttery fruit.

Roussanne

High quality, herb- and flower-scented Rhône variety enjoying a mini revival – and it would probably be a maxi revival if it were an easier grape for the grower and winemaker. It appears in white Châteauneuf-du-Pape, Hermitage and other Rhônes, Savoie (as Bergeron), and increasingly in new creations from Languedoc, Provence, and California. Australia can't be far behind.

Scheurebe

The best of Germany's many crossings. More Riesling-like than most, but with a distinctive and delicious pink grapefruit flavour, especially in the Pfalz. Known as Samling 88 in Austria, it makes impressive sweet wines.

Silvaner

Still quite widespread in Germany and Central Europe, Silvaner (or Sylvaner) produces generally neutral wines with a light mineral/stoney character. It is at its best in Franken in Germany, the Valais in Switzerland (under the name Johannisberg), Italy's Alto Adige, and, if treated with care, in Alsace.

Torrontés

Possibly of Spanish origin, but now an Argentine speciality: often highly aromatic, floral, spicy, Muscat-like dry wines with a crisp finish, despite sometimes high alcohol.

Trebbiano/Ugni Blanc

You don't often see this on labels, but it is by far the most common white grape in both taly and France. Common by name, common by nature, it produces neutral, high-acid wines in both. Best blended with more interesting varieties.

Verdejo

A high quality Spanish grape and the principal component of Rueda. It's not as aromatic as Albariño (or as trendy), but has a leafy, nutty character and ageing potential.

Verdelho

Renowned as the tangy, medium-dry style of Madeira, Verdelho is also making a name for itself as a full, dry lime-flavoured Australian white wine .

Verdicchio

The most interesting white grape of Italy's Marche region, and especially notable in the lemon- and almond-scented Verdicchio dei Castelli di Jesi.

Vernaccia

There are a lot of very different Vernaccia wines in Italy, but the best known is Tuscany's much-needed fresh, nutty Vernacccia di San Gimignano.

Other red grapes often seen

Aglianico

A classy southern Italian variety, particularly at home in volcanic soils. Its best wines, with strong, berry fruit and a smoky, gunflint character, are Aglianico del Vulture and Taurasi. Expect to see some in Australia soon.

Baga

On the one hand Baga produces some of the raw material for sweet, pink Mateus. On the other, it produces dark, tannic, high-acid, berry-flavoured red grapes for Bairrada, Dão, and several other Portuguese reds. Taming the tannins and acidity are the key to making modern style Portuguese reds.

Barbera

The standing of Italy's second most common red grape has been much improved in recent years, especially in Piedmont, by cutting yields and using oak to soften the fruit's natural astringency and complement its sharp cherry and damson flavours. It is also an important variety in California and Argentina, although until now has mostly been used for everyday wines, and is catching on in Australia – like all things Italian.

Blaufränkisch

Limberger in Germany, Kékfrankos in Hungary, and Lemberger in Washington State, but best known as Austria's Blaufränkish. When treated with respect, especially in Burgenland, it can produce high quality, oak-matured wine with pronounced red fruit flavours and peppery tones.

Cabernet Franc

Cabernet Franc is the less aristocratic first cousin of Cabernet Sauvignon and is part of the traditional red Bordeaux blend. It is softer and less tannic with a fruitiness that is more raspberries than blackcurrants. In the Loire, where it stands alone in Chinon, Bourgueil, and Saumur-Champigny, it has an additional mineral flavour, often with some currant leaf or green pepper flavours and a hint of chocolate. The few pure Cabernet Francs from California and Australia are weightier; those from northeast Italy (often in fact Carmenère) tend to be light and grassy.

Carignan

Widely planted in the South of France and much maligned because of its astringency, but old vines planted in the hills, in Fitou for example, can produce attractively deep, spicy, herby wines.

Carmenère

An old, abandoned Bordeaux grape that made its home in Chile under false pretences. In the 1990s it was discovered that much of the country's so-called Merlot was Carmenère, a variety that produces riper, sweeter-tasting wines with additional flavours of blackberry jelly, coffee, soy, spice, and red capsicum. A great revival.

Dolcetto

The trendy third grape of Piedmont in Italy and called "little sweet one" (dolcetto), not because it is, but because it is less tannic than Nebbiolo and less naturally acid than Barbera. The best wines are full and dry with cherry, almond, and bitter-chocolate flavours. Appears in California as Charbono.

Dornfelder

True, there is not much competition, but this is one of Germany's most successful red grapes, with good colour, fruitiness, and acidity, especially in the Pfalz and Rheinhessen.

Gamay

Gamay is the grape used exclusively for Beaujolais and for the lesser red burgundies of the Mâconnais region. A little is also grown around Touraine on the Loire. Its charm is its fresh, fruity, uncomplicated style for immediate drinking, although there are some more serious Beaujolais, named after their individual locations: Fleurie, Morgon, Moulin-à-Vent et al, which are fuller and more flavoursome.

Lambrusco

Forget the cheap, sweet stuff sold in large screw-cap bottles, this is the grape, with many subvarieties, that produces authentic Lambrusco – red, foaming, dry, and refreshing.

Malbec

To most non-French wine drinkers, Malbec now means Argentina, but it originated in southwest France and is the principal grape of Cahors, a traditionally fairly austere wine with a dry mineral character and inky, spiced-blackberry fruit. Argentine Malbec is richer and more exuberant, with ripe, spicy, mulberry, and blackberry flavours, and, often, more evident oak.

Mourvèdre/Monastrell

For a long time little regarded except in Bandol in Provence, the muscular, herby, sometimes quite pungent-smelling Mourvèdre has benefited from the vogue for full, dark, spicy red wines. It gives backbone to southern Rhône wines, such as Châteauneuf-du-Pape, is specifically recommended in Languedoc-Roussillon and has been brought back to life in California and Australia, where, known as Mataro, it had been losing out to Cabernet Sauvignon. Even in Spain, where, as Monastrell, it has been valued mainly for its sturdy tannin and alcohol, growers are giving it more attention.

Montepulciano

Nothing to do with the classy Vino Nobile di Montepulciano, but an important grape in central and southern Italy for producing chunky, but velvety, usually inexpensive reds.

Negroamaro

The name "blackbitter" makes this powerful southern Italian grape sound worse than it is. It is dark and there is a bitterness to the perfumed damson fruit, but there are also dark chocolate, roasted chesnut, and savoury leathery flavours.

Petite Sirah

Partly because the name was originally applied to several varieties in California, it is not always clear what Petite Sirah is. What is not at stake is the style of wine it produces: dark, tannic, and brawny. In California, it is often blended with Zinfandel. It is also grown in Mexico and South America.

Petit Verdot

A minor and temperamental Bordeaux variety appreciated for its deep colour and scent of violets, especially in the wines of Margaux. Several California and Australian producers also use a little in their Cabernet-based wines and it is has begun to appear as a varietal wine, especially in Australia.

Pinotage

The jury is still out as to whether Pinotage is South Africa's trump card or its Achilles heel and still out as to the best style for it. The wines vary from light and fruity to strapping, oak-aged, and tannic, but all should have a distinctive fruit flavour reminiscent of squashy marshmallow sweets. New Zealand has a little Pinotage, but there is no general rush to plant it.

Saperavi

An important, hardy Russian variety with high acidity and tannin which make it tough when young, but capable of long ageing. Blends with Cabernet Sauvignon can work well.

Tannat

Like Malbec and Carmenère, Tannat is another of the varieties from southwest France that has made good in South America. It is the robust, tannic grape of Madiran and, equally, the softer blackberry and raspberry perfumed grape of Uruguay's best reds.

Touriga Nacional

A deep-coloured, intensely flavoured Portuguese variety which has always been an essential ingredient in top quality port and is now increasingly being used for table wines in the Douro and in Dão.

THE MAIN CLASSIC WINE STYLES, AND
ALTERNATIVES

 IF THE WINE WORLD HAS BEEN MOVING FASTER THAN EVER BEFORE IN THE LAST FEW DECADES, THIS IS THE CHAPTER THAT DEMONSTRATES IT ABOVE ALL. UNTIL THE LATE 1960s YOU COULD DIVIDE WINES INTO TWO BROAD CATEGORIES: THE GREAT, ALMOST EXCLUSIVELY FRENCH, CLASSICS; AND THE MYRIAD LOCALIZED REGIONAL STYLES. THERE WAS A DEGREE OF CROSS-FERTILIZATION, AND CUTTINGS AND WINEMAKERS DID SOMETIMES TRAVEL, BUT IT WAS ALL VERY LIMITED; WINE STYLES, WHETHER CLASSIC OR OBSCURE, BELONGED TO THEIR REGIONS. BUT THAT BEGAN TO CHANGE AT THE END OF THE LIBERATING SIXTIES, FIRST IN CALIFORNIA AND THEN, AS THE MOVEMENT GATHERED MOMENTUM, IN OTHER COUNTRIES AND CONTINENTS.

The new producers, sometimes in virgin vine territory, created a new category of wines: wines made anywhere in the world in the image of the great classics – Cabernets that sought to emulate clarets, Chardonnays that modelled themselves on white burgundy, sparkling wines that wanted to be mistaken for Champagne.

The key to the change was grape varieties. The pioneers of these new wines had their own climate, their own soils; all they needed, they decided, was the same grape varieties. If they wanted to make a white burgundy type, they planted Chardonnay. If they wanted an ersatz claret, they put in Cabernet Sauvignon (few of them bothering with the less aristocratic Merlot and Cabernet Franc, even though these were – and

are – the essential blending partners of Cabernet Sauvignon in Bordeaux). And in doing all this they actually simplified rather than complicated the wine world they were expanding by giving us "varietals" – wines made from, and named after, single grape varieties.

Obvious as such a strategy may seem now we are familiar with seeing grape varieties on labels, at the time it was a novel approach. Traditional European wines were, and still are, named after their place of birth – whether a vast area like Bordeaux, or one of its small, high quality subregions such as St-Julien. (True, Alsace is an exception as its wines are named primarily after their grape varieties, but even here the trend has been towards greater locational identification, with the recognition in the 1980s of fifty small top-quality sites or *crus*.) The result of this purely regional focus was that previous generations of wine drinkers seldom knew or cared which grape variety a wine was made from, just so long as it was made from grapes not banana skins.

But the new producers had not been brought up in this traditional atmosphere, born of hundreds of years of experience, where the primacy of terroir (*see* pages 82–83) was unquestioned, and indeed, enshrined in the rules of each appellation, and where, equally, any grape variety that was not officially prescribed was therefore proscribed. As the new producers saw it, so long as the climate was comfortably warm, which of course it was in places like California's Napa Valley, they did not need to worry about its precise details and they certainly did not pay much attention to soil character. If they had the grapes, then the winemaker in his spanking new high-tech winery could do the rest.

The choice of grape variety in these new count-ries is still the choice of the grower, but the pendulum has swung back. Without actually learning to revere dirt, producers have begun to respect it a little more. They still do not give much for its mineral and its microbial content (unless they are organic or biodynamic producers – *see* page 87), but they do lay great store by soil temperature, drainage, and water-holding capacities. They also spend a great deal of time seeking out the perfect, cool mesoclimate within their macroclimate (and usually refer to it as the microclimate, but this is not strictly accurate – *see* page 83).

The descriptions of the classic styles and the new alternatives that follow are inevitably broad brush-stroke portraits. In so vast a continent as Australia, where Cabernet Sauvignon is the second most planted red grape, there could never be one single, narrowly defined style; there isn't one California style either – any more than there is just one for Bordeaux itself. Moreover, in many places, specific regional styles have still to emerge – and in some cases probably never will, because the absence of restrictive appellation rules means that producers are free to make any style of wines that they wish. In other regions, the traditional ones where quality has improved, the style of the wines is also changing: red Bordeaux is generally riper and fuller than it was in the 1970s.

Wines and grapes mentioned in this chapter are described in more detail in the final part of the book (pages 94–157) and in "The Importance of Grapes" (pages 50–59).

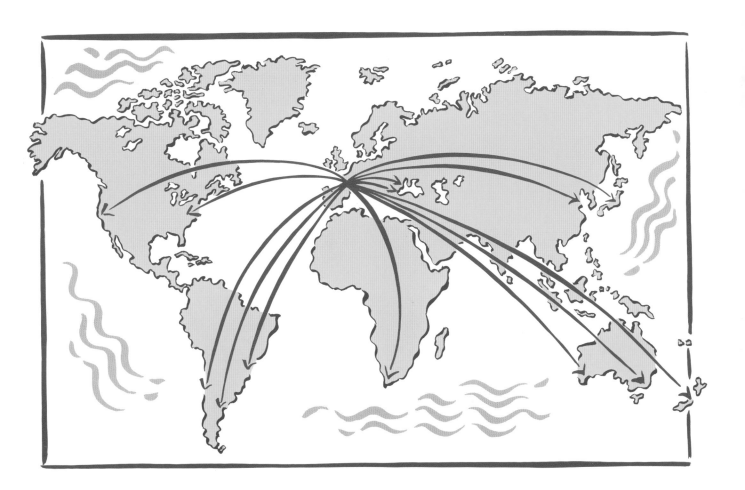

(Below) **The influence of the great classic wine styles of Europe – above all France – is felt in hot-seats of wine learning and hotbeds of wine production in countries and continents in both hemispheres.**

(From left to right) **The classic, high-shouldered red Bordeaux bottle used for Cabernet Sauvignon, Merlots, and blends such as Cabernet/Shiraz all around the world; the sloping-shouldered burgundy bottle used for most of the world's Pinot Noirs (but not Alsace's); two versions of the sloping shouldered bottle, here used for white burgundy and Pouilly-Fumé; the tall, slim green bottle used for German Mosel (a taller, slimmer version is used in Alsace and a brown version is used for Rhine wines); the heavy glass bottle, designed to withstand the pressure within, used for Champagne and other bottle-fermented sparkling wines; the high-shouldered Bordeaux bottle in colourless glass for Sauternes; a typical *fino* sherry bottle; the heavy, dark – almost black – glass of a vintage port bottle; and the sloping-shouldered bottle as used throughout the Rhône.**

RED BORDEAUX

Small wonder that red Bordeaux – claret to the British – should have been the first and most copied of the classics. Bordeaux is the world's largest fine wine region, and, quite simply, the best wines taste sublime – even if you do sometimes have to wait ten or more years for them to reach peak maturity. With such a large region there are variations in taste, but in many ways this is more a question of different levels of quality (the higher the quality, the greater the concentration of flavours, the more new oak barrels used, and the greater the complexity) than it is of diversity of style. There is really only one stylistic divide then, and that concerns grape varieties.

Claret is popularly thought of as a Cabernet Sauvignon wine – and it is certainly the grape variety almost all the new overseas producers planted when they were setting out to make their copies, because it is the major variety in all the illustrious names of the Haut-Médoc (on the left bank of the Gironde estuary), and the red wines of Graves to the south. But red Bordeaux is never a varietal, it is always a blended wine (from Cabernet Sauvignon, Merlot, Cabernet Franc, and sometimes Malbec and Petit Verdot) and Cabernet Sauvignon does not dominate overall. That distinction goes to Merlot, the predominant variety of the right bank appellations such as St-Emilion and Pomerol and of almost all the lesser clarets, from plain Bordeaux to

Premières Côtes de Blaye and Côtes de Castillon. Cabernet and Merlot are similar in taste and are beautifully complementary – as the Bordelais discovered a century ago on replanting their vineyards after the devastating phylloxera plague – and blended together have a characteristic and identifiable taste. As well as the keynotes of blackcurrant, cedar, and pencil, look for the typically deep colour which changes from purple to brick red with age (*see* Why and how to taste, pages 10–21); expect to find the taste of new oak and tannin in the better young wines; and don't be surprised to find mulberry, dark chocolate, tobacco, green pepper, mint, minerals, olives, and cloves. In older wines the complex flavours include autumnal undergrowth (even mushrooms), dried fruit, and fruit-cake.

Broadly speaking, the alternatives to claret come from warmer, drier climates and, because they are usually made from only one grape, are simpler wines. They may have greater power, equal or more obvious fruit, and enough tannin and acid to guarantee a lifespan of five or more years, but a varietal Cabernet or Merlot seldom scales the heights of complexity, elegance, or longevity of a great Bordeaux – which is why aspiring producers elsewhere are increasingly adding a little Merlot and even a spot of Cabernet Franc to their Cabernet Sauvignon.

The USA

In 1976 a California Cabernet Sauvignon from Stags' Leap Wine Cellars in the Napa Valley beat four of Bordeaux's five First Growths (top

(Below) The pretty town of St-Emilion presides over the appellation of the same name on Bordeaux's right bank. Here, where Merlot dominates the vineyards, the wines are slightly softer, broader, and more spicy than those of the Médoc across the river.

château wines) in a competition in Paris, judged predominantly by French tasters. There have been similar sensations since and the French riposte is invariably that the California style – all power and upfront fruit – simply overwhelms the more refined, slower-to-mature French style, and would equally overpower most food and the palate of any drinker who tried a second glass. There is a certain truth in this: California Cabernets and Merlots, despite being toned down since those early days, tend to be big, ripe, oaky, and often quite tannic. But the very best – which include some of those now using the classic Bordeaux blend of grape varieties – do rank with fine claret. (As well as names like Opus and Dominus, look for the marketing name "Meritage" used by some winemakers to indicate the traditional Bordeaux combination.)

There is no fail-safe way of distinguishing a California Cabernet from, say, an Australian one, but if the power, weight, and tannin of the wine are especially striking, I'd plump for California. The Washington State style of both Cabernet Sauvignon and Merlot is a little lighter than California's and in that respect is closer to Bordeaux. It differs in having a more vibrant blackcurrant flavour, whether the wines are soft, easy-drinking styles or more concentrated serious ones.

Australia

Australia specializes in Cabernet/Shiraz blends, as well as pure Cabernet Sauvignon, and a handful of pure Cabernet Francs, and, most recently, Petit Verdots. You might expect Shiraz (the same grape as Syrah of France's Rhône Valley) to give quite a different style of wine, but in fact it marries very well with Cabernet, enhancing the spice and chocolate elements and often giving a sweet blackberry note to the fruit. The Australian style of Cabernet is ripe, full, and fruity, and often has a delicious supple mint flavour (in regions such as Coonawarra). It is softer and less dry-seeming than Bordeaux and less tannic than most California Cabernets. Merlot, a relative newcomer, has been planted so enthusiastically that it is now the third most important red variety, but it has yet to establish a really clear style, partly because the vines are young, partly because yields are often too high and partly because winemakers are still getting to grips with its style and potential.

New Zealand

The comparatively cool climate naturally yields a lighter style than in Australia and brings out the grassy character of Cabernet Sauvignon, but riper, fleshier wines, usually blends with Merlot, are being made in the warmer North Island, especially on the Gimblett Gravels in Hawke's Bay, and on Waiheke Island. They will always be limited in number, but they are in the classic claret mould.

South America

Chilean Cabernets and Merlots are medium to full bodied with a softer texture and more insistent cassis fruit than red Bordeaux. The best are well structured, but many wines are made from high yields to meet supermarket price points and are not

(Below) **Blackcurrants, green pepper, and chocolate are keynotes of all but the oldest red Bordeaux.**

intended to be aged at all. The latest string to the Chilean bow is Carmenère, which is an abandoned Bordeaux variety that, when fully ripe in Chile, gives wines with spicier, sweeter fruit than Cabernet. In Argentina Cabernet is often blended with Malbec, another refugee from South West France and Argentina's answer to Carmenère. Here, Malbec produces rich, mulberry and blackberry flavoured fruit and altogether fuller-bodied wines with more spice than in Bordeaux. Sometimes it has echoes of St-Emilion, but in a bigger, weightier format. Pure Cabernet Sauvignon is still finding its style, but at the top end, grown at high altitude, there are some very impressive, classically styled wines.Cabernet Sauvignon is at home in most countries of South America and in Mexico. Uruguay produces good Cabernets and Merlots and also has its own speciality, Tannat. This is yet another variety from south west France which has settled in South America. It is more tannic than Cabernet Sauvignon, but produces less tannic reds than in its native Madiran.

South Africa

South African red wines have been changing for the better very rapidly in the last few years, largely as a result of new plantings, replacing the old virus-affected vineyards, but also because the South Africans have shaken off the bad winemaking habits that built up during the years of international isolation. There are still Cabernets and Merlots that suffer from astringent acids and tannins, hard green flavours and burnt rubber/soot/tar flavours, but they are disappearing as fast as they lose friends and markets. The best of the new wave are full-bodied with clear blackcurrant fruit and some savoury, cedary, slightly leathery richness, and the potential to develop with a few years' age.

Eastern Europe

Wine from Eastern Europe has been ousted from our affections by New World wines, but we know from the Bulgarian Cabernet Sauvignons that were so popular in the the 1980s and the Moldovan reds that enjoyed the limelight briefly in the early 1990s that there is potential. There is certainly no shortage of Cabernet Sauvignon in the former Eastern Bloc, and some Merlot too. The problem is that tastes have changed: wines have become fuller, softer, and fruitier, and Bulgaria, for one, has not been able to adapt sufficiently. It is making some newer-style wines, complete with a veneer of vanilla-scented new oak, but these tend to fall between two stools: they have lost their similarity to Bordeaux, but haven't the fruit of the New World.

(Above) **More sunshine, blending Cabernet with other grape varieties, such as Sangiovese, and ageing in different kinds of oak can give gently spicy or, in the case of Provence, aromatic herby wines.**

France

The only French alternatives to claret used to be those from the satellite appellations of Bordeaux, the further reaches of the southwest, and from the Loire. The former included the blackcurrant reds from Bergerac and Côtes de Duras, the slightly firmer, more claret-like Côtes de Buzet, and a couple of altogether tougher wines – the Malbec-based Cahors and the Tannat-based Madiran – neither of which resemble Bordeaux very closely. The Loire reds were the light- to medium-weight Cabernet Franc wines of Chinon, Bourgueil, and Saumur-Champigny, with their mineral, currant leaf character and, in good vintages, raspberry fruit and gentle chocolatey tones – but they were only ever loosely related to red Bordeaux.

All these still exist as alternatives, and some of the new Bergeracs are very serious indeed, but there are now a multitude of enjoyable, if not particularly complex, full, fruity Cabernets and Merlots from the Mediterranean south: intense, aromatic, herby Cabernets from Provence; full, ripe Vins de Pays d'Oc varietals, sometimes enriched by oak ageing; and many other vins de pays from the formerly scorned Midi. In style they tend to fall somewhere between the restraint of Bordeaux and the exuberance and ripeness of Australian Cabernet.

Italy

Northeast Italy has long produced light, grassy Merlots and Cabernets which bear little relation to red Bordeaux, but further south in Tuscany there are some superb Cabernets and Merlots, and blends with Sangiovese (the so-called super-Tuscans). With the concentration and youthful austerity of fine claret, they usually combine more weight and fullness, and a slightly smoky spice character.

Spain

Spanish Cabernet first hit the headlines in 1979 when a Penedès wine, Torres' 1970 Mas La Plana, was voted best red by a sixty-strong international (but French dominated) blind-tasting jury in Paris. This classic, rich, tannic wine spawned several good followers. There are silky, oak-matured Cabernets and Merlots made in both Navarra and Somontano.

Portugal

Portugal wisely concentrates on its own fascinating grape varieties, but these, in the Douro (the port producing district), can produce very fine reds with claret-like finesse and length of flavour, if slightly more exotic flavours.

RED BURGUNDY

If claret is by far the most widely mimicked of red wines, burgundy is the one that has most challenged – and frustrated – those who have tried to replicate it elsewhere. The extremely fussy Pinot Noir has belligerently thwarted most attempts to make it behave well abroad. As it is the only red grape variety of mainstream burgundy (that is the Côte d'Or with all its famous and famously tiny villages and vineyards), its conduct has very effectively limited the development of convincing red burgundy-style wines. And, while Cabernet Sauvignon is capable of developing regional characteristics, depending on climate or terroir, few new regions have yet shown that they can consistently give some desirable different dimension to Pinot Noir.

This is great news for Burgundians, but not for all the rest of us who would love to be able to experience more of, and more cheaply, those ethereal scents and silky textures: that signature combination of elegance and gorgeous pure fruit flavours (raspberries, strawberries, cherries, violets...) with, as the wine matures, burgundy's unique *goût de terroir*, the strange, decadent, gamey, or farmyardy richness.

The principal difficulties with growing Pinot Noir are its sensitivity to climate, clonal variation, and its penchant for limestone soils, which are scant in the New World. Pinot Noir is so prone to mutate that many of the early overseas growers originally planted disease-resistant, high-yielding, but poor quality clones; and they tended to plant just one, instantly reducing their chances of achieving complex wines. Having sorted out climatic and clonal requirements, Pinot Noir needs to have its yields carefully controlled and be harvested at exactly the optimum moment. It then needs to be handled in the winery with particular care – that is to say as little as possible.

All that said, the end of the 1990s saw breakthroughs in several parts of the world, so much so that many Burgundian producers have responded to the challenge by striving to improve the quality of their own wines. The result is rising standards of Pinot Noir in both the Old World and the New.

The USA

The discovery of some ideally cool, sea-breeze-chilled pockets in California – especially Carneros, the valleys of Santa Barbara County, and the Russian River Valley in Sonoma County – has transformed the quality and style of the state's Pinot Noirs. Their number will always be limited, but the best wines are beautifully aromatic, have a great purity of fruit, and, with punctilious oak ageing, develop some silkiness and complexity. This is not (yet?) the decaying, farmyardy complexity of great mature burgundy, but not all California's Pinot Noir producers consider this a cause for regret.

In the mid-1980s, before California Pinot Noir had found its feet, cool-climate Oregon in the Pacific Northwest was being touted as the promised land. It could yet turn out to be. Certainly Domaine Drouhin, scion of the Burgundy house of Drouhin, has been producing very convincing Burgundy-style wines and some others have achieved classic, refined Pinot Noir fruit,

(Below) **The pure fruit flavours of cranberries, raspberries, and cherries are signature notes of great red burgundy.**

but quality generally is uneven from vintage to vintage, as well as winery to winery.

Australia

Pinot Noir has a longer history here than in California, but as a source of alternatives to burgundy, Australia lags behind. As in the USA, the seeking out of cooler climates has brought what success there is, particularly in the Yarra Valley, Mornington Peninsula, and Geelong (all around Melbourne), but even here the wines – expensive by Australian standards – tend to have the delicious fruit of young burgundy, but not its breadth and velvety depth. Tasmania has the potential to produce top wines, but probably only every few years in the warmer vintages, like 2000. Most Western Australian attempts at Pinot still leave me wondering whether it is ever going to be really at home here.

New Zealand

The cool climate and southerly latitude make highly promising Pinot Noir territory. Initially, the main plantings for red wine (as opposed to sparkling) were in Martinborough at the south of the North Island, but in the last few years there has been an explosion of plantings on the South Island in Central Otago, Marlborough, and Waipara in Canterbury. The wines have deep colour and a deep fruitiness; some also hint tantalizingly at a savoury Burgundian quality. We shall be hearing more of New Zealand Pinot Noir.

France

Côte Chalonnaise wine is hardly an alternative to burgundy; it is burgundy, but from the rather underestimated region south of the Côte d'Or where the villages of Givry, Mercurey, and Rully produce good value wine with plenty of fruit, but less complexity than the classic style. They are, however, much closer in spirit (as well as geographically) to the Côte d'Or than the Pinot Noirs of Sancerre and Alsace: red Sancerre (and its less fashionable neighbour Menetou-Salon) and Alsace are altogether paler, lighter, and thinner than burgundy. Beaujolais is also technically part of Burgundy, but its wines, made from the Gamay grape, are quite different – with the occasional exception of Moulin-à-Vent, the most powerful of Beaujolais wines and one that, from a good vintage, can become increasingly burgundian after five or so years.

The rest of the world

Germany will never be a profound red wine producing country, but a small band of new wave producers is showing that Pinot Noir (called Spätburgunder), especially when lightly oaked, need not be pale and vapid.

Austria, too, is producing some good, if sometimes rather oaky, Pinot Noir (or Blauburgunder). It also has a grape variety, Sankt Laurent, which, if its yields are kept in check, can make wines that taste remarkably burgundian.

In the southern hemisphere, a handful of producers in South Africa, predominantly in the Walker Bay region, have proved beyond doubt that, in the right place, Pinot Noir can be coaxed into producing wines with seductive, silky-sweet burgundian fruit, and some complexity. Chile is not yet achieving the complexity, but some of its Pinot Noirs have enticingly authentic, gently sweet, aromatic fruit.

(Above) The village of Vosne-Romanée in the heart of Burgundy's Côte de Nuits is famous for its Grand Cru vineyards – Romanée-Conti, La Tâche, and Richebourg among them – which produce the most splendidly aromatic, rich, and velvety of red burgundies.

WHITE BURGUNDY

Great white burgundy doesn't come in just one style. It doesn't even come in just two – the wine of every village has its characteristic nuances – but it is possible all the same to differentiate between two distinct styles: those of Chablis and the Côte d'Or. The Chablis area, Burgundy's cold, frost-susceptible northern outpost, produces a wine that is minerally, steely, streamlined, and bone dry. It shares little with mainstream white burgundy from further south other than a hard-to-define savoury, almost vegetal complexity which both acquire with age. Chablis is the style of white burgundy that has almost totally eluded the rest of the world (the reason seems to be Chablis' rare soil type). In contrast, the Côte d'Or style – epitomized by the rich, buttery, walnuts-and-cinnamon Meursault wines and the similarly full-bodied, but slightly tauter, firmer, fleetingly smoky character of Puligny-Montrachet – has proved to be more promiscuous (even if the quality of its very greatest examples has yet to be matched). The reason is Chardonnay. Chardonnay, from which almost all white burgundies and certainly all the great ones are made, despite being appreciated for the full-bodied, flavoursome wines it mostly produces, doesn't actually have much personality. That is its virtue. It can be moulded pretty much to order, which means winemakers in the New World can, if they wish, play down their non-burgundian tropical fruit flavours and enhance the savoury, buttery, nutty ones that mark the burgundian end of the spectrum.

(Below) **The richness of the great white burgundies is expressed in aromas of walnuts and hazelnuts, toast and butter.**

(Left) **Looking down on to the mist-filled valleys of Burgundy: the best vineyards are on the slopes rather than the valley floor. This is Vézelay, south of Chablis, the home of the drier, steelier, more minerally style of white burgundy.**

Chardonnay's malleability means that in many cases regional styles may be even more blurred than for other varieties: a style can so easily be less a reflection of a particular terroir and more an indication of the producer's financial resources and intended market. To get the creamy, nutty flavours of fine burgundy, for example, the winemaker needs to mature the wine on its flavour-giving lees in a proportion of, if not all, new French oak barrels that cost approximately 400–500 euros each; he must also have fermented it in the same barrels rather than in huge, easy-to-monitor-and-maintain stainless steel tanks. There are shortcuts, but these tend to give simple, flattering tastes in the short term but not the depth, texture, complexity, and longevity of great burgundy. For these there is no way round time, effort, and expense.

The USA

The keynotes of the California Chardonnay style are very similar to the Cabernet ones – ripe fruit, power, oak. But the better Chardonnays – coming from newer, cooler regions south of San Francisco, as well as the traditional high quality areas of Napa Valley, Sonoma, and Carneros – are not the alcoholic overweights they once were. Nor are they the lean,

ascetic aberrations that appeared in the 1980s when the pendulum swung, mercifully briefly, too far the other way. Their fruit flavours, even from the cooler vineyards, are always likely to be riper, slightly more exotic than burgundy's; the oak taste is nearly always more prominent (whereas in fine burgundy oak is used more to give structure and ageing potential than specific flavours); the acidity is lower; and California Chardonnay is made to be drunk within a few years, although that doesn't stop the best wines from developing some complexity. The less good are over-filtered, with fruit, oak, high alcohol, and nothing else (all other flavours having been stripped out by over-zealous use of new technology in the winery), and cheap California Chardonnay usually has a sweetness that palls very quickly.

Of the other states producing Chardonnay, New York – especially Long Island with its mild, maritime climate – is producing some wines with a nutty, yet elegant richness that more than fleetingly resembles that of Puligny-Montrachet. One or two producers in Oregon have also succeeded in producing top quality, burgundian Chardonnay, but most of the output is rather lean. Washington State has more success – with a bright fruit, more California style. Another two regions to watch, perhaps surprisingly, are British Columbia and Ontario in Canada.

Australia

Australia doesn't produce Chablis-like Chardonnays, or light, aromatic, flowery ones like those of Italy's Alto Adige, but most other permutations can be found and if, early on, they all seemed to taste of oak, that is no longer the case. Oak is more judiciously used now and unoaked or unwooded Chardonnay is a fashion in its own right. The warm areas, such as Barossa Valley and above all Hunter Valley, produce the fattest styles – packed with ripe fruit and a butterscotch richness. Cooler areas, such as Adelaide Hills, Eden Valley, Padthaway, Yarra Valley, Margaret River, and Tasmania are capable of more European-style Chardonnays – oak-fermented, concentrated, and racy, with well-defined fruit and acid. But the Australian wine industry is the one most geared to producing whatever style of wine is required by the buyer, so these are by no means hard and fast styles.

A speciality, and a curiosity, is traditional, unoaked Hunter Valley Semillon which develops a rich, toasted, honeyed character in maturity that is more than a little burgundian.

New Zealand

New Zealand is at the forefront of the world Chardonnay stage. The relatively cool climate in both North and South Islands can ripen Chardonnay to perfection, giving fruit flavours of great clarity and concentration, but not the tropical fruit of hot countries. When high natural acidity and alcohol are complemented by full, buttery richness and toasty oak, results can be impressively Meursault-like.

South America

The average Chilean Chardonnay is cheaper than those of California, Australia, or New Zealand and is unlikely ever to be mistaken for burgundy. But things are developing, especially in cool – and fashionable – Casablanca Valley. It is still early days, but it is clear that this area is capable of sophisticated, well-structured Chardonnays.

South Africa

Chardonnay only really began to take off in the second half of the 1980s with the availabiliy of better clones, and at first many producers were heavy handed with oak. Since then, a character has evolved which is less ebulliently fruity, more European than Californian or Australian. Some of the wines are very good indeed.

(Above and below) **New World Chardonnays are usually much more boldly fruity than white burgundy.**

France

As with red burgundy, the lesser known southern areas of Burgundy itself are a good starting point in the search for alternatives – the Mâconnais for creamy, appley Chardonnays and Côte Chalonnaise villages for slightly fuller-bodied ones. Chardonnay from the Ardèche region to the south, as made by Burgundian Louis Latour, is also convincingly burgundian in a creamy, savoury way. Other French Chardonnays tend to fall into one of two main categories: crisp, fruity, flowery, and unoaked (Haut-Poitou, Vin de Pays du Jardin de la France, and Savoie), a style which bears little resemblance to any burgundy, apart perhaps from having the crispness of Chablis; and the riper, fuller, often oaky vins de pays of the south (particularly Vin de Pays d'Oc) which have a lot of the New World in them.

Italy

There are three contrasting styles of Chardonnay in Italy. There are the indigenous, crisp, aromatic wines of the far north (Alto Adige and Friuli) for drinking within two to three years. There are the big, rich, oak-aged wines made (as *vini da tavola*) by famous names in the red wine areas of Chianti, Brunello di Montalcino, Barolo, and Barbaresco. These are designed to compete with the world's best and are mostly very impressive, if occasionally a little too oaky and very expensive. And then there are the new Chardonnays of the far South – of Puglia and Sicily. One or two of Sicily's are particularly ambitious creations; but in general the South, and Puglia in particular, produces moderately priced, oak-influenced Chardonnays in the New World idiom.

The rest of the world

Austria aims for class – particularly burgundian class – with its Chardonnays. Sometimes it succeeds, but there has been a tendency to overdo the oak element. Austria also has Grüner Veltliner: in youth, this tends to be more like Riesling, but, given age, the best Grüner Veltliners, especially from the Wachau, Komptal, and Kremstal regions, can develop a deep nutty characteristic reminiscent of burgundy. Chardonnay has not penetrated much of Spain, but where it has, it has mostly been very successful, especially in Penedès, Navarra, Somontano, and Raimat in Costers del Segre. Bulgaria, Hungary, Portugal, Israel, China, and even England and Germany have all produced creditable Chardonnay – and, no doubt, yet more will join this still rolling bandwagon.

SANCERRE AND POUILLY-FUMÉ

Sauvignon Blanc, the only grape of the Loire wines Sancerre and Pouilly-Fumé, is both assertive and uncompromising. In at least ninety-five per cent of cases, these, its classic manifestations, are wines to enjoy when young – when intensely aromatic, pungent, mouth-wateringly crisp, and bone dry, with the smells and flavours of newly cut grass, gooseberries, currant leaves, (sometimes even blackcurrants) and often a flinty, stony, or slightly smoky quality. But Sauvignon is fussy about its climate. If, as happens periodically in the Loire, it sees too little sun, and particularly if this is exacerbated by the vines being allowed to over-produce, it will be mouth-puckeringly tart and thin. However, if it sees too much sun, as it tends to in California and Australia, or it is allowed to develop too much foliage, it will develop a clumsy, herbaceous character with unattractive flavours of tinned asparagus and green beans, rather than the racy, fresh, herbaceousness. It is fussy, too, about its soils, performing best in limestone and flint soils (as in the Upper Loire) and least well in rich, fertile soils.

(Below) **Textbook Sancerre and Pouilly-Fumé have the unmistakeable Sauvignon aromas of freshly cut grass and gooseberries and a slightly smoky, flinty character.**

(Above) **Sauvignon Blanc is much less easy to please than Chardonnay, but it is at home in the cool of Château de Nozet in Pouilly-Fumé.**

Sauvignon is no more flexible in the winery, although having few options at least makes the winemaker's life simple – provided he is skilled at handling those few options. On its own (that is without Sémillon, its traditional partner in white Bordeaux) it seldom takes to oak, although Californians who are fond of their own oaked Fumé style would disagree. The successes with oak tend to be where the wine has been fermented, as well as matured, in barrels and these are the only wines with the potential to develop with age.

New Zealand

France and New Zealand are the two countries that produce outstanding Sauvignon Blanc in any quantity, but New Zealand, which only began producing it commercially in the eighties, is the more consistent, because of its climate. The New Zealand style, epitomized by the Marlborough region, is almost explosively intense and vibrant: vividly grassy, with crunchy gooseberry fruit, sometimes more tropical, passion fruit flavours, and tangy acidity. Only a few examples have the Loire's minerally pungency.

The USA

There is a handful of fine California Sauvignons and Fumé Blancs. The fruit flavours are concentrated, steely, and crisp and oak, if used, has lent structure and depth, but most of the rest lack charm, varietal character, and acidity – and are not helped by a sweetness of residual sugar. Partly this is a matter of taste: Americans like Fumés like this – *i.e.* quite unlike Sancerre and Pouilly-Fumé; European palates do not. Partly it is a matter of economics: Sauvignon commands much lower prices than Chardonnay, so yields have to be large. Livelier, more classic styles come from Washington State, but Sauvignon is losing vineyards to Chardonnay and red varieties.

Australia

Sauvignon Blanc is one of the few varieties that Australia's varied vineyards and talented winemakers struggle with. In most parts the climate is just too hot, but the Adelaide Hills has been notably successful with a crisp, but less pungent style than New Zealand. Margaret River produces some excellent, intense, bright Sauvignon/Semillon blends.

South America

Most Chilean Sauvignon is a wishywashy imitation of the New Zealand style. This is partly a reflection of big crops and low prices, but it's also because much of Chile's so-called Sauvignon is in fact the inferior Sauvignonasse grape. Casablanca Valley, Chile's sought-after cool region, yields the country's best Sauvignons – and they are the real thing.

South Africa

The Cape is the hot new property where Sauvignon Blanc is concerned. Producers who have sought out cool regions or higher altitudes are making some textbook, verdant wines. The style generally leans to the Loire, but with a smidgen of New Zealand's more powerful fruit thrown in. The best of both worlds? That's what's worrying the New Zealanders.

France

Fashionable Sancerre and Pouilly-Fumé have three small near-neighbours and followers – Menetou-Salon, Quincy, and Reuilly. Menetou-Salon and Quincy come closest in style and quality to Sancerre, but happily at lower prices. Sauvignon de Touraine and Haut-Poitou's Sauvignon are lighter and less concentrated, but, at best, good value, zingy whites.

Sauvignon in Bordeaux, whether or not blended with Sémillon, has improved hugely. Like the Sauvignon from Bergerac and Côtes de Duras on the Dordogne to the east, it is now, more often than not, light and attractively gooseberry flavoured. It also gives a boost to many *vin de pays* blends in the southwest and appears in varietal form as Vin de Pays d'Oc. The latter never have quite the verve of Sancerre, but can be good.

Italy

There are a few pockets of Sauvignon scattered in Italy, few are coherent styles (it is blended with other varieties). The principal exception is the wines of Collio in Friuli, which have more concentration than those of Alto Adige, and have the penetrating intensity of Sancerre, but slightly sweeter fruit.

Spain

The wines of Rueda can be pure Sauvignon or a blend with Verdejo. Either way, they provide Spain with a convincingly verdant Sauvignon style of wine.

The rest of the world

Bright, fruity, clean-cut Sauvignons come from many parts of Central and Eastern Europe including Hungary, Slovenia, the Czech Republic, and Moldova. Austria, particularly Steiermark, produces fuller, more intense Loire-like wines.

GERMAN RIESLING

So unfashionable and so abused was the name Riesling by the 1990s that some British wine merchants encouraged Australian producers to abandon the traditional tall slim Riesling bottle in favour of a burgundy or Bordeaux shape. Some producers went further and dropped the name Riesling altogether. This did nothing to restore the reputation of the classic German Riesling styles, but it seems to have made some reluctant converts to the joys of the grape itself. Certainly, by the turn of the century there were signs of a modest Riesling renaissance, and even of a German Riesling renaissance, in some countries, including the US.

Ironically, the name was most abused on its home territory – by the rising tide of ever blander and more dilute, semi-sweet Liebfraumilch, Bereich Nierstein, Bernkastel *et al*. These wines were increasingly made from lesser grape varieties, such as Müller-Thurgau, and unfortunately consumers erroneously associated them with Riesling. Elsewhere it suffered from imposters – most importantly in Europe from Welschriesling (variously called Laski Rizling, Olasz Rizling, or Riesling Italico), but also in California, from Gray Riesling (or Pinot Gris) and Emerald Riesling, in

(Above) **Steep slopes in the chilly northern climate of Germany's Rheingau region are ideal for picking up the best of the sun.**

(Below) **German Riesling flavours range from crisp, green apple in the Mosel to sweet peaches and apricots in the warmer Pfalz.**

Australia from Semillon, and in New Zealand from "Riesling/Sylvaner" (Müller-Thurgau).

In fact German Rieslings span the spectrum of bone-dry to extremely sweet, but the classic styles are the medium-dry to sweet *Kabinett, Spätlese, Auslese,* and so on (for more on the official classification of German wines *see* Germany, page 110–11). Even among these, the fruit flavours range from the crispest and crunchiest of apples with a twist of lemon (Mosel), to the riper, spicier flavours of the Pfalz and the honeyed apricots and peaches of the sweet wines. With age Riesling develops a distinctive petrol (or kerosene) character and honeyed notes, but for those who don't care for petrol, one of the great joys of the variety is that, despite its longevity, Riesling is also scintillating in its youth.

Australia

Riesling and Australia have gone hand in hand since German settlers in the Barossa Valley arrived with cuttings. Today it is a high quality and commercially important variety in many regions, but the best wines come from Clare Valley, Eden Valley (the hills above the Barossa), and a sprinkling from Mount Barker and Frankland in the West. These are inevitably bigger and more alcoholic than German Rieslings, but their flavours are not dissimilar. The distinctive Australian character is a mouth-watering lime flavour, often with a touch of passion-fruit or guava. With age, the best develop a honey-and-toast, occasionally a petrol, character, but petrol is less sought by Australians. Excellent sweet botrytis wines, too.

New Zealand

While most winemakers have been concentrating on Sauvignon and Chardonnay, those who have put effort into Riesling have shown that New Zealand's climate makes it well worth while. The style is more Germanic than Australia's – crisp, fragrant, and fruity, but less steely or minerally. There are very good late-harvest (sweet) wines too.

The USA and Canada

The majority of California Rieslings are off-dry, fairly bland, commerical wines, although there are some exceptions, both dry and sweet, from higher and cooler parts. Washington State and Oregon are climatically more suited and Washington in particular has produced good wines, in all styles from dry to lusciously sweet, but much of its Riesling has been replaced by other varieties. Perhaps the best American Rieslings – certainly the most Germanic – are those from the Finger Lakes in New York State.

Canada's dry Rieslings are well worth trying, but its justly famous Rieslings are the intensely sweet and concentrated Icewines made, like German *Eiswein*, from winter-frozen grapes.

France

Alsace, at one time annexed to Germany, is the only region of France to grow this German grape variety and the wines are altogether bigger, drier, and more alcoholic in style than their German counterparts. At their best (from limited yields) they have marvellous, slightly spicy apple flavours and distinct minerally notes which need time to show through an initial austerity. Cheaper versions can have a rather dilute, apple-pips-and-skins character. In good vintages, some grapes will be picked late in the autumn to make *Vendange Tardive* and *Sélection des Grains Nobles* styles. These are rich, ripe, and concentrated, although in the case of *Vendange Tardive* not necessarily very sweet. They are also bigger and more alcoholic than their late-picked and botrytized counterparts from Germany.

Austria

Rieslings from Austria, especially the Wachau, are one of the wine world's great secrets, perhaps because the Austrians drink most of them. If you do get the opportunity, expect to taste top quality, dry, steely, but gloriously fruity, aromatic, and quite weighty wines.

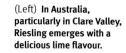

(Left) **In Australia, particularly in Clare Valley, Riesling emerges with a delicious lime flavour.**

CHAMPAGNE

Champagne producers are still convinced – or at least they say they are – that to make an equivalent sparkling wine it is not enough merely to plant the same grapes (Chardonnay, Pinot Noir, and Pinot Meunier) in a comparable cold climate (assuming such exists) and to reproduce the Champagne method (*méthode traditionelle* or *classique* when used outside Champagne – in which a second fermentation and maturation on lees take place in bottle). These new sparkling wines tend to be more overtly fruity with softer acidity and less structure than Champagne, which makes them ready to drink sooner, but also shorter-lived. The trend is towards greater elegance, but most still lose out to Champagne when it comes to complexity, underlying intensity, (as opposed to upfront flavour) and length of flavour. There are three facets of Champagne's character that prove hard to reproduce, or at least match: the subtle but rich, biscuity, bready, yeasty flavours that it develops from ageing on its lees (undergoing the process called yeast autolysis); the toasted, nutty character that comes not from oak but simply from maturing Chardonnay; and the gorgeous raspberry fruit of good Pinot Noir-based Champagnes. Other sparkling wines do not match up to Champagne, the Champenois maintain, because they do not come from the same type of chalk soil. It is true that there is little chalk or limestone in New World vineyards. But growers counter that it is not the chemical properties of the chalk and limestone that are significant but their physical properties – they drain well, but also retain moisture at depth without becoming waterlogged – and these physical properties are certainly not the exclusive preserve of French chalk/limestone soils.

Whatever the truth is, for sheer finesse and complexity, the finest Champagnes still have the edge over the best of all the rest – and so they

should when they cost so much more. But, the best Australian, New Zealand, California, and English sparkling wines (several of which, ironically, are made by, or in conjunction with, Champagne houses) are superior to the worst Champagnes selling at much the same price. Moreover, although the quality of the poorest Champagnes improved during the 1990s as a result of more rigorous production laws introduced in 1992, the standards of New World sparkling wines are improving with every vintage as winemakers master the processes, as grape quality rises with increasingly mature vines and as stocks are built up of the older "Reserve" wines that are so fundamental to Champagne.

(Above) **The Aube, the southernmost of Champagne's subdivisions, concentrates on the red grapes Pinot Meunier and Pinot Noir.**

(Below) **The rich, biscuity, hazelnuts character of Champagne is the aspect that is hardest to reproduce – elegantly – elsewhere.**

The USA

In California several Champagne houses started making sparkling wine in the 1980s, either on their own or in partnership with local firms. Although some have now retreated, the wines continue, with results that range from quite good to very good indeed when leaner fruit flavours are matched by some creamy depth. There are also particularly good wines from some of the Californian producers without Champagne connections. Cooler areas like Anderson Valley, Carneros, and Sonoma clearly favour sparkling wines, but there are top results from the warmer Napa Valley as well. Considering Oregon's climate and its established Pinot Noir vineyards, it is surprising that so little serious attention has been paid to sparkling wine – all the more so considering the quality achieved by the leading player, the Australian-backed Argyle winery.

Australia

Alongside masses of admirably cheap, cheerfully clean, soft, and fruity sparkling wines that don't have much in common with Champagne, Australia has an increasing number of high-class Chardonnay and Pinot Noir blends from cooler areas such as the Adelaide Hills, southern Victoria, (especially Yarra Valley), and the even cooler, wind-swept Tasmania. With usually slightly more fruit flavour (apple, citrus, melon) and a little less creamy depth than Champagne, the Champenois cannot afford to feel complacent – as those who have invested there, such as Moët et Chandon, know only too well.

New Zealand

With sparkling wines, as with still white wines, New Zealand has come a long way in a short time and has made the world sit up. The climate, especially in Marlborough, is well-suited to making high-acid base wines, as the Champagne house Deutz has acknowledged by its investment there. If there is a New Zealand style – at the top end – it is slightly fatter and creamier than Champagne, but several of its sparkling wines come very close to their French role model.

France

The closest French approximations to Champagne are Crémant de Bourgogne and Crémant de Limoux, but that isn't saying much. Neither is very like the real McCoy, although the quality of both has risen markedly in recent years – Crémant de Limoux especially (not to be confused with its sibling Blanquette de Limoux which is made predominantly

from the apple-flavoured local Mauzac grape). Saumur and Vouvray from the Loire, made from the Chenin Blanc grape, have a different style. They tend to be quite acid, and in mediocre years rather stalky, but in good vintages Vouvray in particular can have a lovely sweet-fruit and toasted-nut character. Crémant d'Alsace, usually made predominantly from Pinot Blanc, has a more flowery fruity style than Champagne, as does Seyssael Mousseaux, the light-bodied sparkling wine of the Savoie region.

Spain

Spain, particularly Penedès, turns out a sea of inexpensive *cava* (sparkling wine) and a few more expensive, more refined versions. Producers have worked hard at improving its simple, fruity, if rustic flavours, but there is only so far they can go with the undistinguished local grapes. Adding some Chardonnay undoubtedly helps. Meanwhile, sales, based on low prices, go from strength to strength.

Italy

Italy produces vast quantities of sparkling wines, some using the *metodo classico* (*méthode traditionelle*), but most not Champagne-like. The exceptions, from Franciacorta and Trento in the north, range in style from much crisper and leaner than Champagne to richer and fatter, occasionally impressively toasty. Asti and Moscato d'Asti – sweet, feather-light, and grapey, are very different.

UK

A handful of English wine producers has identified sparkling wine as a subject suited to their cool maritime climate and soils. Some make wines that are typically English – light, aromatic, and crisply fruity. One or two have made serious challenges to Champagne.

India

The Omar Khayyam brand of sparkling wine is proof that you can do anything if you are determined enough. The vineyards are in the hills of Maharashtra, the Indian owner brought in Champagne expertise and the quality of the wine was good at first, but was left behind when the New World progressed.

(Left) Melon flavours are typical of the more fruity style of Australian sparkling wines.

SAUTERNES

Although most countries have a tradition of making sweet wines, there are not all that many close copies of Sauternes, the glorious, golden, naturally sweet wine of Bordeaux – but given the way it is made and the recent history of Sauternes, perhaps that isn't surprising. Great Sauternes, with its luscious taste of honey and *crème brûlée* offset by flavours of apricot, peach, and pineapple, and its lanolin texture, is the product of Sémillon and Sauvignon Blanc grapes which have been horribly shrivelled and dehydrated by a fungus (*Botrytis cinerea* or "noble rot") that only appears in particular warm, humid autumn weather conditions. Some years it doesn't arrive at all, in which case, if you are lucky, you will be able to make a very good sweet wine, but not one with the extraordinary honeyed opulence, unctuousness, and longevity of a classic vintage. In addition, because of the dehydration of the grapes, you need at least twice as many to produce each

bottle of wine as you do to make red or dry white Bordeaux of comparable quality. As for history, Sauternes was in the doldrums for decades until the eighties. Unfashionable, unloved, and neglected, prices had dropped until it was scarcely economic to produce a fine wine, which meant that producers didn't try and standards were often very low. No wonder there were few pioneers of the Sauternes style elsewhere. The turn-about came in 1983 with a long overdue outstanding vintage (rapidly followed by very good ones in 1986, 1988, 1989, and 1990). Wine drinkers suddenly realized what they had been

(Above) **Morning mist and afternoon sun are the ingredients Sauternes properties such as Château Guiraud hope for in the autumn to induce "noble rot".**

(Below) **Honey, apricots, and pineapple – some of the flavours that give great Sauternes its lusciousness and intensity.**

missing. Sauternes became fashionable, expensive, and sought after and was tentatively followed by a few more winemakers elsewhere.

The USA

In California, as in Australia, most botrytis-affected wines are made from Riesling, but even these, because of their more powerful style, are sometimes as Sauternes-like as they are Germanic. There are also some excellent Sémillon/Sauvignon botrytis wines being made in the classic way – although it is more usual to induce botrytis artificially either in the vineyards or after picking. The clue to most sweet wines is the description "late-harvest".

Australia and New Zealand

Ever since De Bortoli caused a sensation with its first vintage, 1982, of a Sauternes-style botrytized Semillon, there has been a slow trickle of similar wines. It's perhaps surprising that there have not been more, considering how much Semillon is planted and that De Bortoli's wine achieved such success as the product of the mass-market Murrumbidgee region, rather than a fashionable and expensive cool climate area. The Australian style is sweeter, fatter, and more overtly fruity than Sauternes, with a little less complexity. There are also some high-quality botrytized Rieslings in both New Zealand and Australia. These are made in a Germanic style, in that they are concentrated, sweet, and fragrant with more penetrating acidity and lower alcohol than the Semillons, but they are altogether bigger wines than German Rieslings.

France

Cérons, Premières Côtes de Bordeaux, Ste-Croix-du-Mont, Loupiac, and Cadillac are Bordeaux appellations not far from Sauternes that have the potential to make wines in the same manner, but in a lighter style. Quality varies, but the best, especially from Ste-Croix-du-Mont and Loupiac, are convincing

(Left) **The sweet wines of the Chenin Blanc grape in the Loire have a glorious honeyed, apple taste.**

cheaper alternatives. The same applies to the sweet wines of Bergerac from the Dordogne region to the east. Some of the Monbazillacs and Saussignacs are exceptional.

Moving north, botrytis sometimes affects Chenin Blanc grapes in the Loire Valley, giving to wines such as Coteaux du Layon, Bonnezeaux, Quarts de Chaume, Vouvray, and Montlouis a wonderful depth of honeyed fruit (apricot, apple, nectarine...) and a flavour of almond marzipan, always underpinned by the high acidity of the Chenin grape. They never have the opulence and fat of Sauternes, but they have such intensity they can last an extraordinarily long time. Vouvray and Montlouis can also be dry, or medium-dry wines (as well as sparkling) so look for the word *moelleux* (sweet) or some indication of a special *cuvée*, or selection.

In Alsace, when noble rot strikes, producers make *Sélection des Grains Nobles* wines. Those made from Gewurztraminer grapes are highly individual, aromatic, and spicy, but they share with Sémillon an oily character, which can make them surprisingly similar in weight and texture to Sauternes.

Germany

It doesn't make sense to leave out Germany's superb *Beerenauslese* and *Trockenbeerenauslese* wines – made from nobly rotten Riesling grapes in fine vintages – but they are quite different in style from Sauternes. Intensely sweet, fragrant, and honeyed, they have great ageing potential because of their higher acidity, but are much less fat and alcoholic than Sauternes.

Hungary

Hungary's historic sweet wines, Tokáji (or Tokay), Aszú, and Eszencia, are like no other wines, but they deserve a place here all the same. Fabled for their curative and life-giving properties – as well as their own, apparently indefinite, lifespan – they are made from botrytized grapes, idiosyncratically processed, then matured in barrel. The result is a cornucopia of flavours – tangerine, apricot, candied peel, dried figs, stem ginger, coffee, and spice.

Austria

Austria's botrytized sweet wines, mostly from Burgenland on the Hungarian border, are more similar to Sauternes than the German style. They may be made form Germanic grapes and have Germanic labels, but they are altogether bigger and richer with an extraordinary concentration of fruit and botrytis aromas and flavours.

HERMITAGE AND COTE-ROTIE

(Above) **The steep Hermitage hill on the east bank of the Rhône is difficult to work, but worth the trouble because of its favourable exposure to the sun and granitic soil.**

Despite the fact that Hermitage and Côte Rôtie were as highly prized as the best clarets and burgundies in the nineteenth century, these great red Syrah wines from the northern Rhône were not much emulated until relatively recently. Until the 1990s, the tide was against wines with such colour, body, and tannin. It was against wine like Hermitage, the more massive and famous of the two, which took time to show its enticing berry aromas and rich gamey complexity through a mask of often tarry, leathery tannins. And, although it seems hard to believe now, contemporary taste was against the rich, spicy flavours of the Syrah grape. The aristocratic Cabernet Sauvignon was still the unchallenged red king – and if any red could be regarded as the crown prince it was the softer Merlot.

Even Australia, which has always had a great deal of Syrah under the name Shiraz (planted originally for fortified "port" styles), didn't treat it with much respect. In the mid-1980s, with Chardonnay all the rage, there was such a surplus of Shiraz that growers were selling their grapes to

(Below) **The Syrah grape gives the wines of the northern Rhône tantalizing berry aromas and great power.**

the makers of muffins. Worse still, in 1986, the government instituted a "Vine Pull" scheme, paying growers to pull up their vineyards. Inevitably, they chose the least popular varieties and their old and least productive vineyards. Mostly, this meant old, unirrigated Shiraz vineyards that gave low yields of magnificently concentrated wines – but wines for which there was little demand. The complementary varieties, Grenache and Mataro (aka Mourvèdre) suffered similarly, although on a smaller scale because there were fewer of them at the outset.

Oddly, all this went on at a time when Australia's most revered wine was a dark, full-bodied red called Grange Hermitage (it has since dropped the Hermitage moniker, but remains a wine of iconic status). And yet it is not so odd when you know that Max Schubert, the wine's creator in the 1950s, was not inspired by Hermitage but by red Bordeaux. He had never been to the Rhône. He used Shiraz grapes because those were what were available in the Barossa Valley where he was Penfold's winemaker, but he aimed to copy what he had seen at leading Bordeaux châteaux on a study visit to the region. The result was a wine with the complexity and longevity of top Bordeaux and Hermitage, but with the colour and body of Hermitage and flavours like those of the Rhône.

When the pendulum first began to swing towards bigger, riper, spicier styles in the 1990s, it was Grange that was the inspiration for the vast majority of Australian winemakers. Some looked to the Rhône, particularly those in cooler regions, but Australia was rapidly establishing a new style and standard for the variety. After an exceptional 1990 vintage, the Rhône's fortunes also looked up, but it was not this so much as seeing the success of Shiraz in Australia that encouraged its feverish planting in many other countries from the mid-1990s. Some of the new growers use the name Syrah, indicating where their allegiances lie, but most have looked more to Australia and label their wines Shiraz.

Australia

Generally, the Australian Shiraz style is bigger, riper, and softer than the wines of the northern Rhône, with more overt berry fruit, a rich chocolatey taste, and a flavour of mixed spice, rather than the freshly ground pepper that is more typical of the Rhône. In some regions (such as Coonawarra and Langhorne Creek), there can be a characteristic minty flavour, although, when present, it is not exclusive to Shiraz. Oak flavours, especially the distinctive spice and vanilla of American oak, have been a trademark of much Australian Shiraz, but there has been a trend in recent years, in the Barossa for example, to the more subtle flavours of French oak barrels. The Clare and Eden Valleys produce a slightly inkier, dark-chocolate style, while the warm, wet Hunter produces chunky, traditionally more leathery wines. In cooler regions, such as the Grampians in Victoria and Mount Barker in Western Australia, there is a more restrained, peppery style that is closer in spirit to the Rhône. Some producers in the Barossa are now adding small amounts of the white Viognier grape to their Shiraz in the same way that the producers of Côte-Rôtie traditionally include a smidgen of the perfumed Viognier to give their wines the fragrance that distinguishes them from Hermitage. Others are using Grenache and Mourvèdre to add a bit more interest and complexity.

The USA

California has had its cultish Rhône Rangers since the 1980s. This is a not entirely serious name given both to the wines made from Rhône grape varieties (Syrah especially, but sometimes blended with its classic French partners, Grenache, Viognier, and Mourvèdre) and their undeniably serious winemakers. Some of the wines are outstanding, especially from slightly cooler regions such as Santa Barbara and western Paso Robles, and often they are in the perfumed, more elegant Côte Rôtie mould rather than the Hermitage one. For now, they are made in small quantities at inevitably high prices, but that may change. California, like other countries, has been planting vast tracts of Syrah, some of it called Shiraz, indicating the intention to produce a fruitier, more Australian style – one that will compete head-on with the Australian wines that have been unwelcome inroads into the California markets.

The other serious contender in the US is Washington State, where Syrah is now close to being the most important red grape and where powerful, but stylish wines being produced.

France

At their best, Syrah *vin de pays* from the south of France are good value. They have the typical berry fruit and peppery spice and a decided succulence and texture, but they don't have the weight, depth, complexity, or tannin of northern Rhônes – and nor are they priced as if they had.

South America

It is early days for Syrah in Chile, and it's on a small scale, but there have already been some promising results in a style that is New World in its fruit profile, but a little less rich and fleshy than Australian Shiraz. Argentina also has Syrah – more than Chile – but not many producers are yet taking it seriously enough to keep yields in check. Those who are show how much potential Argentina has with this variety.

South Africa

Shiraz plantings are still limited in South Africa, but it is a variety that is gaining ground. Most producers are aiming at a more Australian than Rhône style and there have already been some very good results, especially in Stellenbosch.

The rest of the world

Switzerland has long had Syrah in the Valais region and can make good, deep-coloured wines, as can Austria's Burgenland, a more recent recruit. There are promising outcrops in New Zealand (warmest parts) and in Spain and Italy. There are also some young vineyards in Morocco that have the potential to produce good wine as the vines mature, providing yields are regulated.

(Below) The fuller styles of sherry – *amontillado* and *oloroso* – share with tawny port a nutty character; vintage port is intensely rich and fruity with the flavours of blackcurrants and plums as well as dried fruits.

SHERRY AND PORT
– the two great fortified wines

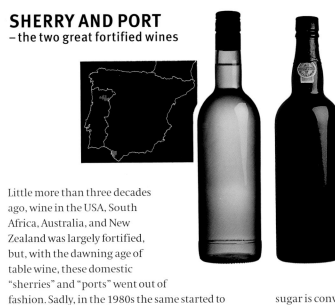

Little more than three decades ago, wine in the USA, South Africa, Australia, and New Zealand was largely fortified, but, with the dawning age of table wine, these domestic "sherries" and "ports" went out of fashion. Sadly, in the 1980s the same started to happen to sherry – the real thing from Jerez in Spain.

The dryness of classic sherry seems austere to palates brought up on the typically ripe, soft, fruity wines of today; so sherry nowadays is a taste that often has to be acquired. And yet it doesn't help that a great deal of sherry exported to Britain is sweetened. Many people never experience the real things: *fino* and *manzanilla* that are mouthwateringly crisp and dry, with a yeasty tang and sea-salty freshness; *amontillado* that is equally bone dry, but darker, fuller and nutty; and *oloroso* – still dry, but richer, fuller, warmer, and nutty but not yeasty.

Of the lingering imitations, Australian sherry styles come closest to their role models, with some particularly good *fino* styles. South Africa produces reasonably good sherry types, although never achieves the finesse of Jerez. Spain's own Montilla is a much-improved cheaper alternative to sherry.

When sherry was the classic aperitif, port was the classic wine for late on in a meal and sipped for long after it. There are several styles, but the main divide is between bottle-aged, epitomized by vintage port, and wood-aged tawny. Vintage port, made only in the best years and seldom ready before it is at least ten years old, is deep-coloured, intensely sweet, fruity (blackcurrants, plums, dried figs), rich, chocolatey, and, when young, peppery, and undrinkably tannic. The aptly named tawny is mellow, nutty, and slightly woody, with dried-fruit, derived from long ageing in wooden casks. Unlike vintage port, it should be served cool and can make a good aperitif.

In theory, both are copied in Australia and South Africa. In practice, the tawny styles predominate, but they tend to be much fuller, fruitier, and more powerful than genuine tawny. The most successful vintage styles are made in tiny quantities in Australia and are usually based on the Shiraz grape, which gives a more aromatic, sweeter wine. In Europe, sweet red fortified wines are traditional in the South of France in Banyuls, Maury, and Rivesaltes. Made largely from Grenache and, lower in alcohol than port, they can be intense and long-lived. Italy's answer to port is Recioto della Valpolicella. This is unfortified, but high in alcohol because the harvested grapes are left to dehydrate and become more concentrated before fermentation. As not all the sugar is converted into alcohol, the resulting wine is sweet and concentrated, with complex, bitter-cherry fruit and herby, spicy, sometimes gamey flavours.

(Below) **The chalky *albariza* soil of Jerez that suits the Palomino grape so well.**

THE VINEYARDS:
WHERE AND WHY

GRAPES ARE CERTAINLY THE PRINCIPAL INFLUENCE ON THE STYLE AND QUALITY OF A WINE, BUT THEY ARE ONLY THE STARTING POINT — AND AS GROWERS IN THE NEW WINE WORLD HAVE DISCOVERED IN THE LAST QUARTER OF A CENTURY THEY ARE NOT NECESSARILY THE BEST PLACE TO BEGIN.

In contrast to France, where any wine aspiring to a status above basic plonk (*vin de table*) has to be made from grape varieties specifically authorized for the relevant region or appellation, the general modus operandi of the new pioneer producers was to acquire a plot of land in sunny California, Australia, or wherever and choose their grape variety, or varieties, according to whim and/or sales aspirations. After all, vines grow in any temperate climate and flourish with plenty of warmth, water, and space, so why worry about the type of soil, topography, or nuances of climate – all those factors (and more) that the French combine under the name terroir and believe in with near religious fervour?

Why? Because flourishing vines are not necessarily the key to great or even good wine. They tend instead to produce large quantities of dilute, flavourless grapes which naturally produce dilute, flavourless wine – the vinous equivalent of large woolly-textured Mediterranean apples. Whether, as Western European tradition has it, vines really need to "struggle" to yield grapes with the quality potential to make great wine is debatable, but there is no doubt that, with few exceptions (Coonawarra being one), for wines with any pretensions to quality, they need to be planted in soils where they can put down deep, nutrient-searching root systems.

And they don't do that if everything is presented on a plate (irrigation, fertilizers, superabundant sun, and so on) at more or less surface level. They go into overdrive producing excessive foliage and unripe, or at best bland, grapes.

(Above) **Spraying water on the vines is, perhaps surprisingly, an effective way of warding off frost damage in Chablis.**

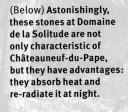

(Below) **Astonishingly, these stones at Domaine de la Solitude are not only characteristic of Châteauneuf-du-Pape, but they have advantages: they absorb heat and re-radiate it at night.**

Soil

Looking at the ideal conditions for vine cultivation – so far as such an ideal exists – it is no coincidence that the long-established European vineyards are on land where very little else thrives. Vines do, it seems, like poor soil – but there is more to it than that. Whether or not growers in the past identified the relevant factors, European experience over centuries has shown that the best soils are those that encourage root penetration, are well drained and yet at the same time are capable of holding water without becoming water logged. Limestone, as found in Burgundy and Champagne, but, tellingly, very little in the New World, fits this prescription perfectly; so do other rocky and gravelly soils such as those in the finest claret vineyards of the Haut-Médoc in Bordeaux. Stony soils (sometimes incredibly stony, as in Châteauneuf-du-Pape) are in fact the best all-rounders across a range of climates, for they have the advantage of being easily warmed and the capacity, through their stones, to re-radiate the heat at night, they are not too fertile and they do not readily erode. Moreover, stony soils are mostly found on lower slopes and foothills, a position which often also has distinct climatic advantages such as good air drainage and exposure to the sun.

Whether in addition to a soil's physical properties, its chemical composition (mineral and microbial) influences the taste of the wine it produces is a moot point. Basically the French believe it does; the New World will have none – or not much – of it. While there is no scientific evidence to support the French view, there is no arguing that certain soils are associated with particular grape varieties and, more to the point, with particular wine styles and tastes. Plenty of experienced tasters find a slaty taste in many Mosels, an earthy taste in red Graves and a gun-flinty, steely character in Chablis, all of which they attribute to the soils (slate, gravel, and Kimmeridgian limestone respectively.

Climate

Although to the French, with their notion of terroir, the influences of climate and soil are inextricably bound, the role of climate is actually more clear-cut. Put very simply, growers in the Old World are often near the limits of successful vine cultivation and so they live with the annual prospect of too little sunshine and too much rain to produce a perfectly ripe and flavoursome crop. They also get much greater variation in quality and style from vintage to vintage. Those in much of the New World live with the prospect of too much warmth and too little rain to produce grapes with subtlety and balanced fruit, acid, alcohol, and tannin. With the aid of irrigation, however, (still largely banned in Europe), they do get more consistent results.

The outcome of all this is that, to date, the world's greatest wines have come from the hotter years in the best European vineyards, for Europe, it appears, has greater quality potential, but, ironically, less likelihood of it being realized.

But growers in the New World are not taking this lying down. Increasingly, in California, Australia, South Africa et al, the emphasis is on microclimate (strictly speaking, mesoclimate), the localized climate within a climate reflecting the lie of the land – the pocket sheltered from the prevailing wind, the slopes catching cool sea breezes, fogs, an extra hour of sun, or cooler night-time temperatures. Not surprisingly, the "perfect" spots being sought out are essentially closer in spirit to the cooler climatic conditions of their European role models (even though, in Australia in particular, irrigation is nearly always essential). The results, already, are some great wines – both subtle and complex – but, as in Europe, there is less certainty of greatness being produced every year.

(Below) **Cooling fog, drawn in off the Pacific, is a familiar – and welcome – sight on hot days in the Napa Valley.**

CHOICES IN THE VINEYARD:
TENDING VINES

HAVING APPROPRIATE GRAPE VARIETIES IN SUITABLE SOIL UNDER A FAVOURABLE CLIMATE DOES NOT, ALAS, GUARANTEE YOU GOOD WINE — AND IT IS NOT ONLY THAT YOU NEED A GOOD WINEMAKER. WELL BEFORE THE WINERY AND CELLAR STAGE, YOU NEED TO HAVE CARED FOR YOUR VINES PROPERLY — TRELLISED, TRAINED, PRUNED, TREATED FOR DISEASE AND INCLEMENT WEATHER, AND PICKED THEM TO THEIR BEST ADVANTAGE.

The value of careful husbandry was one of the great lessons that producers in the New World began to learn in the late 1980s. Until then, they had put almost all their efforts into what happened in the winery, believing that science and technology were sufficient to ensure good wine. What they found of course was that they ensured sound, technically correct wine, but, as any cook could have told them, the end result could only ever be as good as its ingredients. Today the pendulum has swung firmly towards the vineyards.

Pruning and training

Looking at the neat rows of trellis-trained vines in many a modern vineyard, it is perhaps hard to visualize how, left alone, most vines would become rambling masses of branches, shoots, and leaves climbing up any available trees. The more luxuriant they became, the more the grape bunches would be shaded from essential sunlight and the more erratic their growth would be. This is the view that explains the norm of hard pruning, whether by hand or machine, during a vine's winter dormant period.

(Below) **Some New World producers have begun to question the value of hard winter pruning, but in the Old World it remains a key stage in the vineyard year, as shown here in Champagne.**

But this tradition (like so many others) has been challenged in the New World, particularly in Australia, where some growers have abandoned the expensive practice of winter pruning altogether (they do a minimal amount of summer pruning) and have apparently found that, contrary to previous evidence, unpruned vines show considerable self-discipline: they not only keep their vegetation growth in check, but they produce bunches on the outside of the canopy where there is maximum exposure to sun. Supporters of such "minimal pruning" say that, although yields increase, so does quality. The majority of producers have yet to be convinced and it is certain that pruning will remain a primary quality controller for the time being.

Another hot topic, related but less controversial, is "canopy management" – the canopy being the potentially sunlight-blocking foliage. The aim of this practice is simply to allow leaves and fruit the best possible exposure and aeration by using a combination of techniques including new trellising systems, shoot thinning, summer pruning, and leaf removal.

Yield

All the above practices affect the grape yield (output) and the yield affects wine quality – high yields adversely so – which is why the French *appellation contrôlée* system (*see* France, page 96), and appellation systems based on it, specify maximum yields and ban or tightly regulate irrigation. But the equation isn't as simple as that. While there is no denying that there comes a level of output above which quality deteriorates (basically all the flavours are diluted), there are all sorts of variables to consider.

Grape variety is the obvious one: the quality of Pinot Noir grapes begins to suffer at lower yields than Chardonnay, for example. Place is another: a harsh climate will naturally produce lower yields than a more moderate one. The density of planting is yet another and particularly tricky one: yields are often measured in volume per hectare, but the number of vines planted per hectare varies enormously – being much lower, for example in the New World, where mechanical harvesters are widely used (and need room to move up and down the rows) than in regions such as Burgundy where mechanization is very limited. Generally speaking, wide spacing is thought to be less good for quality because the vines' roots tend to spread lazily horizontally rather than down through layers of soil containing different nutrients. Finally, there is the unarguable, but seemingly irreconcilable, fact that in Bordeaux, Burgundy,

Why vine age is important

You may have seen the words vielles vignes *(old vines) on a wine label. This is because the age of the vines, in tandem with other factors such as the number of bunches of grapes produced (yield), has a critical influence on the quality and character of a wine. Vines usually begin to fruit in commercial quantities and are entitled to appellation contrôlée status from their third year, but grape quality and intensity of flavour improve as they age.*

The exception to this is that some young vines do produce very high quality. Both the world's most sought-after port, 1931 Quinta do Noval Nacional, and the fabled 1961 Château Pétrus were made substantially from the grapes of five- to six-year-old vines.

The clue to such quality from young vines seems to be restricting yields. In fact the yield of all vines begins to decline eventually (it depends greatly on variety, but often from about fifteen to twenty years old), although quality may continue to improve – hence the grower wishing to draw attention on labels to his old vines.

So why would any grower advertise the fact that his are jeunes vignes *(young vines)? In fact the growers who occasionally do this are trying to tell you something quite different. They are trying to let you know that, were the vines older (they are probably under three years), they would be entitled to a superior appellation.*

(Below) **"Pergola" training with local granite supports in Galicia, northwest Spain – a traditional system in this lush, green region.**

and Champagne since 1982 some of the best vintages have been some of the largest.

There is no neat formula. In the end it has to be the responsibility not of the law but of the individual to produce the yield he or she deems appropriate to the quality of wine intended (not everyone, after all, is aiming for the stars). This might be done by a combination of pruning (winter, spring, and summer), "green-pruning" (removal of excess bunches in summer), and by considered use of fertilizers and other treatments. Which brings me neatly to another contentious area: products applied in the vineyards.

Going "green"

In fact this is not nearly as controversial as it would have been fifteen or twenty years ago. The great "nurture versus nature" debate has almost become the great consensus. From growers through to academics, buyers, and sellers, in the New World and Old, the mood is very much greener than it was. Certified organic growers are still a small minority, but there has been a huge increase in growers following *lutte raisonnée*/ sustainable agriculture/integrated management systems. These are not officially regulated, but the idea is to use natural methods and treatments (such as cover crops and insect predators) rather than chemical treatments, unless absolutely necessary to save a crop or a livelihood. Yields are usually lower, but that can be considered a positive effect. In many cases the same additive-free thinking extends to the processes in the winery, although there is a marked reluctance all round to jump headlong into the organic camp.

Ripening and picking

You might think that deciding when to pick would be the easiest of decisions – you harvest, surely, as soon as the grapes are ripe. Well, yes and no. The grape is quite a complex fruit and deciding when it is at the optimum point of ripeness for the intended style of wine can be nail-biting (even without worrying about such threats as impending storms). Leave it a fraction late and acidity will begin to drop, resulting in increasingly flabby, short-lived wines – whites in particular. Pick a little too early and the sweetness of the fruit will be muted and probably dominated by unripe, green flavours and acid, giving a tart taste (especially to white wines), and/or tannin, which gives to red wines a harsh, dry, bitter taste and feel.

The difficulty is exacerbated by the fact that physiological and chemical ripeness can get out of

(Above) *Biodynamie*, practised here at Coulée de Serrant in the Loire, means rigorously traditional cultivation methods.

sync. In Bordeaux in 1989 – theoretically an excellent vintage – some Merlot grapes were found to be ripe in every respect except for their tannins. When growers waited for the tannins to ripen, acid levels began to drop menacingly.

Overall, though, the art and science of harvesting at the best possible time has improved in the last decade or so, largely because of advances in winemaking. To take but one example, since winemaking is the subject of the following chapter, red grapes in Bordeaux are now generally picked later and riper than they were before control of fermentation temperatures was widely exercised, because, with such control, the higher sugar levels in the grapes need not cause fermentation to overheat and stop early. Riper grapes mean sweeter, richer fruit flavours and riper, more attractive tannins. The other critical decision is whether to pick by hand or by machine. In some regions, Champagne and Sauternes for

From organic to biodynamic

Only a few years ago, "Biodynamie", organic vine growing taken a stage further into the realms of the cosmos, as inspired by Rudolph Steiner, still looked distinctly cranky. But the 1990s saw some of France's most celebrated wine estates, especially in Burgundy, taking an interest, then taking the plunge into this most rigorous of cultivation systems. Biodynamie is much more than soil management and crop cultivation using only natural treatments. Practitioners avoid clonally bred vines and use a range of specially prepared organic, herbal, and mineral treatments in homeopathic quantities. These include dung that has been buried in a cow's horn from one equinox to the next and infusions of valerian and horsetail. But its most important function, to quote one its most impassioned disciples, Nicolas Joly of Coulée de Serrant in the Loire, is to "support the life of the soil by reinforcing its links with the solar system and its cosmic background" – i.e. what is actually happening in the sky. In practice this means working the vineyards and the wine according to the moon and stars. Cranky? French growers have been doing this to some extent for generations, bottling wine in the spring in accordance with the phase of the moon, for example.

example, mechanical harvesters are banned; in others, such as Bordeaux and Burgundy, they are allowed but are little used – at least by the top properties; and in others, vertiginous slopes or closely planted rows of vines make machine access impossible. Hand-picking is gentler and more discriminating, say its advocates. A human picker can be trained to pick only the healthy bunches, or to pick only those thoroughly affected by "noble rot", leaving the others to develop it before the next selective picking. But in Australia, where mechanical harvesters (and pruners) prevail, their supporters say the most sophisticated modern machines are sufficiently gentle and have the added advantages of being much faster than humans and available without complaint at all hours.

(Right) **Mechanical harvesters are unusual in Burgundy, where landholdings are often tiny: rows of pickers bent double are a far more common sight.**

THE WINEMAKER'S ROLE

IN SOME WAYS WINEMAKING IS THE EASY BIT. IF NATURE AND NURTURE HAVE PROVIDED RIPE, HEALTHY GRAPES, THERE REALLY IS NO EXCUSE FOR POOR WINE, AS THE PROCESS BY WHICH GRAPE SUGARS ARE CONVERTED INTO ALCOHOL AND CARBON DIOXIDE DURING FERMENTATION IS AS SIMPLE AND NATURAL AS IT HAS ALWAYS BEEN. INDEED, WINE WILL MAKE ITSELF, PROVIDED THE WEATHER IS REASONABLY WARM AND THAT NATURAL YEASTS ON THE GRAPE SKIN (AND IN THE WINERY) HAVE NOT BEEN KILLED OFF BY CHEMICAL SPRAYS IN THE VINEYARDS. THAT PRESUMABLY WAS HOW IT ALL STARTED.

It would be daft, though, to imply that winemakers were in any way redundant. Wine left to make itself would in most cases soon be bacterially spoiled – on its way to vinegar – because once it has finished fermenting it needs to be protected from oxygen. But, as the pendulum has swung more towards the role of the grower in the vineyard in determining quality, so it has swung away from the winemaker as interventionist wizard, a role which reached its apogee in some of the high-tech wineries of California and Australia in the 1970s and 1980s.

MAKING RED WINE

Crushing

Once picked, the aim is to get all grapes to the winery as quickly and as smoothly as possible – ideally, although this is usually more important for white grapes, transported in stacks of small plastic crates, rather than in one heavy mass in the back of a huge truck where the bunches at the bottom will get squashed by those above. At the winery most red grapes are put through a "crusher" to break the skins and gently release the juices ready for fermentation, and, depending on the grape variety and region, to remove all or some of the bitter, tannic stems (some are often left on in Burgundy, but they are almost always removed in Bordeaux).

The principal exceptions to the crushing rule are red grapes for sparkling wines, Beaujolais, and other bright, fruity reds intended to be drunk young, and some burgundy. Here the whole bunches are fermented. The best red grapes of the Douro, destined for long-lived vintage port, are also treated differently. Many port producers, having tried mechanical alternatives, have come back to old-fashioned treading – by warm and gentle human feet – although some find that

> Wines and grapes mentioned in this chapter are described in more detail in the final part of the book (pages 94–157) and in "The Importance of Grapes" (pages 50–59).

feet are even more effective if the grapes have been given a swift preliminary pre-crush by machine.

Fermentation

After crushing, the "must", the pulp of skins, and juice, is fed into fermentation containers which vary from traditional open-topped wood vats to glass-lined cement and fibreglass (neither usually associated with the highest quality wines) to giant, stainless steel tanks to, in a few cases, wooden barrels. A small amount of sulphur dioxide, as protection against oxidation and as an antiseptic, may be added if it was not added at the crusher stage, but this is more especially needed for white wines. In cooler climates, such as the main French wine regions, sugar (*chaptalization*) or concentrated grape must (enrichment) may be added to both reds and whites to bring the potential alcohol up to a reasonable level. And in many regions, particularly warm New

World ones, acid may be added, although, again, this balance adjustment is more usually applied to white wines.

To get fermentation started immediately a winemaker has several options. In cool climates, he might heat the must, and he might use yeast activators and/or cultured yeasts. These are much more reliable than wild strains, but the argument against them is that, in dispensing with the indigenous yeasts in favour of laboratory-cultured ones, you lose some of the regional individuality of wine. (This is particularly the case with the malleable Chardonnay grape, for which there are some very popular – in the New World – Burgundy-type cultured yeasts giving extra rich, buttery flavours and others that give notably fruity flavours.)

When fermentation is underway, stopping the temperature from rising too high is crucial. Over-hot musts produce coarse, stewed-tasting wines and, if the temperature gets completely out of control, the yeasts will be killed off before

Improving on nature?

In the past, growers were stuck with what nature provided. Nowadays, if winemakers don't get the grapes they want, there are a number of processes available to those who have the (often expensive) equipment. Concentrating the must – removing water from juice and pulp – is one which is increasingly used in this era of strapping, high alcohol wines. There are three main methods: producers of sweet wines favour cryoextraction, in which the grapes are chilled until the watery juices freeze, leaving the sugar- and acid- rich juice to flow when the grapes are crushed; red wine producers favour either evaporating the must under vacuum or reverse osmosis. But just because it's possible, it doesn't mean everyone approves.

Red wine: the vital stages

1 TREADING OR CRUSHING THE GRAPES
Treading, the traditional method for vintage port, is not just a quaint custom put on for the benefit of visitors, but the best way to extract the maximum colour and tannin from the skins in a short time.

2 FERMENTATION
Either in closed vats or open-topped vessels. Temperatures may be carefully controlled or they may not. Whichever approach, this is the stage where yeasts convert grape sugar into alcohol and therefore juice into wine.

3 SUBMERGING THE SKINS
During fermentation a "cap" of skins rises to the top of the bubbling mass and has to be pushed down regularly, either mechanically or by prodding with a pole, to ensure colour leaches out of the skins into the liquid.

4 PRESSING
Red wine grapes are crushed before fermentation but pressing is carried out afterwards. The left-over pulpy grape mass is put through a press to yield tannic "press wine" – which may or may not be blended in to improve the final wine.

5 MATURATION
Most of the better red wines – especially those intended to improve with age – are at least partially aged in new oak barrels for depth and complexity. A new trend is to ferment, or partly ferment, them in these barrels.

6 RACKING
As they mature, red wines drop a sediment – they are removed from this in a process called racking, in which the wine is moved gently from one barrel to another clean one... the final transfer is to the bottling line.

they have finished converting sugar into alcohol. Most reds are therefore fermented somewhere between 25–30 ˚C (77–86 ˚F). The other essential during red wine fermentation is to keep the skins submerged, so that their colour (the flesh of most red wine grapes is as colourless as that of white grapes), tannin, and flavours are leached out into the liquid. Carbon dioxide given off by the yeasts constantly pushes the skins to the top, so they need to be pulled down again regularly, either by pumping the juice up and over or by punching them down by hand or mechanically.

Fermentation may take only a few days, but if so, the results will be light reds for early consumption. More serious reds are more likely to take two weeks and may be left macerating with their skins for three or more. The wine will then be drawn off the skins (although this can also be done part way through fermentation to make a less tannic wine) and the skins will be pressed. The winemaker may then add some, or all, of this sturdy, tannic "press wine" to give the original wine more body, or he may leave the decision until spring.

Malolactic fermentation

The final stage of fermentation for all reds (but only some whites) is the "malolactic fermentation", the conversion of astringent malic acid into softer lactic acid. Nowadays this is usually induced (by adding appropriate bacteria) straight after the alcoholic fermentation, but some traditional and non-interventionist winemakers allow it to happen of its own accord when temperatures begin to rise in the spring. In theory the wine is now ready to drink. In practice most red wines need time to soften, but those intended for immediate drinking will be fined and filtered to remove sediment and any other foreign bodies prior to bottling.

Oak

Most of the world's serious red wines are matured in new oak barrels for between four and twenty-four months to soften the tannins and develop that elusive attribute – complexity. And preferably the oak is French, because France, with everything else going for it, also manages to have the finest oak, from forests such as Allier, Nevers, and Limousin. New oak gives flavour (especially vanillin) and tannin, and, being porous, allows limited, but significant, beneficial interaction between wine and air.

The age of the barrel is fundamental: the newer the barrel, the more it gives to the wine, so after three or four years it has little left to impart. Another important variable is its charring, or "toast": the higher the toast the more toasty the flavour.

Compared with French oak, American tends to be less subtle, with a stronger vanilla-and-spice taste, as does Slovenian. The advantage of these and other woods such as chestnut and acacia is that they are cheaper. But nowadays there are cheap ways to get new-oak flavour: oak chips and oak staves canbe suspended in stainless steel tanks or old oak vats to give a quick oak fix. It doesn't make for subtlety and is much frowned on in classic European regions, but gives a simple toasty-oak flavour to wines for early drinking.

Final stages

During wood ageing, the winemaker still has a few crucial tasks. Most barrels need to be topped up periodically to compensate for evaporation and the wine must be "racked". This is the drawing off of wine from one barrel to a clean one, leaving behind the sediment that has been deposited (the number of rackings depending on the duration in barrel and the type of wine). Some wines also need to be blended. This may be because they are made from more than one grape variety (claret, for example), or because the winemaker has so far kept wine from different vineyards separate. Before bottling, the wine will be fined to remove impurities, either traditionally with egg white or with a commerical clarifying agent such as bentonite. Most wines will also be filtered, to further ensure their stability, although top producers, especially in Burgundy, the Rhône, and California, often dispense with filtration on the grounds that it strips wines of character.

Tannin

There is much debate in the wine world about whether today's great red wines from the classic regions – claret, burgundy, Rhône, Barolo – will last as long as their predecessors, and the ripeness, or softness, of the tannins is at the heart of the debate. Tannin, the dry, slightly bitter, mouth-coating substance that makes cold tea so unpleasant, is essential for wine, especially red, that is going to be aged (whites rely more on acidity), but winemakers since the 1980s have been aiming for less aggressively tannic wines – wines, simply, that are suppler and ready for drinking sooner. They achieve this by picking the grapes later, so that the tannins in the skins, stalks, and pips are all riper; by removing the stalks, which contain tannins that are more bitter than those in the skins; and by crushing gently, so that the pips, which contain the harshest tannins of all, are not split.

And, if maturing the wine in wood, which is another source of tannin, they make sure that they buy good barrels, made from well-seasoned, properly toasted oak, and they are careful not to leave the wine in them for too long. But none of this answers the fundamental question as to whether contemporary classics will last as long as their predecessors. The winemakers say they will, because tannins are present, although different, but they would say that, wouldn't they? Only time will tell.

MAKING WHITE WINE

White winemaking is essentially the red wine process without the grape skins. The grapes (which may be white, red, or both), are crushed, destemmed, and pressed before they are fermented, although a few winemakers practise "skin contact", a period of a few hours' pre-pressing when the juice is left on the skins to draw additional aromas and flavours from them. Before fermentation the juice may be clarified, either by allowing natural cold settling, by filtration or by centrifuge, but the latter two methods are harsh, taking away more than just the residue of skins, pips, and stalks.

Both the duration and the temperature of fermentation vary considerably, but are directly related. Modern, light-bodied, and aromatic whites are often fermented very slowly for up to four weeks in stainless steel tanks at temperatures as low as 12°C (54°F) – to retain all the freshness of the grape. Most will then be racked, filtered, cold stabilized (so that if subjected to cold later in their lives they do not turn cloudy in the bottle) and bottled within three to six months of the harvest. Traditional European and full-bodied whites tend to be fermented more quickly at higher temperatures – up to 20°C (68°F) – in barrel, to give bigger, richer flavours. Whether whites undergo malolactic fermentation is the winemaker's choice. Most burgundy and champagne does, and it adds to their complexity, but in warmer climates where acidity is naturally lower it is usually prevented (with extra sulphur dioxide, or filtration).

Some wines will then be aged in new oak; some will get a quick, cheap dose of oak chips; and the finest full-bodied whites, especially Chardonnays and Sauternes, will have already been fermented in new oak barrels because this gives even greater depth and complexity (light and aromatic styles are seldom oak-fermented). In addition, the lees (dead yeast residues) may be left in the barrel to be stirred up regularly over several months to give creamier tastes and textures. Oak-matured whites are then usually racked, filtered, (although not invariably) and bottled at between four and twenty months.

Rosé wine

Making rosé is more or less a half-way house between white and red wine. In a very few instances, the law allows winemakers to make rosé simply by blending finished white and red – eg. pink champagne – but the colour of most still rosés comes directly from the skins of red grapes. This may be before fermentation, either by crushing the grapes and leaving them to macerate for up to thirty-six hours, or by very gently pressing whole bunches to release delicately tinted juice, or from a brief fermentation with the skins. Whichever the method, after fermentation rosé is handled very much in the manner of white wines.

White wine: the vital stages

1 ARRIVAL AT THE WINERY
Perfect grapes, especially white grapes, can be spoiled by delays and heavy handling between vineyard and winery, so speed is of the essence: harvesting, transport, and crushing must take place quickly and carefully.

2 PRESSING
After crushing – or even sometimes nowadays without crushing – white grapes are pressed to release all their juice. It is important to press before fermentation so contact between juice and the skins, pips and stalks is minimized.

3 FERMENTATION
The face of the ultra-modern wine industry: stainless steel vats are good for white wine fermentation as they enable efficient temperature control and therefore control over yeast activity and the style of the finished wine.

4 FILTERING THE WINE
Carried out before fermentation, to clarify juice, and/or afterwards, to make sure the wine is clear and stable. Some say it strips wine of flavour, but those in favour say the best filters (below) are quite gentle enough.

5 WHY FILTER?
Before and after – two glasses of the same Chardonnay: the one on the left is unfiltered, that on the right has been passed through the vacuum filter seen left.

6 MATURATION
Full-bodied white wines are then frequently aged in new oak barrels to give richness of flavour and texture. (The best wines might also have been fermented in the barrels.) Bottling may either be from vat or from barrel.

Sparkling wine

If yeast and sugar are added to finished wine, fermentation will start all over again, and if the carbon dioxide given off has no means of escape it will be trapped as bubbles in the liquid – thus sparkling wine. But there is sparkling wine and sparkling wine. The quality and style of the base wine are critical: the finest, notably those for Champagne, are very pure, but thin, acid and fairly neutral – the result of scarcely ripe grapes, hand picked and pressed very gently in whole bunches. The nature of the container in which the second fermentation occurs is no less important. The best results – the most complex and subtle – are achieved when it takes place in the original bottle and the wine is then left there for some time (a minimum of fifteen months in Champagne) with its lees: the dead yeasts gradually break down giving the typical creamy, bready, brioche character of fine Champagne. This is the traditional method and there is no matching it, but it is expensive and time-consuming – the removal of the sludgy yeast sediment, before the wine can be topped up with a dose of wine and sugar ready for release and sale, being not the least part.

An easier way of dealing with the sediment – one often used in the New World – is to transfer the now sparkling wine to a large tank where the sediment is removed, usually by filtration. The wine is then given its *dosage* of wine and sugar and bottled once again. This method can produce good sparkling wines, but they lack the finesse and complexity of the bottle-fermented Champagne method. Less good again, but cheaper, is the *cuve close* or tank method where the second fermentation takes place in a vast tank. Finally, for the lowest grade of fizz, there is carbonation, where carbon dioxide is simply and very cheaply pumped into still wine.

Sweet wine

Excluding fortified wines, the vast majority of sweet wines are white, and their sweetness is natural grape sugar – from unusually sweet, ripe grapes – that has not been converted into alcohol, or, as for some German wines, has been enhanced by the addition of sweet grape concentrate (*Süssreserve*). At high sugar levels yeasts struggle to work and may give up at eight to nine per cent alcohol (as in great German wines) or may struggle on until they are killed at fifteen to sixteen per cent. More commonly winemakers halt the fermentation themselves (with sulphur dioxide, refrigeration, racking, or centrifuging) at the point when they feel sugar, alcohol, and, no less important, acid levels are all in harmony.

The grapes for sweet wines, picked late in the autumn, are essentially dehydrated (to a greater or lesser extent), hence the high levels of sugar and acidity. They may actually be shrivelled – "raisined" – on the vine, as happens in Jurançon in South West France in the best years; they may be spread out and dried (raisined) on mats, or hung up to dry, as with Italy's *passito* and *recioto* wines; or, most significant of all, they may be shrivelled on the vine by a grey mould called noble rot (*Botrytis cinerea*). In certain warm, humid weather conditions this ugly but benificent mould appears in Sauternes, Germany, the Loire, Alsace, Tokay, and Austria, and is responsible for all the greatest sweet wines. In less favourable conditions, in the New World, noble rot may be sprayed onto grapes in the winery.

Another way of producing immensely concentrated sweet wines is to freeze the water out. In Germany and Canada grapes are left on the vines – occasionally into the New Year – to make *Eiswein* or Ice Wine. Simulating this process in their cellars, some Sauternes châteaux freeze excess water out when the grapes have been swelled – and diluted – by rain before or during picking.

(Left) *Remuage*, or riddling, is the critical process of gradually turning and upending the maturing bottles of champagne, so that the sediment slides down into the neck of the bottle.

Fortified wine

Wines that have been fortified (usually with grape spirit) are also often sweet, because the fortifying alcohol is added to the fermenting wine before all the sugar has been converted. Port is the classic example; others include Muscat de Beaumes-de-Venise and other southern French *Vins Doux Naturels*, Australian liqueur Muscats, Bual, and Malmsey madeiras. But the spirit can also be added at the end of fermentation to produce a dry fortified wine, for example sherry (the sweet styles being sweetened later, as also with Sercial and Verdelho madeira).

Much of the character and quality of the major fortified wines – port, sherry, and madeira – comes from their long years spent peacefully maturing in bottle or wood, further details of which are outlined in the Styles chapter (page 81) and the Spain and Portugal chapters (page 128 and pages 132–33).

Organic winemaking

There is a global trend to reducing the chemical input in vineyards and wineries and yet fully fledged organic winemaking is far less evident than the organic viticultural practices to which it is the natural corollary. The main reason is that, although levels of sulphur dioxide usage have been going down, it is very hard to make stable wine without using any at all (see Winemaking page 89). The other reason is that, legally, in the EU there is no such thing as organic wine: it is "wine made from organically grown grapes", because the bureaucrats have yet to decide what constitutes organic production. The USA has defined both organic wine and wine made from organically grown grapes. For a wine to be labelled organic in the USA, it must have a negligible under 10ppm sulphites. The Soil Association in the UK has also ruled on the production process. As well as forbidding the use of copper sulphate in the vineyards (because it builds up toxically in the soil), it has set permitted levels of sulphites in the finished wines at markedly lower levels than those allowed by the EU.

(Left) **Luscious sweet wines are produced in Italy from grapes which have been laid out to dry – to "raisin" – in airy rooms on straw mats.**

WHERE THE BEST
WINES ARE MADE

3 The world wine map has changed almost beyond
recognition in the last quarter of a century. Countries,
and even whole continents, have opened up to
produce exciting, high quality wines. In the Old World
– slow to respond to the challenge from the New World at first –
run-down vineyards have been revitalised, new regions and
wines have been developed, and wines that never used to travel
beyond their local bars and restaurants are now sold in cities
thousands of miles away.

FRANCE

Italy produces more wine than France, Australia produces it more reliably, Bulgaria produces it more cheaply – and yet, for centuries, France has been regarded as the source par excellence of high quality. Even today, with the best producers of the New World challenging France at every turn, the challenge is still essentially on French terms. If France didn't exist, the wines of almost every other country in the world would be vastly different.

It is the distinctly unpromising climates of France's greatest wine regions that, paradoxically, are critical to quality, because, although wine can be made anywhere warm enough to ripen grapes, fine wine is made at the margins, where it is only just warm enough and, in poor years, not warm enough at all; Champagne, Burgundy, the Loire, and even Bordeaux specialize in this kind of knife-edge climate.

France's other secret is its soils. They are varied enough to suit just about any grape variety of almost any quality – which means that, although the country's reputation inevitably rests on its finest wines, it also produces everyday wine to satisfy the smallest pocket. And nowadays, with improved winemaking skills finding their way into the backwoods, *appellation contrôlée* (or AC) wine no longer has a monopoly on quality and excitement.

It was this realization that led recently to a fundamental change to the *appellation contrôlée* system. AC wines are at the top of the pyramid, but until 2001 AC did not set out to guarantee quality. By regulating grape varieties, yields, minimum levels of alcohol and maturation periods, it guaranteed origin and style. But in an increasingly competitive world this was not enough. Stung by falling exports and growing criticism of quality, the regulatory authority introduced measures to control and

(Right) **With its "varietal"** *vin de pays*, **Languedoc has been dubbed the "New World" of Europe, but it is also a region where tradition dies hard – and the traditional wines from old vines and low yields can be sensational.**

monitor vineyards and winemaking – and thus, it is hoped, make AC a guarantee of quality, as well as origin and style.

Between AC and *vin de pays* is *vin délimité de qualité supérieure (*VDQS*)*: a small group effectively in the AC waiting room. *Vin de pays* (literally, "wines of the countryside"), of which there are about 150, also come from specified areas and grape varieties, but these can be very wide-ranging indeed. The catch-all regional *vin de pays* are: du Jardin de la France (Loire), du

Comté Tolosan (Midi-Pyrenees), des Collines Rhodaniennes (Rhône-Alpes), and, by far the most important, Vin de Pays d'Oc (Languedoc-Roussillon). Within these four are many much smaller *vin de pays* with much more tightly defined local styles.

ALSACE

Unlike most areas of France, the warm, dry, and sunny region of Alsace in the northeast identifies

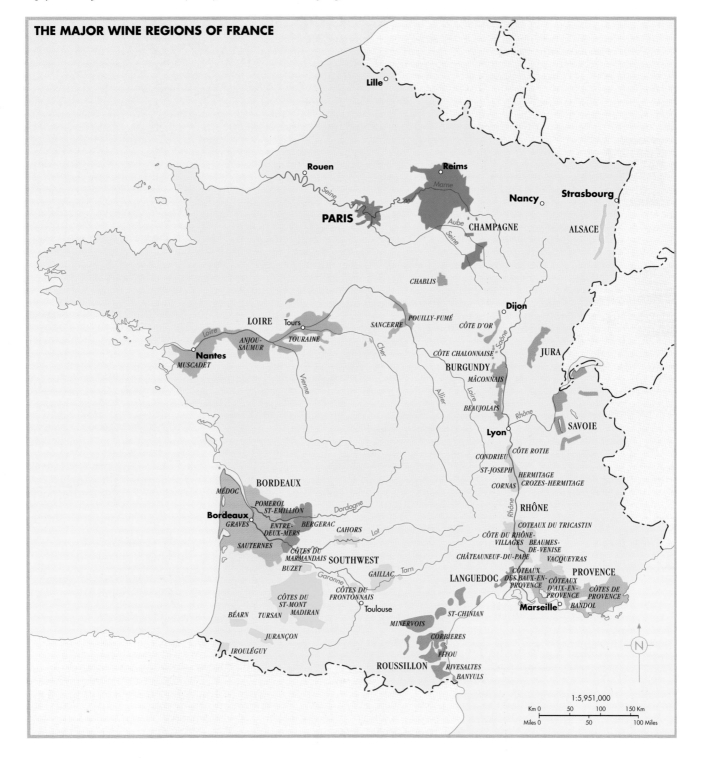

(*Right*) **Riquewihr – picture-book Alsace, with its cobbled streets and half-timbered houses, and textbook Alsace wines, especially Riesling.**

Alsace vintages		
2002	8	▼
2001	7	★
2000	9	★
1999	7	★
1998	9	★
1997	8	★
1996	8	★
1995	8	★

Key
0–10 quality rating
(10 = top wine)
▲ should drink
★ can drink, but no hurry for the top wines
▼ must keep

(*See* also **When to drink**, pages 44–47)

its aromatic white wines (and limited output of red wines) primarily by grape variety – and this includes the small percentage of production that comes from the fifty individual vineyards now designated Grand Cru. Grand Cru wines, which generally may only be made from the region's four best white varieties (Riesling, Tokay-Pinot Gris, Gewurztraminer, and Muscat), have greater depth and ageing ability.

Accounting for a larger proportion of the bottles on our shelves are producers' own "prestige" labels, given various Réserve or Cuvée names. While these indicate a quality higher than the individual producer's average, there is no structure for comparing one producer's Cuvée with another's Réserve. The other indicators to look for on labels are *Vendange Tardive* or *Sélection des Grains Nobles*. These are high quality, concentrated wines made from sugar-rich late-picked grapes in good vintages. *Vendange Tardive* wines are semi-sweet to sweet depending on the year and producer. *Sélection des Grains Nobles*, made only from the four top grape varieties, are sweeter and richer because they are made from grapes that have been affected by botrytis.

The wines

Crémant d'Alsace

The *méthode traditionnelle* sparkling wine of Alsace (made by the same method as Champagne) can be good value. It is usually made from Pinot Blanc, sometimes with Riesling, and it is best drunk young.

Edelzwicker

Often now sold simply as Alsace, Edelzwicker is the inexpensive, often attractive everyday white blended from Sylvaner, Pinot Blanc, and Chasselas.

Gewurztraminer

Grown nowhere else in France, this grape gives full-bodied, exotic, scented wines, with a slight oiliness. The best sweet wines are drunk locally with foie gras.

Muscat

Little-grown but delicious. Young Muscat wine, with its dry, rose-petal freshness is an excellent aperitif.

Pinot Blanc

Perfumed but lighter and less spicy than Tokay-Pinot Gris, Pinot Blanc (aka Clevner or Klevner) is usually straightorward, refreshing, scented, and appley.

Pinot Noir

Alsace's only red grape is often little more than a shadow of its burgundian self, but served young and cool, it makes a very good summer red. A few producers are producing very serious wines.

Riesling

In Alsace, the classic Riesling of Germany gives wines of greater body and ripeness, whether dry or late-picked. Grands Crus and producers' special labels can be austere early on but often live for years; lighter versions are best young.

Sylvaner

Simple, appley dry wine, mostly used for blending.

Tokay-Pinot Gris

This is how Pinot Gris is known in Alsace, but the Tokay part is soon to be dropped. It makes rich, spicy, sometimes honeyed and nutty wines, including superb sweet ones.

BORDEAUX

Bordeaux in southwest France is the world's largest fine wine region and red Bordeaux – or claret – has always dominated the international wine market. The top seventy or eighty wines, many of them ranked in the famous 1855 Classification, may take ten or even fifteen years to mature and then remain at their peak for many more. But Bordeaux is more than illustrious names (and phenomenal prices). This large region is home to over 12,000 producers (châteaux both great and humble, and cooperatives) and no fewer than fifty-four appellations, rising from the catch-alls Bordeaux and Bordeaux Supérieur (the latter has slightly stricter production rules and half a degree more alcohol) to the individual communes, such as Pauillac and Pomerol, which boast the great names and the highest price tags. There are also white wines, dry and sweet, some *crémant* (sparkling), and even some rosé and *clairet* (light red, from which the English "claret" derives).

Classifications, rankings, and categories

Wines have been classified and ranked in various parts of the Bordeaux region since the last century and there are now several classifications (*see* Graves, St-Emilion, and Sauternes), but first and foremost is still the 1855 Classification of the Médoc. This ranked the top fifty-nine châteaux as *crus classés*, "classed growths", in five ascending tiers from Cinquièmes Crus (Fifth Growths) to Premiers Crus (First Growths), simply according to the prices they fetched. The First Growths were Châteaux Lafite, Latour, Haut-Brion (actually in the Graves), and Margaux. Mouton-Rothschild had to wait another 118 years to join their ranks and its promotion is the only change there has ever been to the classification. No one doubts, however, that, were it revised now, there would be more changes: the internationally loved Lynch-Bages, for example, would certainly be raised from Fifth Growth – probably to Second.

A handful of the 200 Médoc properties that call themselves Crus Bourgeois would also almost certainly find themselves, by virtue of their fine vineyards and no-expense-spared winemaking methods, elevated to Cru Classé, but the majority are properties of lower aspirations. They aim for wines above average in quality with the potential in good vintages to improve with a few years in the cellar. Crus Grands Bourgeois and Crus Grands Bourgeois Exceptionnels are superior subdivisions. Below the Crus Bourgeois come the myriad unclassified properties. Dubbed "*petits châteaux*", these are everyday clarets that can usually be drunk within a

(Left) **Not every part of France is wine growing country: the sand of Les Landes is not ideal for wines, although in some parts of the world, such as the Sables du Golfe du Lion in the south of France, sand planted with vines has the advantage of being phylloxera-free.**

Bordeaux vintages (red)		
Médoc & Graves		
2002	8	▼
2001	8	▼
2000	9	▼
1999	7	★
1998	7	★
1997	6	★
1996	8	★
1995	8	★
1994	6	★
1993	5	▲
1992	4	▲
1991	4	▲
St-Emilion & Pomerol		
2002	8	▼
2001	8	▼
2000	9	▼
1999	7	★
1998	9	▼
1997	6	★
1996	7	★
1995	8	★
1994	7	★
1993	5	▲
1992	4	▲
1991	3	▲

(*See* page 98 for key to symbols)

year or eighteen months of the vintage and seldom benefit from much more than three years' keeping.

There are also brands (the most famous of which is Mouton-Cadet). The Bordeaux merchants and cooperatives that make most of these are aiming for consistent taste and quality year in year out, so the wines are often blends from anywhere in the Bordeaux region and may be a blend of years. Generic wines – those simply called Médoc, St-Emilion, etc – are more specific regional blends, and occasionally they may come from a named property.

The so-called Second Labels are in a different league. These are the wines from major châteaux which have been rejected as not quite good enough to go under the main château label and bottled separately under a different, but often recognisably linked, name (eg. Carruades de Lafite, Les Forts de Latour) and sold more cheaply. So long as you are wary of poor vintages, these can offer an earlier-maturing taste of the château style. *Vins de garage*, or garage wines, so-named because they are made in tiny quantities and often on land where there is no château, rose to fame and fortune in the 1990s. Most come from around St-Emilion and Pomerol, the Merlot-dominated right bank. The essential features – minute production, low yields, very ripe grapes, and huge amounts of new oak – produce a style that is very concentrated, ripe, and rich. And very expensive. Whether they will prove more than a passing fad is yet to be seen.

Grapes

Virtually all red Bordeaux is a blend of grape varieties: Cabernet Sauvignon (the most famous) and Merlot (the most widespread and the chief variety in simpler, early-drinking clarets), together with Cabernet Franc and sometimes some Petit Verdot and Malbec. The whites, both the sweet and the dry, are based on Sémillon and Sauvignon Blanc, sometimes with a little of the aromatic Muscadelle.

Wines and regions

Graves

To the south of the Médoc and the city of Bordeaux, the slightly warmer climate and distinctive gravel soils of the Graves region produce Bordeaux's best dry whites, and clarets with a spicy/tobacco, even earthy characteristic. All the classed growths (the Graves was classified in the 1950s) are in the northern third, which has its own AC – Pessac-Léognan – but there is good value to be found under the Graves appellation. There is also a little-used AC for sweet whites: Graves Supérieures.

Médoc

The vineyards of the Médoc run in a long, narrow strip along the left bank of the Gironde, north of the city of Bordeaux, and out towards the coast. The Bas-Médoc, nearer the sea, is the area of lesser quality, while the thinner, more gravelly soils of the Haut-Médoc to the south are home to some of Bordeaux's finest red wine châteaux, including of course the *crus classés*. These lie in the six communes that have their own appellations: Margaux, St-Julien, St-Estèphe, Pauillac, Moulis, and Listrac.

Pomerol

Pomerol is a tiny region of tiny estates with outsize reputations commanding outsize prices: its famous Châteaux Pétrus and Le Pin are two of the world's most expensive wines. The appellation lies on the right bank of the Dordogne where the cold, water-retaining clay soils suit Merlot better than Cabernet Sauvignon. The high Merlot content gives wines that are fleshier and more voluptuous than the typical Médoc claret, but no less concentrated. The wines of the larger Lalande de Pomerol appellation just to the north are less concentrated but, equally, much cheaper.

St-Emilion and satellites

This compact appellation south of Pomerol makes Merlot-based red wines that are generally softer and earlier-maturing than those of the Médoc, and often have a more spicy quality. The best wines are classified as Premier Grand Cru Classé, followed by Grand Cru Classé, and this is the only Bordeaux classification to be regularly revised. There are also five "satellite" villages which may add the name of St-Emilion to their own – St-Georges, Montagne, Puisseguin, Lussac, and Parsac.

Sauternes and satellites

Great Sauternes, made from botrytis-affected Sémillon and Sauvignon Blanc grapes in the south of the Bordeaux region, is one of the world's most opulent sweet white wines which, from a good vintage, will last for two decades or more. There are twenty-five classified châteaux, with just one Premier Grand Cru (the fabled Château d'Yquem) and the rest divided fairly evenly between Premiers Crus and Deuxièmes Crus. Sauternes is made in five villages, but one, Barsac has its own AC which means the wine can, confusingly, be labelled either Barsac or Sauternes. Among the satellites, Cérons and Cadillac make the least interesting wines, while Loupiac and

Ste-Croix-du-Mont on the other side of the Garonne produce some convincing cheaper alternatives to Sauternes.

Other regions

Entre-Deux-Mers (between the rivers Dordogne and Garonne) is the largest and one of the prettiest regions in Bordeaux. The AC is for dry whites only – basically crisp, Sauvignon-influenced, modest wines. Reds from the region, sold as Bordeaux or Bordeaux Supérieur (very occasionally, somewhat confusingly, as Graves de Vayres), are similarly basic, simple clarets for drinking young. The adjoining Premières Côtes de Bordeaux, which runs along the east bank of the Garonne, has more potential and is beginning to fulfil it: reds, both oaked and unoaked, are worth seeking out;

Bordeaux vintages (white)		
Sauternes		
2002	7	▼
2001	9	▼
2000	7	▼
1999	8	★
1998	7	★
1997	8	★
1996	8	★
1995	7	★
1994	5	▲
1993	4	▲
1992	3	▲
Graves & Pessac-Léognan		
2002	8	▼
2001	8	▼
2000	8	★
1999	9	★
1998	8	★
1997	5	★
1996	9	★
1995	8	★
1994	8	★
1993	6	▲
1992	4	▲

(*See* page 98 for key to symbols)

(Left) **St-Emilion, to the north of the Dordogne river, is quite different in feel and in its wines from the Médoc: properties are much smaller; the soils have more clay and sand; and Merlot predominates over Cabernet.**

the sweet whites are sold under the AC Cadillac. The Côtes de Castillon and Côtes de Francs in the east are near St-Emilion both geographically and in style, and are a useful source of good value, solid, Merlot-based reds. Simlarly, Fronsac and Canon-Fronsac, just to the west of Pomerol, provide a good quality, more affordable alternative to Pomerol itself. The larger regions of Côtes de Bourg and Premières Cotes de Blaye, to the north, generally make simpler, fruity, early drinking reds at modest prices, with a small amount of white in Blaye.

BURGUNDY

Compared with the appellations of Burgundy, even Bordeaux's "tiny" Pomerol looks big. Burgundy, running down eastern France from Chablis to Lyon, is about one-fifth the size of Bordeaux, and its classifications, its whole structure and mentality are different. Despite its much smaller area, it has far more appellations than Bordeaux, with parcels of a few hectares (which would fit into a Bordeaux château's vineyards many times over) having their own AC status, each divided among many growers. There are no châteaux in the Bordeaux sense – just growers and *négociants* (merchants who buy wine or grapes, blend, mature, bottle, and sell the result under their own label). The latter used to be more important, but interest in, and regard for, the more individual wines of growers has increased. Merchants, as a consequence, have made efforts to get away from their strong "house styles" and let the characteristics of the different vineyards and villages show through.

Classifications

At the top of the tree are the thirty or so Grands Crus, which are individual vineyards with their own appellations (Le Montrachet and Bâtard-Montrachet, for example). The next best, Premiers Crus, are also individual vineyards, but they attach the name of their village to their own name (eg. Puligny-Montrachet-Les Pucelles). Below this come the village wines (eg. Meursault or Puligny-Montrachet) and then the regional appellations (eg. Bourgogne or Bourgogne Hautes-Côtes de Nuits).

Grapes

Burgundy not only differs from Bordeaux in its grape varieties, but in the way it uses them: burgundy is almost never blended. The great reds are made from Pinot Noir, the great whites from Chardonnay, Beaujolais and much red Mâcon is made from Gamay, and the incidentals are Sauvignon Blanc for Sauvignon de St-Bris and Aligoté for Bouzeron and Bourgogne Aligoté. Passe-Tout-Grains, a blend of Gamay and Pinot Noir, is the insignificant exception.

Wines and regions

Beaujolais

The southernmost area of Burgundy produces the familiar, juicy, fruity red wines of Beaujolais. The two simplest are Nouveau, released a few weeks after the harvest each November, and basic Beaujolais (often

Burgundy vintages (white)		
2002	9	▼
2001	8	★
2000	9	★
1999	7	★
1998	7	★
1997	7	★
1996	9	★
1995	9	★
1994	7	▲
1993	6	▲

Burgundy vintages (red)		
Côte d'Or		
2002	9	▼
2001	7	★
2000	7	★
1999	9	★
1998	7	★
1997	7	★
1996	9	★
1995	9	★
1994	5	▲
1993	8	▲

Beaujolais Crus		
2002	8	★
2001	6	★
2000	9	★
1999	9	★
1998	8	▲

(*See* page 98 for key to symbols)

(Left) **Corton, the Grand Cru of Aloxe-Corton in the Côte de Beaune, produces both red and white burgundies of great power and richness.**

the same wine released later). Beaujolais-Villages from thirty-nine better villages should be slightly fuller and last a couple of years, and Beaujolais from the ten top villages, the "Crus", should be meatier and capable of at least three years' age. The "Crus" are Brouilly, Chénas, Chiroubles, Côte de Brouilly, Fleurie, Juliénas, Morgon, Moulin-à-Vent (the biggest and longest-lived), Régnié, and St-Amour. Beaujolais Blanc is usually sold as St-Véran.

Chablis

Chablis is the crisp, dry white from limestone soil to the far north of the region. Traditionally it has a characteristic whiff of gun-flint, though nowadays some is aged in new oak *barriques* and is fatter and more nutty. There are seven Grands Crus (eg. Les Clos) and seventeen Premiers Crus (eg. Vaillons); Petit Chablis, generally inferior, comes from lesser sites.

Côte Chalonnaise

The four villages at the southern tip of the Côte d'Or – Mercurey, Givry (both producing nearly all red wine), Rully (red and white), and Montagny (all white) – are ACs in their own right, but are also entitled to the AC of Bourgogne Côte Chalonnaise.

Both reds and whites can be impressive "mini Côte d'Or" wines at a fraction of the price. The village of Bouzeron has its own AC for Aligoté, in recognition of its superior conditions for growing this slighty tart, but drily flavoursome grape variety.

Côte d'Or

The Côte d'Or, a string of hills running north-south and divided into the Côte de Nuits in the north and the Côte de Beaune in the south, is the heart of Burgundy; the fabled names – Vougeot, Vosne-Romanée, Volnay, Beaune, Pommard et al – roll off the hills. The Côte de Nuits produces mostly red wines – bigger, more substantial ones than the Côte de Beaune which makes whites such as the famed Meursault and Montrachet as well as reds. Wines from the Côte de Beaune-Villages, Côte de Nuits-Villages, and Hautes-Côtes are well worth looking at in good vintages, as is the basic generic Bourgogne from a good grower in a famous village such as Chambolle-Musigny.

Crémant de Bourgogne

Burgundy's *méthode traditionelle* Chardonnay and Pinot Noir sparkling wine can be a useful half-price Champagne-substitute – but don't try to age it.

(Above) **From the gentle inclines of the Grand Cru Grands Echézeaux in the Côte de Nuits come some of the most elegant yet long-lived of red burgundies.**

(Left) **If the sun shines in the autumn as the leaves are beginning to turn, Champagne's gently rolling vineyards look beautiful, but once winter sets in in this northerly region, it can get very cold.**

Mâconnais

Both reds and whites are produced in this area in the south of Burgundy, but the reds (made from Gamay) are in decline while the quality of the whites has been improving, especially those from the forty-two superior villages. These are labelled Mâcon-Villages or Mâcon with the specific village name (eg. Mâcon-Milly or -Lugny). St-Véran, Pouilly-Fuissé, Pouilly-Vinzelles, and Viré-Clessé are ACs in their own right. The best have Côte d'Or richness, if not quite its finesse.

CHAMPAGNE

Champagne comes from just one place, a region about ninety miles (145 kilometres) northeast of Paris with Reims and Epernay at its heart. The chalky soil and chilly climate combine to give ideal conditions for ripening Chardonnay, Pinot Noir, and Pinot Meunier just sufficiently to make the sort of acidic still white or rosé base wine to turn into fine sparkling wine.

Styles and quality

In fact the climate is so marginal that most Champagne is non-vintage: instead of being the product of a single year which might well taste thin and sharp, it has some older Champagne blended in to give it roundness. In good years, however, vintage Champagne is made: this is kept longer before it is released (at least three years and commonly five) and will have more depth and the potential to age for several years, even a decade or more. Most, but not all, so-called prestige *cuvées*, the sort of top quality Champagnes that sell under a fancy name at a very fancy price (Dom Pérignon for example), are vintage. *Blanc de blancs* is made from white grapes (Chardonnay) only and is an elegant and increasingly fashionable style. The less common *blanc de noirs* is white Champagne made from black grapes only and is usually more full bodied. Pink Champagne can be made with a large proportion of Chardonnay or none at all, so it can be quite a delicate style, or a full, fruity one if mostly Pinot. *Brut*, the style we see mostly in Britain, is very dry; Extra Dry, confusingly, is slightly less so. A Champagne which is advertised as "recently disgorged" (*récemment dégorgé*) has been aged for an extra-long time and has only recently been taken off its lees (*see* page 92); as ageing is one of the keys to Champagne quality, recently disgorged wines (which will be expensive) can have more depth and, because they have spent time on their lees, more freshness as well. (Bollinger has cleverly registered the initials RD as one of its own trademarks, leaving everyone else to cope with the unwieldy full-length.)

Grand Cru and Premier Cru on labels are not the guarantee of quality that one might expect: Grand Cru means that the grapes used are the region's most expensive, coming only from the seventeen finest villages; Premier Cru is applied to the next best forty villages and the grapes from them are therefore the next most expensive. But good grapes alone do not make good Champagne and the Grand and Premier Cru classifications do not impose production rules. The two terms are most often seen on small-scale Champagnes made by growers (rather than by houses such as Moët & Chandon, which buy in most of their grapes or still wine from several sources, or by cooperatives), and the quality of these ranges from superb to dire. Fortunately they are usually

Champagne vintages		
2002	9	▼
2001	non vintage	
2000	7	▼
1999	7	▼
1998	7	★
1997	6	★
1996	9	★
1995	8	★
1994	non vintage	
1993	7	★

(*See* page 98 for key to symbols)

relatively cheap, so there is more incentive to take a risk. The tiny letters RM, for *récoltant manipulant*, on the label indicate one of these growers. If you don't want to take a risk, UK supermarket own-labels are reasonably reliable, if never thrilling, cooperative produce. The brands of the large houses (the famous names) are more expensive, but they should be of consistent high quality, each with its own house style. Mostly they are, but a minority spoil the show.

LOIRE

We tend to think of the Loire as white wine country, but in fact an enormous variety is made: as well as whites in all permutations of sweetness and dryness, there are rosés, reds, and sparkling wines too. The one thing that links them all, apart from the meandering Loire river, is that the fairly northerly location means that they are generally light-bodied – a few reds and the very sweet wines being exceptions.

Wines and regions

Muscadet

This light dry white from the Loire's cool Atlantic coast, is the antithesis of bold, full flavoured New World wines, but Muscadet has its place, so long as it is well made and reasonably priced (neither of which it always is). The best area is Muscadet de Sèvre-et-Maine which fortunately accounts for most of production, but what gives Muscadet character and freshness is the "*sur lie*" method – leaving the wine on its lees (*see* page 91) until it is bottled. This term appears on labels, but bear in mind that it is sometimes abused by big merchant companies – estate-bottled wines are the safest bet. Gros Plant, Muscadet's VDQS sibling, is even lighter, drier, and sharper and tastes better in france – with oysters.

Anjou-Saumur

Upstream from Muscadet in Anjou-Saumur the main white grape is Chenin Blanc. The best wines are the nervy, minerally, dry Savennières, and the sweet, nobly-rotten (and immensely long-lived) Coteaux du Layons. The latter include the distinguished *crus* of Bonnezeaux and Quarts de Chaume.

The principal red grapes, Cabernet Franc and Cabernet Sauvignon, make Anjou and Saumur reds and rosés. The best is the raspberry-perfumed, slightly earthy, red Saumur-Champigny; the most familiar is the usually unexciting, sweetish Rosé d'Anjou. Cabernet d'Anjou and Rosé de Loire are better.

Touraine

Fresh, raspberry-scented Cabernet Franc is the star of this eastern half of the central Loire. Chinon, Bourgueil, and St-Nicolas-de-Bourgueil are the best reds – best drunk young and cool except when from the ripest vintages when they can improve for five years. Touraine's other great wines are Vouvray and Montlouis which are made from Chenin Blanc grapes and may be dry (*sec*), semi-sweet (*demi-sec*), or immensely sweet (*moelleux*), depending on the vintage (and not always saying which on the label); and they may also be sparkling.

Loire vintages		
Coteaux du Layon		
2002	8	▼
2001	6	★
2000	6	★
1999	6	★
1998	6	★
1997	9	★
1996	9	★
1995	9	★
Sancerre		
2002	8	★
2001	7	▲
2000	9	▲
1999	7	▲
Red wines		
2002	8	▼
2001	6	★
2000	7	★
1999	7	★
1998	7	★
1997	8	★

(*See* page 98 for key to symbols)

(Left) **Wending its way for the best part of 600 miles (966 kilometres) from the middle of France to the sea in Brittany, the Loire is home to an array of different wines: Saumur is famous for its sparkling wines, but the reds can be delicious.**

(Above) **Châteauneuf-du-Pape has not only given the world a famous red wine – its wine regulations, drawn up in 1923 by Baron Le Roy of Château Fortia (above), formed the basis of France's entire** *appellation contrôlée* **system in 1936.**

Sancerre, Pouilly-Fumé, and the Upper Loire

Way upstream, deep in France, the Loire grapes change to Sauvignon Blanc in the renowned Pouilly-Fumé and Sancerre ACs and their cheaper, but sometimes good satellites Menetou-Salon, Quincy, and Reuilly.

VDQS Sauvignons of Haut-Poitou (an area of good-value Gamay and Chardonnay too) are lighter, but often delicious. Red and rosé Sancerre, made from Pinot Noir, can be stunning in ripe vintages, but is always expensive. Red Menetou-Salon is a worthy substitute.

Sparkling wines

Méthode traditionelle sparkling wine is made all along the Loire (but not in Muscadet). It can be good and crisp, and is made mainly from Chenin Blanc. The most general AC is Crémant de Loire, but Saumur is

the one most often seen. Vouvray and Montlouis can be attractively soft, fruity, and nutty.

Other ACs

The Loire abounds in self-explanatory ACs such as Sauvignon de Touraine (in a good vintage, good value at half the price of Pouilly-Fumé) and Cabernet d'Anjou. Less known wines worth investigating include the refreshing Gamay-based reds of Côte Roannaise and the dry whites and light reds of Cheverny.

RHONE

The Rhône, rather like the Loire, yields a host of different types of wine – red, white, and rosé, still and sparkling, dry and sweet – but, whereas the Loire's bias is towards light and white, in the much warmer, more southerly Rhône region big, magisterial, long-lived reds dominate. Viticulturally,

(Left) **Whereas the northern Rhône is renowned for its precipitous slopes and single red grape variety, Châteauneuf-du-Pape, anchor of the south, is in all ways more expansive – with no fewer than thirteen grape varieties in its much flatter, boulder-strewn vineyards.**

the Rhône starts south of Lyon and runs south to Avignon, but in doing so it divides into two distinct areas. In the hilly, rocky north, where vineyards perch on terraces chiselled out of near-vertical granite, just one grape is grown for red wines: Syrah. In the south, where the river and the land broadens, so, too, does the range of vines: Syrah is joined by Grenache (the most widely planted), Carignan, Cinsaut, Mourvèdre, and several others. And to the white grapes of the north – Marsanne, Roussanne, and Viognier – the south adds Grenache Blanc, Ugni Blanc, Clairette, and Muscat.

Wines and regions

Northern Rhône

The dark, muscular, tannic reds of the northern Rhône often need five or even ten years to soften and develop their fascinatingly complex flavours – their extraordinary combination of gamey, leathery, or tarry richness, fragrance, and ripe berry fruit. The two stars are Côte-Rôtie, the most perfumed, and Hermitage, the most majestic. Crozes-Hermitage is the much improved, earlier-drinking cousin of Hermitage. St-Joseph is similarly less long-lived, but it has a seductive, smooth, black fruits flavour which can be enjoyed from youth to about eight years; Cornas is bigger, blacker, and more tarry, but give a top producer's wine ten years and it might rival the more expensive Hermitage. Traditional white Hermitage lives for decades, its austere, herby, almost medicinal character mellowing to honeyed, nutty, straw flavours; the modern style – fruity and perfumed – can be drunk young, as can

the whites of St-Joseph and Crozes-Hermitage. The rare and costly Condrieu, made from Viognier, has an extraordinarily heady bouquet and voluptuous, silky, yet dry palate. It should be drunk young.

Southern Rhône

Standards throughout the southern Rhône improved greatly throughout the 1990s. The dominant appellation, after the catch-all Côtes du Rhône, is Châteauneuf-du-Pape, a large area making warm, richly fruity, spicy reds largely from Grenache. They can be drunk as soon as they are released and usually provide pleasurable drinking for five or six years; those from the best estates last ten or fifteen. The smaller nearby appellations of Gigondas, Vacqueyras, and Lirac produce similarly spicy red wines that don't have keeping qualities of the best Châteauneuf but are decidedly cheaper.

Progress in the general appellations of Côtes du Rhône and Côtes du Rhône-Villages (the latter covering the sixteen best villages) means that there is a much greater chance now of finding a peppery, plummy Côtes du Rhône or a slightly fuller Villages wine. Among the best villages, which can be named on the label, are Sablet, Séguret, Valréas, and, above all, Cairanne. Other reds to look out for are the full-bodied Côtes du Ventoux and Costières du Nîmes (the latter straddling the southern Rhône and Languedoc) and the lighter Coteaux du Tricastin, Côtes du Lubéron, and Côtes du Vivarais. This is quintessential red grape country, but there are a few white wines, including the powerful, herby Châteauneuf and slightly lighter Lirac, and they too have improved, becoming altogether fresher.

Rhône vintages (red)		
north		
2002	6	▼
2001	9	▼
2000	8	▼
1999	9	▼
1998	8	★
1997	8	★
1996	7	★
1995	9	★
1994	7	▲
1993	4	▲
south		
2002	3	▼
2001	9	▼
2000	9	▼
1999	8	★
1998	9	★
1997	7	★
1996	7	▲
1995	9	★
1994	7	▲
1993	6	▲

(See page 98 for key to symbols)

Rosé, sparkling, and sweet wines

The famous rosés of Tavel are full-bodied, powerful, and spicy, while those of Lirac and Costières du Nîmes are slightly lighter; all should be drunk young.

The Rhône's most delicious sparkling wine is the idiosyncratic Clairette de Die, a fragrant, grapey, semi-sweet, Muscat-based wine, refreshingly low in alcohol. Crémant de Die Brut is less interesting, and so is the north's rather unrefined St-Péray.

Beaumes-de-Venise is one of the red wine villages in the Côtes du Rhône, but it is famed for its golden, grapey, barley sugar-sweet, fortified Muscat which has its own AC as a *Vin Doux Naturel*.

THE SOUTH WEST

The South West covers a large, disparate area between Bordeaux, the Massif Central, and the Pyrenees where wines divide into two distinct traditions: the Bordeaux look-a-likes – red, dry white, and sweet – based on the Bordeaux grape varieties; and the often little-known but potentially more exciting wines made from unusual local grapes such as Manseng (both Petit and Gros), Fer-Servadou, Tannat, Duras, and Négrette.

Bergerac, a continuation of St-Emilion on the Dordogne, is the Bordeaux side of the coin. It produces large quantities of red and white, most of which are for early drinking and very reliable, but a few estates make some that are more serious and oak-aged. Other names to look for include Buzet, Côtes du Marmandais, and Pécharmant for reds, Montravel for dry whites, and Côtes de Duras and Côtes de St-Mont for both. Monbazillac and Saussignac are sweet wine enclaves of Bergerac, now producing some excellent wines.

Cahors, from the Lot Valley to the south of the Dordogne, shows the southwest's wilder side. These days it is not the black, tannic wine of legend, but the Auxerrois grape (alias Malbec) still makes it a chunkier, more austere wine than claret or Bergerac. It usually takes three or four years for its mineral, blackberry fruit to shine and the best last several years. The Tannat-based Madiran is another traditionally big, sturdy wine that has benefited from producers' efforts to bring out fruit flavours without losing essential personality.

Other characterful local wines include Gaillac, Béarn, Irouléguy, and Côtes du Frontonnais among the reds, Gaillac and Pacherenc du Vic-Bilh among the whites, and Jurançon, a distinctive, vibrant white that ranges from dry to very sweet and can be excellent in all forms. But of all the southwest wines it is simple Vin de Pays des Côtes de Gascogne that is the commercial success story. What was the base wine of the Armagnac region, is now a fruity, light, grassy, dry French white. Equally appetizing aperitifs are the new *vin de pays* rosés – du Quercy and du Lot.

THE SOUTH

Two decades ago Languedoc-Roussillon, the vast region running from the Spanish boarder to Nîmes, was known for little but the poorest plonk. Today it is one of the most progressive of regions, rightly tagged the New World in France. Producing almost twice as much wine as Australia, it is still the source of most of France's *vin de table*, but the ratio of quality wines has soared. Vineyards on unsuitable land have been razed and the overwhelming dominance of the rustic red Carignan grape has been lowered by replacing it with officially recommended "improving" varieties: Grenache, Syrah, and Mourvèdre have increased in the appellation wines such as Corbières, Minervois, Faugères, St-Chinian, Collioure, and the umbrella ACs

READING FRENCH LABELS

On the whole the French still prefer fairly classic labels, as do the consumers who choose French wines.

From top to bottom: Domaine de Molines is the name of the producer and the name of the wine (domaine and château are often fairly loosely applied in France); *réserve* means whatever the producer chooses: there are no controls over the use and other terms that seem to imply superior quality; *mis en bouteille à la propriété* means bottled at the property, but oddly enough this can mean at the local cooperative; 1998 is the vintage (year of harvest); this wine is a blend of Merlot and Cabernet (with, if any difference in proportions, more of the former than the latter); it is a Vin de Pays d'Oc, literally a wine of the countryside of the Oc region (now known as Languedoc); 13% is the alcohol content, measured as a percentage of the volume; 750ml is the bottle size.

(Left) In Roussillon, close to the Mediterranean coast and the Spanish border, gnarled old Grenache vines produce the distinctive Banyuls wines, France's answer to port.

of Coteaux du Languedoc and Côtes du Roussillon; the international favourites Cabernet and Merlot have appeared in *vin de pays*. And Carignan itself is better cared for. Old vines up in the hills, in the Fitou appellation for example, are now nurtured to produce low yields of well-balanced grapes and in modern, well-equipped cellars the Carignan is vinified specifically to bring out its fruit and soften its tannin and acidity.

The warm Mediterranean climate ensures that red wines predominate, but the rise in quality of the reds has been followed by that in the traditional whites.

The other triumph for Languedoc-Roussillon is its *vin de pays* which now provide some of the best value wines – reds, whites, and rosés – in France. These range from small-scale wines from dynamic estates in the numerous small *vin de pays* (Coteaux de Murviel to name but one), to modern oaked and unoaked varietals – especially Chardonnay, Sauvignon Blanc, Viognier, Cabernet Sauvignon, Merlot, and Syrah – in the all-embracing Vin de Pays d'Oc. These latter, often coming from hitherto down-at-heel cooperatives, compete head on with wines from Australia and the rest of the New World – and it is no coincidence that many of the winemakers here are Australian or Australian-trained.

The situation with Provence was different. Quality was seldom bad, but it was mostly of a mediocrity that didn't justify the prices based on proximity to fashionable Mediterranean resorts. The wines will never be cheap, but the rosés are now fresher and fruitier, and there are some impressive reds. Bandol's are especially good – deep, spicy, herb- and berry-flavoured with the potential to age a decade. Bandol rosés and whites are attractive, too, but expensive, as are those of Cassis, Bellet, and Palette. In ascending order of quality, the ACs of Côtes de Provence, Coteaux d'Aix-en-Provence, and Les Baux de Provence are increasingly making herby, blackcurranty reds (often benefiting from some added Cabernet and Syrah) and nicely structured rosés; the whites are generally clean, but unexciting.

Sparkling and fortified wines

Crémant de Limoux proves that, if the acidity of the Mauzac grape is combined with Chardonnay and the *méthode traditionelle*, the south can make very creditable sparkling wine. The South is also the home of Roussillon's *Vins Doux Naturels* – sweet wines made from semi-fermented grape juice fortified with brandy. These can either be made from Muscat (as in the Rhône's Beaumes-de-Venise) and made to be drunk young, like Muscat de Frontignan, de Rivesaltes, and de Lunel, or they can be based on red Grenache and long-aged. Some are aged in wood deliberately to develop a maderized, *rancio* character – for example in Banyuls, Maury, and Rivesaltes.

SAVOIE AND JURA

The crisp, racy, white wines from eastern France's Alpine Savoie region almost all find their way to the local ski resorts, but are well worth trying. They are mostly made from Jacquère, Chasselas, Chardonnay, and Roussette. Look out for Roussette de Savoie, the more general Vin de Savoie, Crépy, Seyssel (especially the sparkling), and Bugey.

The main varieties of the Jura region include Chardonnay and the strange, nutty, resiny white Savagnin; the reds are Pinot Noir and local Poulsard. The main appellations are Arbois and Côtes du Jura. The speciality of the region is the intense, dry, sherry-like *Vin Jaune*, made from Savagnin and matured under a film of *flor* yeast for at least six years in barrel.

(Left) **The Alpine vineyards of the Savoie region near Grenoble and Lake Geneva produce zesty, fragrant, dry white wines.**

GERMANY

German wine is like no other. Although the grape varieties are not unique to the country, the wines have a particular blend of fragility and strength, of delicacy and concentration, that marks them out from the Cabernet, Shiraz, and Chardonnay bandwaggon rolling across the rest of the wine world.

German wine is ruled by its climate. That might seem an obvious statement, but nowhere else (except Austria, which uses a similar system) is the wine law based on the simple premise that a ripe grape makes better wine than an unripe one. There are of course territorial designations. For "quality wine" (*see* below), the country is divided into thirteen regions, and these are subdivided into *Bereiche*, which are subdivided into *Grosslagen*, or large sites, which are in turn split into *Einzellagen*, or single sites (in other words, single vineyards, which may also be described as *Gutsabfüllung* if their wines are estate-bottled, rather than from a cooperative; cooperatives may use the term *Erzeugerabfüllung*). Thus the label will give the geographical origin of a wine, often in minute detail – but the ripeness of the grapes remains the crux of the matter.

At the bottom of the scale, usually only accounting for about two per cent of output, is *Tafelwein*. This is very basic table wine, invariably chaptalized (*see* page 89) and blended. *Landwein*, a step above, is supposed to be the equivalent of French *vin de pays*, but it has never attracted the same attention or generated the same interest and production is negligible. The bulk of German wine usually – although it depends on the vintage – comes into the next category, *Qualitätswein bestimmter Anbaugebiete* (QbA); this is "quality wine" from one of the thirteen regions.

So far so simple. But to rise above this (usually fairly basic) level, a wine must come not from a superior patch of land, but must be made from properly ripe, or even overripe grapes. This, in a land whose most northerly vineyards may have trouble ripening at all in a cool summer, is considered to be the key. *Qualitätswein mit Prädikat* (QmP) is the term given to any wine ranking higher than QbA and production is usually, although not always, less. QmP means quality wine with special attributes, and it falls into six categories, none of which may be *chaptalized*.

Kabinett is the lightest; above it comes *Spätlese*, which means "late-picked". *Auslese* is made from specially selected bunches of grapes; *Beerenauslese* is made from individually selected berries, often affected by noble rot. *Trockenbeerenauslese* is made from selected berries that have been shrivelled on the vine by noble rot and therefore make intensely sweet wine. *Eiswein*, made from grapes frozen solid on the vine during Germany's icy winters, is also very sweet – and rare. *Beerenauslese* is sweet too; in the vast majority of cases *Auslese* is sweet, although less so than *Beerenauslese*, and *Spätlese* can be anything from dry to semi-sweet.

After a shaky start in the 1980s, with some thin, tart wines, dry styles have become a permanent and increasingly impressive element in the German wine repertoire. The idea was, and is, to

(Below) **The Rheingau in the heart of Germany is a small region with an outsize reputation for long-lived Rieslings – and for aristocratic estates. Schloss Vollrads, although now owned by a bank, is one of the oldest and finest.**

THE MAJOR WINE REGIONS OF GERMANY

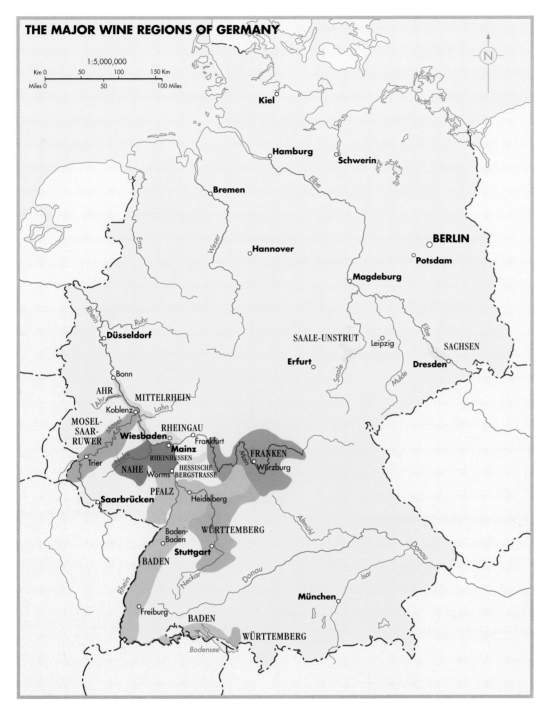

1:5,000,000

Km 0   50   100   150 Km
Miles 0   50   100 Miles

J.L. WOLF

1998
Jesuitengarten
RIESLING

PFALZ

READING GERMAN LABELS I

A modern minimalist German label aimed at attracting, rather than deterring, non-German speakers. The essential information has been pared down to the minimum on the main label.

From left to right, top to bottom: J.L. Wolf is the producer; 1998 is the vintage (year of harvest); *Jesuitengarten* is an *Einzellage* (*i.e.* a single vineyard); Riesling is the grape variety; Pfalz is the region (one of Germany's thirteen).

produce wines that go with food. That's not to say that the traditional light-bodied, sweet styles aren't suitable wines for the table, but there was clearly a gap for a drier, fuller style that was only partially being filled by the established dry wines of regions such as Franken and Baden. Until recently dry wines were always labelled *Trocken* or *Halbtrocken* (dry or half-dry), but two new categories – Classic for dry wines from a single variety and region, and Select for single variety wines from a specific vineyard – may not be labelled with any additional "dry" designations.

As well as the wine law classifications, there are several producer groups which embrace their own sets of high standards: the two most important are Charta and VDP. Charta is an organization of Rheingau growers aimed at promoting traditional, high quality, dry Rheingau Riesling wines: bottles bear an embossed double or triple arch, the latter reserved for vineyards classified as *Erstes Gewächs* ("first growths"). VDP, *Die Prädikatsweingüter*, to give it its full name, is a nationwide group of nearly 200 top, environmentally aware estates. Bottles carry the VDP's eagle logo and vineyards are classified in three tiers with, at the top, *Grosses Gewächs* or *Erstes Gewächs* (depending on region). These are the equivalent of Burgundy's Grands Crus and come in embossed bottles.

Grapes

Riesling is unquestionably Germany's finest grape, even though Weissburgunder (Pinot Blanc) and Ruländer (Pinot Gris or Grauburgunder) can producer finer wine in the warmest regions. Riesling is also once again the most widely planted grape, having overtaken the inferior and declining Müller-Thurgau.

Red grapes account for barely a fifth of the vineyards, but this is considerably more than a few years ago. Spätburgunder (Pinot Noir) leads the way in both plantings and quality, followed the more ordinary Portugieser and Dornfelder.

Among the varieties that have been losing out are Silvaner and several of the many crossings developed in the twentieth century when yield was more important than quality. Kerner, Scheurebe, Bacchus, Faber, and Morio Muscat are still widespread, the first two, in particular, deservedly so.

Wines and regions

Ahr

This cold, northerly region, one of Germay's smallest, is almost perversely dedicated to the production of red wines, mostly from Spätburgunder, which is gaining at the expense of Portugieser. The traditional style is lightweight and medium sweet, but dry, *barrique*-aged Spätburgunders are increasing.

Baden

The Baden region, the southernmost and third largest, specializes in two things: red wines and dry wines – all more alcoholic than the German average. It faces Alsace across the Vosges mountains, and enjoys similarly balmy, if slightly wetter, weather; and like Alsace it specializes in the Pinot family of grapes, here known as Weissburgunder, Ruländer, and Spätburgunder. The soils are very varied and the hills rolling rather than steep. Most of the wines are made by the local cooperatives, which turn out reliable, good value wines.

Franken

Dry Silvaner is the speciality of this region, traditionally bottled in the squat, flagon-shaped "*Bocksbeutel*", but increasingly now in the classic French shapes. Characteristically it is fairly full-bodied with rapier-acidity and an earthy taste which can be extremely attractive. Because of the short growing season in this easterly region, Riesling doesn't do well, leaving the bland Müller-Thurgau as the most widely grown grape variety.

Hessiche Bergstrasse

A tiny region that produces fine, dry Riesling, which at its best is comparable to Riesling from the Rheingau, a small quantity of *Eiswein* and a small, but growing, volume of Spätburgunder.

Liebfraumilch

Always a blended wine, always sweetish, usually completely bland and among the cheapest of

(Below) **The vineyards of the Mosel – often terraced to make cultivation possible – are some of the steepest in the world, but the angle gives them good exposure to the sun.**

Germany's offerings, Liebfraumilch conquered export markets in the 1970s and 1980s and helped to ruin Germany's vinous reputation. It also destroyed the reputation of the Riesling grape, although Riesling hardly ever entered a bottle of Liebfraumilch. Riesling's good name is now being restored, while Liebfraumilch is on the wane.

Mittelrhein

Another region the wines of which are seldom seen abroad. It makes good, steely Riesling, two-thirds of it dry, but viticulture is on the decline.

Mosel-Saar-Ruwer

This is one of Germany's most famous regions, and with good reason: a Mosel-Saar-Ruwer wine from a top grower is light and delicate but with a thread of steel running through it; high acidity is matched by appley, peachy, fruit, and it will live for years. The Riesling grape is king here, and the best wines are grown on the precipitous slate slopes of the river banks. The Saar and the Ruwer are both tributaries of the Mosel, and produce wines that are yet leaner and steelier – but which soften and open out in good years. These wines don't deserve to be cheap, and it's worth paying the extra for an individual grower's from a village like Brauneberg, Bernkastel, or

READING GERMAN LABELS II

German labels are no easy read, but, if taken step by step, they do reveal most of the vital information – and there has been a welcome trend away from elaborate Gothic script.

From left to right, top to bottom: **Weingut Toni Jost** is the producer (*weingut* means estate); Hahnenhof is the estate name (it comes from the outstanding vineyard – *see* below); Mittelrhein is the region (one of Germany's thirteen); 1999 is the vintage (year of harvest); Bacharacher is the village; the word ending in er is always the village and distinguishes it from a larger, less fine area, such as a *grosslage*; following the village name, in this case Hahn, is the vineyard, thus pinpointing the wine's origins (a further indication of quality); the grape variety is Riesling and the quality/ripeness level is *auslese*; *gutsabfullung* means the wine was bottled at the estate (*erzeugerabfüllung* means estate-bottled, but can, misleadingly, be used by cooperatives); 8% is the alcohol content, measured as a percentage of volume (8% is low and indicates a traditional *auslese*, as opposed to a drier, higher alcohol wine); 500ml is the bottle size; *Qualitätswein mit Prädikat*, or QmP, is the broad quality category: the description *auslese* has already given the precise level; the AP number is the official test number of this batch of wine (all quality wine has one); the producer's name and address appear at the bottom of the label.

Vintages

Rhine (QmP)

2002	8	★
2001	9	★
2000	6	★
1999	8	★
1998	8	★
1997	8	★
1996	8	★
1995	8	★
1994	6	★
1993	8	★

Mosel (QmP)

2002	9	★
2001	9	★
2000	7	★
1999	9	★
1998	8	★
1997	8	★
1996	7	★
1995	9	★
1994	7	★
1993	8	★

Key

0–10 quality rating
(10 = top wine)

▲ should drink

★ can drink, but no hurry for the top wines

▼ must keep

(*See* also **When to drink,** pages 44–47)

Graach, or Urzig rather than settling for something less exciting. And how do you spot the dull ones? Not easy, but price should be a guide – as can the words "*Winzergenossenschaft*" or *Winzerverein*, which mean "cooperative".

Nahe

There are splendid Rieslings from this region, especially from the towns of Bad Kreuznach and Schlossböckelheim. The latter is the name of the village's most famous estate, as well as of the village itself; it is also the name of a *Bereich* covering half the Nahe, and *Bereich* wines are likely to be less interesting than those of the village or the estate. Generally Nahe wines come somewhere between the lightness of the Mosel and the weightiness of the Rheingau in style.

Pfalz

The Pfalz, Germany's second largest and sunniest region, has been its most dynamic in the last decade. It falls into two distinct parts: the northern is the area of great estates and includes the Mittelhaardt with such renowned villages as Deidesheim, Forst, and Bad Dürkheim; the southern part is a region of mixed farming and fewer famous names – but while standards have risen dramatically in the Pfalz as a whole, it is the south that has seen the most changes.

Riesling is the Pfalz's most planted grape, giving impressively steely, yet rich and sometimes

(Right) **Assmannshausen is unusual in the Rheingau for specializing in Spätburgunder to produce red wines.**

spicy, wines, but it has no monopoly on quality. Germany's finest Scheurebe comes from the Pfalz – concentrated and high in life-enhancing acidity – and the Pinots, Spätburgunder, Weissburgunder, and Grauburgunder, are all significant, as are sparkling wines.

Rheingau

The Rheingau has long been recognized for producing Germany's finest wine, although these days the Pfalz region is mounting a serious challenge. Rheingau's reputation rests on its Riesling which, grown on its steep river banks and on an enormous variety of soils, gives wines of weight and ripeness, balance and depth. It is warmer here than in the Mosel, so the grapes ripen more easily, and in good years can reach *Trockenbeerenauslesen* levels, although the trend has been to dry wines. It's also a region characterized by a proliferation of aristocrats: every other property seems to be owned by a Prinz or a Graf. The best villages include Hochheim (which gave its name to the English term for all Rhine wines – hock), Eltville, Erbach, Hattenheim, Johannisberg, and Rüdesheim. Assmannshausen specializes in red wines from Spätburgunder (Pinot Noir) grapes.

Rheinhessen

There are some very good producers here in the country's largest wine region– mostly in the Rheinterrasse area, a string of riverside villages around Nierstein – but the bulk of Rheinhessen is soft, agreeable… and dull. It is one of the main sources of Liebfraumilch. The name Nierstein is used not just for the village (which has some splendid vineyards) but also for the *Bereich* of Nierstein Gutes Domtal, the wine of which is cheap and not always cheerful. Apart from Nierstein itself, the best villages are Oppenheim, Bodenheim, and Nackenheim. As well as Riesling, the grape varieties to look for on labels include Silvaner, Scheurebe, and Rivaner.

Saale-Unstrut and Sachsen

These two small, northeasterly regions, which joined the wine fold from the former East Germany, have benefited from considerable replanting in recent years. Müller-Thurgau dominates in both regions, but other varieties are also significant, including Weissburgunder, Silvaner, Riesling, and Grauburgunder, and the style of the wines is dry, firm, and characterful.

Sekt

The German term for sparkling wine. Deutscher Sekt is made from German grapes, as opposed to Sekt, which is mostly made from imported Italian and French wine and dominates the market. The best Deutscher Sekt is made from Riesling, Weissurgunder, or Spätburgunder, and the label will often indicate this. Sekt bA comes from one of the thirteen quality regions.

Württemberg

There is some very good Riesling from this large southerly region of Germany, but over half the wine is red, from grapes such as Trollinger, Müllerrebe, Limberger, Portugieser, and Spätburgunder, and some of it is very serious. Despite the amount of wine produced, neither reds nor whites are often seen abroad – which is a pity.

(Above) **Enjoying greater warmth and sunshine than Rhine regions to the north, the Pfalz produces fuller, riper, often more spicy wines – some of Germany's best with food.**

ITALY

Italy has been a united country for less than 150 years, so it is not surprising that even today much of its thinking is still regional and that its wines developed for purely local audiences. The effects of this regionalism are to the good in that each part of Italy has evolved its own traditions and flavours, helped by a vast array of characterful indigenous grape varieties, but it also means that many wines are still little known outside their localities. They simply didn't need to travel because vines are grown, and wine is made, almost everywhere.

With such volumes and such diverse traditions, standards inevitably vary enormously, but there is no disputing that there are red wines, especially from Tuscany and Piedmont, to equal any in the world. Talk – and action – turned to quality in the 1980s. Individual vineyards, mesoclimates, and low yields became the buzz words and international grape varieties arrived.

There is no disputing either that in the 1990s Italy became one of Europe's most dynamic wine producers. A new generation of growers, not just in the famous regions, but all the way down to Puglia and

Sicily, brought new skills and dedication. Combining a respect for tradition with an appreciation of modern techniques, they focused on Italian grapes but were not afraid to bring in Chardonnay, Merlot, and so on where they could be useful. At last Italy could shake off its slightly tarnished reputation – the legacy of the poor quality of the familiar wines (the likes of Soave and Chianti) in the 1970s.

In fact, it was the exceptional wines made in Tuscany from Cabernet Sauvignon, sometimes on its own, sometimes blended with the local Sangiovese, that demonstrated that Italy was capable of producing

(Right) **The Tuscan hills are renowned for their great red wines, but the vineyards around the medieval hill town of San Gimignano offer a contrast – a modern white from the Vernaccia grape.**

red wines of world class. The next step was to show that Italy didn't need Cabernet Sauvignon to make wines of this quality: it could make equally fine wines from its own varieties. This it did.

The trouble with most of these new wines, at least as far as the authorities were concerned, was that their use of foreign grape varieties and/or small new oak *barriques* meant that they fell foul of Italy's quality wine laws. They didn't qualify as DOC (*denominazione di origine controllata*), the rough equivalent of French AC, or the newly created DOCG (*denominazione di origine controllata e garantita*), which in theory guaranteed quality as well as origin, grape varieties, and maturation. Instead, their official status was *vino da tavola* – mere table wine. It didn't matter to the

producers, who could command higher prices than for any other Italian wines, but it showed the weakness of the Italian wine law.

It was partially resolved in the 1990s by a new law enshrining many of the previously outlawed elements and making Bolgheri in Tuscany (a hotbed of these wines) a DOC, but some producers choose to stick with their *vino da tavola* status, almost as a badge of honour, and other outstanding wine still fall outside the DOC and DOCG regulations.

The new law also introduced IGT (*indicazione geografica tipica*), a category between *vino da tavola* and DOC that serves as an equivalent to *vin de pays*. Veneto and della Venezie are two of the large IGTs frequently seen.

THE WINE REGIONS OF ITALY

Other classifications and designations that are useful to know are Riserva, indicating a DOC or DOCG wine from a good vintage that has been aged longer than normal before release; Classico, which indicates the heartland, the best part, of a DOC or DOCG; Superiore, which usually means higher alcohol, but can mean a superior subregion; and Vigna or Vigneto, indicating a special vineyard or "*cru*".

Grapes

When it comes to grape varieties, Italy has a cast of thousands – many of them fascinating originals, such as Arneis, Fiano, Picolit, Teroldego, and Schioppettino, capable of high quality but entirely localized. Others such as the red Sangiovese have successfully reached most parts, though Sangiovese's heart remains in Tuscany. The white Trebbiano is similarly well spread, although everywhere could have done with a little less of it: some strains are better than others but all are fairly neutral in flavour. The great Nebbiolo's stronghold is the northwest, but it is not alone: it shares its territory with the likes of Barbera and Dolcetto and more obscure varieties such as Freisa and Grignolino. In the northeast, unusual local varieties, such as Vespaiolo (white) and Lagrein (red) compete with Pinot Grigio and high-class French grapes. The far south has a cast that includes Primitivo, Negroamaro, and Nero d'Avola.

Wines and regions

Aglianico del Vulture

Made from Aglianico in Basilicata, this can be one of the finest, most complex reds. Its deep colour, smoky berry perfume, and tannin give it superb ageing potential.

Alto Adige

This cool, mountainous corner of Italy used to be part of Austria. Its people still, for preference, speak German and call their region the Südtirol. Its twenty grape varieties, mostly white, are mainly sold as varietals, and are light, vibrant, and aromatic. Look for Chardonnay, Pinot Bianco, Traminer, and Rhine Riesling, and, for the red Lagrein Dunkel: dark and fruity with a bitter-chocolate finish. Look also for red Teroldego Rotaliano.

Arneis

The Arneis grape, with its flavours of nuts, herbs, and pears, produces Piedmont's and one of Italy's most characterful dry whites.

Asti

It is much-maligned, but this inexpensive, sweet sparkling Piedmont wine from the Muscat grape is low in alcohol, high in delicate, grapey perfume, and perfect drunk well chilled on a summer's day – just so long as it's very young and fresh. The same applies to the similar Moscato d'Asti.

Barbaresco and Barolo

The Nebbiolo grape in the neighbouring Barolo and Barbaresco regions of Piedmont makes wines that are all tannin and hidden fruit when young, but which mature into intriguingly perfumed, complex, supple, yet always full-bodied reds. Barolo is traditionally the more massive – described as king of Piedmont, where Barbaresco is queen – but in both regions the trend has been towards more approachable wines with greater fruit and riper tannins. Nebbiolo wines that are gentler on the palate and pocket include Carema and Nebbiolo d'Alba, and blends with other grapes in Lombardy and Valtellina.

Barbera d'Alba and Barbera d'Asti

After the prestigious Nebbiolo, Barbera is the main Piedmontese red grape (and Italy's second most

(Left) **The tannic Nebbiolo grape, reaching its apogee in Barolo and Barbaresco, produces wines of phenomenal power and longevity.**

(Right) **An unmistakeably Tuscan vista, but here in Montalcino, south of Siena, an unusual clone of Sangiovese, called Brunello, gives bigger, more muscular wine than in Chianti.**

planted variety). It has damson and cherry fruit with relatively high acid and low tannin, and can be made to be drunk young or in a bigger style and aged in oak – a bit like a mini-Barolo. Alba produces the fullest Barbera, closely followed by the usually slightly softer and fruitier Barbera d'Asti.

Bardolino

Made from similar grapes to those that go into Valpolicella, but on different soils around Lake Garda in the Veneto, Bardolino is a much lighter red – as well as a rosé. Both should be drunk very young while they still have their freshness and cherry-stone fruit, and the red can be chilled.

Bianco di Custoza

On the southern part of Bardolino and west of Soave, the Bianco di Custoza DOC gives crisp, fruity, creamy whites in the Soave mould – but generally cheaper.

Bolgheri

A relatively new DOC on the Tuscan coast, created to give official recognition to red wines that are so sought-after they hardly needed such rubber-stamping. Bolgheri is home to the world famous Sassicaia, a Cabernet Sauvignon wine that spearheaded the move to top quality and to French varieties, although the estate now has its own personal DOC (the first such in Italy). Masseto leads the Merlot wine pack. The DOC also applies, though is less used, for white, rosé, and Vin Santo.

Brunello di Montalcino

Brunello is the Tuscan name for a strain of Sangiovese grown in the Montalcino area south of Siena (and south of Chianti). It makes a rich, dark, concentrated red wine (heavier and more tannic than Chianti) which is aged longer in barrel, and can usually take another five to ten years in bottle. Despite DOCG status, it lived on its reputation for too long, but recent years have seen a raising of standards. Rosso di Montalcino, the soft, plummy, younger version is cheaper and usually better value.

Cannonau di Sardegna

The island-wide appellation for Sardinia's full, dry reds from Cannonau (Grenache). Often good value.

Carignano del Sulcis

A high quality, full-bodied red made from Carignan in southwest Sardinia. The Riserva is particularly good.

READING ITALIAN LABELS

Stylish modern labelling from style-conscious Italy. Not all are in this league, but labelling has improved.

From top to bottom: **Fattoria di Felsina Berardenga** is the producer (*fattoria* is a Tuscan word for a wine-producing estate, often a grand and historic one); this is a Chianti from the Classico zone (Classico is usually the superior heartland of a wine region); 1998 is the vintage (year of harvest); Chianti Classico is a *denominazione di origen controllata e garantita*, or DOCG, the official top quality level of Italian wine; the wine was bottled at source (*all'origine*), *i.e.* on the estate, by the grower (*viticoltore*), Felsina di Berardenga, whose address is given at the bottom; 13% is the alcohol content, measured as a percentage of volume; 75cl is the bottle size; the "e" means only that this is an official EU bottle size.

Carmignano

The small DOCG of Carmignano is an enclave of Chianti, west of Florence that makes a fine Sangiovese-based red that has always contained a little Cabernet Sauvignon. The wines are Chianti-like, but with greater elegance and ageing potential. There is also an attractive DOC *rosato* and a good value, younger, less concentrated version called Barco Reale.

Chianti

In so large a region (it covers much of central Tuscany) standards are bound to vary – and styles too – but at least Chianti is a much more reliable name than it once was – and so it should be as a DOCG. All Chianti is made mostly from Sangiovese and has a characteristic hint of astringency, but there are two broad styles: the lighter, younger, fruity Chianti (which always used to come in straw-covered flasks); and the more serious, expensive type that has real depth of flavour, but also an austerity that needs time to soften (two to four years for non-Riserva and at least four for Riserva). Most of these more serious Chiantis come from the Classico subregion (Chianti is divided into eight such regions) and they are always labelled Chianti Classico. This is the historic central area between Florence and Siena that is peppered with aristocratic estates and estates now owned by rich outsiders. The other important subregion for top quality is the smaller Chianti Rufina.

Cirò

Calabria's most celebrated wine, in an admittedly limited field, is the dark, full Cirò Rosso made from the ancient Gaglioppo grape. There is also a lively, dry Cirò white made from the equally ancient Greco.

Colli Orientali del Friuli and Collio

Adjoining DOCs in Friuli on the Slovenian border, producing around twenty wines (mostly varietals) apiece. Collio is renowned for the quality (and cost) of its dry whites – extraordinarily aromatic, intense, fruity, and beautifully streamlined Pinot Bianco, Pinot Grigio, Tocai Friulano, etc – but reds such as Cabernet and Merlot can be good too. Colli Orientali favours the same whites, plus the local Ribolla Gialla and Verduzzo, but makes more reds – including some impressive Merlot, Cabernet, and local Refosco and Schioppettino. There are also some fine sweet wines including Ramandolo, Verduzzo, and Picolit.

Copertino

A robust, full-flavoured, spicy red made from Negroamaro in Puglia. Often good value.

Dolcetto

Dolcetto is pretty well a Piedmont exclusivity. The best come from the DOCs of Alba, Ovada, and Dogliani, with Asti producing an attractive lighter style. In general they should be drunk young, but there are some producers trying more serious, tannic styles.

Fiano di Avellino

A distinctive, full, dry, aromatic white made from the Fiano grape on the hills around Avellino in Campania. Its aromas can be reminscent of Viognier.

Franciacorta

This DOCG east of Milan accounts for most of Italy's top Champagne-type sparkling wines. The still reds

and dry whites under the DOC Terre di Franciacorta are also made to a high standard.

Frascati

Frascati, the local wine of Rome, is not one of the great Italian whites, except in volumes produced, but it is a much better one than it was a decade or two ago – softly dry and leafily refreshing. Some producers are now also trying their hand at a traditional sweet version.

Friuli Grave

The main DOC of the Friuli region, covering grapes such as Merlot, Cabernet, Pinot Nero, and Refosco for the reds; Pinot Grigio, Pinot Bianco, Tocai, Riesling Renano, Sauvignon, Traminer, Chardonnay, and Verduzzo for the whites. The wines are generally well made, although Pinot Grigio, when overproduced, can be neutral-flavoured and disappointing.

Gattinara and Ghemme

Two Nebbiolo-based Piedmont reds which are both DOCG and at best can rival Barolo. Quality varies, however (more than it should for DOCG) and this best is not seen often enough.

Gavi

Gavi, the fashionable dry white of Piedmont, has more character than Tuscany's Galestro – being made largely from the citrusy Cortese – but it is expensive. Cortese del Piemonte is cheaper and can be as good.

(Above) **White grapes, especially Trebbiano, have been the bane of Chianti in the past, but here, near Panzano, the producer Fontodi is proving that more aromatic varieties, such as Pinot Bianco and Sauvignon, can be worth pursuing.**

Lambrusco

In its truest native form (Lambrusco di Sorbara and Lambrusco Grasparossa di Castelvetro are the best) it is deep red, refreshingly dry, crisp, and juicy. Drunk young and cool, but not chilled, it is the perfect complement to the rich local food of Emilia-Romagna.

Lugana

From south of Lake Garda, this is one of Italy's dry whites of real quality and personality. Medium-full, well rounded, perfumed, and delicately nutty.

Marsala

Sicily's famous fortified wine is now wildly unfashionable, but an old *vergine*, the top quality, bone dry style, is a complex, sherry-type animal. The lesser *fine* and *superiore* categories may be sweetened.

Montefalco

Rosso di Montefalco, Umbria's DOC Sangiovese-based red, is most seen, but it is the powerful red DOCG Sagrantino di Montefalco that is most revered. It comes in both dry and sweet (*passito*).

Montepulciano d'Abruzzo

The Montepulciano grape (no relation to Tuscany's Vino Nobile di Montepulciano) produces generous, solid, spicy red wines here on the Adriatic coast.

Morellino di Scansano

An increasingly popular southern Tuscan red from the Morellino clone of Sangiovese. Robust, yet supple.

Moscato Passito di Pantelleria

An intensely sweet, rich, apricoty wine made from sun-dried grapes on the tiny island of Pantelleria, southwest of Sicily. Quality is high, quantities small.

Orvieto

If heavily based on Trebbiano, Orvieto is pale, dry, and rather bland, but when other grapes are added, particularly in the Classico area, it can develop some nutty character; even so, it is not to be kept. Abboccato is the (now) much less common semi-sweet version.

Pomino

There is a French influence in the wines from this small DOC east of Florence, with Cabernet and Merlot in the Sangiovese-based red and Pinot Bianco in the whites. Results are good, but prices high.

Primitivo di Manduria

The leading DOC for Puglia's widely grown and, thanks to its connections with California's Zinfandel, newly fashionable Primitivo grape. The wines are headily perfumed and alcoholic with spice and ripe fruit.

Prosecco di Conegliano-Valdobbiadene

Sparkling Prosecco (from the Veneto) can be dry or semi-sweet. It is not a Champagne copy, but a fresh, appley, affordable sparkling wine – delicious so long as it is drunk young and well-chilled.

Recioto

Sweet wines made from grapes that have been hung up or spread out to dry. The most renowned, and most complex in flavour, are the red Recioto della Valpolicella and the white (golden) Recioto di Soave.

Rosso Cònero

The full-bodied reds of the Rosso Cònero DOC in the Marches are based on the Montepulciano grape, which gives an appealing, warm, spicy character.

Salice Salentino

Impressive, deeply fruity, chocolatey reds from the Salentino peninsula in Puglia. Can be bargains.

Soave

Soave, like Chianti, was much abused and then much improved. There is still mass-produced dross, but from the Soave Classico heartland in the hills behind Verona there is much that is crisply fruity with the distinctive straw and almond character.

Taurasi

Campania's long-lived DOCG red wine made from the noble Aglianico grape.

Torgiano

Lungarotti is almost the only producer in this Umbria DOC and (for red Riserva) DOCG near Perugia. The red, based on Sangiovese, is like a fleshy, supple Chianti.

Trentino

The southern extension of Alto Adige (*q.v.*) produces roughly similar wines, mostly from

(Below) **Close to the mountains and the Austrian border in the north, the wines of Alto Adige and Trentino are mostly made from single grape varieties – nineteen different ones in Alto Adige.**

single grape varieties, but there are more reds and generally they are riper and broader (eg. Cabernet Sauvignon, Lagrein and the almondy Marzemino). Pinot Bianco, Chardonnay, and Pinot Grigio are successful whites.

Valpolicella

The Veneto's best-known red varies from lightweight, simple wine – best drunk young while its modest cherry-kernel flavours are still fresh – to concentrated, sweet Recioto della Valpolicella (*q.v.*) and equally concentrated dry red Amarone della Valpolicella (both the latter are made from dried grapes). In between the young, light, and the concentrated end-of-dinner styles there is Valpolicella Classico, and single-vineyard wine of medium to full body and high quality.

Verdicchio dei Castelli di Jesi

From near Ancona in the Marches, a crisp, dry, nutty white for drinking young. Traditionally it comes in an amphora shaped bottle.

Vernaccia di San Gimignano

A nutty and honeyed or (more usually) clean, lemony, and straightforward Tuscan white from the Vernaccia grape. Drink young.

Vino Nobile di Montepulciano

This Sangiovese-based red from a region to the south of Chianti was Italy's first DOCG (though more for political than qualitative reasons). In style the wines lie between the elegance of Chianti and the power of Brunello di Montalcino, and quality has improved recently. Rosso di Montepulciano, the younger, lighter version, can be good value.

Vin Santo

Vin (or Vino) Santo can come from anywhere, but most, and the best, is Tuscan. It is an after-dinner sipping wine, made from grapes left to dry on racks until Christmas, then fermented in barrels, sometimes for years. Intense, complex, tangy, with orange, raisin, and apricot flavours, it can be sweet or dry.

Vintages

Barolo & Barbaresco

Year	Rating	
2002	5	▼
2001	8	▼
2000	9	▼
1999	9	▼
1998	9	★
1997	9	★
1996	9	★
1995	7	★
1994	5	▲
1993	7	★

Valpolicella (Recioto & Amarone)

Year	Rating	
2002	5	▼
2001	8	▼
2000	9	▼
1999	7	★
1998	7	★
1997	9	★
1996	7	★
1995	9	★
1994	7	★
1993	8	★

Tuscan reds

Year	Rating	
2002	5	▼
2001	8	▼
2000	9	▼
1999	9	★
1998	8	★
1997	9	★
1996	7	★
1995	8	★
1994	7	▲
1993	7	▲

Key

0–10 quality rating (10 = top wine)

▲ should drink

★ can drink, but no hurry for the top wines

▼ must keep

(See also **When to drink**, pages 44–47)

SPAIN

For centuries Iberia was on the edge of the known world, and Europe came to an end in a waste of barren mountains and plains cut off from France by the Pyrénées. Her more recent history, too, bred a fierce isolationism, which you could taste in the wines with their deeply-etched wood-aged signature. You still can taste it in many Spanish reds, if seldom now in the whites and rosés, but it is no longer a case of blanket coverage. Styles are more diverse – and all the better for that.

While the face of Spanish wine changed enormously in the 1990s, some of the fundamental influences on what can be produced inevitably remain the same. Spain still has more vineyard planted than any other European country, but is only the third largest wine producer after France and Italy. Yields are low partly because even

the mass-producing vineyards are not managed in the same efficient, industrial way as they are in France or Germany, but largely because of the climate. Vines have traditionally been planted very widely spaced because, in so much of the country, the heat and aridity of the summer months deprive them of water. Only Galicia in the Atlantic-influenced

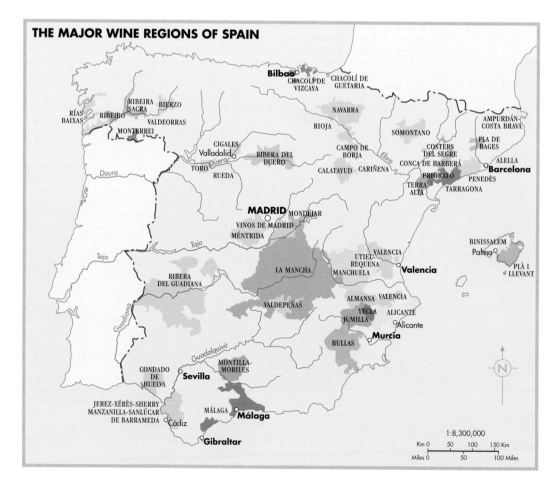

THE MAJOR WINE REGIONS OF SPAIN

northwest can claim to have a cool, rainy climate. Irrigation is now permitted (as of 1996) and has been instrumental in raising both quality and yields, but it requires investment on a scale beyond the means (and often the inclination) of the average small grower.

The climate has meant that Spain's finest wines have always come from the northern half of the country, while the dry and barren centre (Castilla-La Mancha) concentrated on cheap bulk wines and the hot south became famous for fortified and dessert wines. There is still truth in this, but nowadays it is only half the story.

Fifty-five regions, spread across the country, are now classified *denominación de origen* (DO): the equivalent of French *appellation contrôlée*, in which the origin, grapes, vinification, and maturation of the wine are carefully specified. Above them, so far, there is just one DOCa (*denominación de origen calificada*, similar to the Italian DOCG) – and that, unsurprisingly, is Rioja. In 2001 Priorat applied to become the country's second DOCa. It if succeeds, it will have stolen a march on such regions as Ribera del Duero and Penedès.

Below DO is the equivalent of French *vin de pays*, *vino de la tierra*. These range from complete regions (Castilla y León, Galicia, Extremadura, and Andalucia) to the small and obscure. Under the heading *vino de mesa*, table wine, comes much that is fairly basic,

much that is infinitely better than it would have been ten years ago and a tiny minority of top quality wines from producers operating (as in Italy) outside the quality wine regions.

The other significant classification for Spanish wines – especially red – is one according to age and maturation. Details vary from DO to DO, but generally, for red wines, a Joven (young) wine is sold in the year after the harvest; a Crianza is aged for two years, at least six months of it in oak; a Reserva is aged for three years, of which one is in oak; and a Gran Reserva is aged for five years, two of them in oak. The hierarchy is the same for white wines, but with the ageing periods generally shorter.

Grapes

It infuriates Spanish producers to hear this said, but one of their handicaps is their grape varieties. Spain hasn't Italy's advantage of an array of thrilling indigenous varieties. The red Tempranillo (under several pseudonyms) is the star of the cast, aided and abetted by Graciano and Monastrell and by Mediterranean grapes such as red (and white) Garnacha (Grenache) and red Cariñena (Carignan). Among the whites, Albariño, grown in Galicia, can be gorgeous, as can the rare Godello. Verdejo, mainly from Rueda, vies with Albarîno as top white. After

(Below) **Planting vines is not always a simple matter of choosing a well-exposed slope: on the island of Lanzarote vineyards are dug into hardened lava flows, and walls around the vines protect them from wind damage.**

that come Parellada, Xarel-lo, Macabeo, Moscatel, Pedro Ximénez, and Airén, the latter being the least distinguished of all.

Wines and regions

Cariñena

Despite its name, Garnacha, not Cariñena, dominates the vineyards of this, Aragon's largest DO, lying inland in eastern Spain. The wines are typically chunky, ripe, and alcoholic, although modern technology, Tempranillo, and Cabernet Sauvignon are lightening them up a touch.

Cava

Cava is the name given to most of Spain's *méthode traditionelle* sparkling wine. State-of-the-art technology and grapes from the (relatively) cool vineyards of northern Spain (mostly Catalonia) are a promising background. The problems come with the grapes, Xarel-lo, Macabeo (aka Viura), and Parellada, which can have an earthy, rooty dullness. But quality has improved greatly – judicious additions of Chardonnay doing their bit. If in doubt go for youth and freshness and drink it well chilled.

Conca de Barbera

Sandwiched between Penedès, Costers del Segre, and Tarragona in Catalonia, much of Conca de Barberà's production goes to *cava*, but it also makes some fine Chardonnay, Cabernet, Merlot, and Tempranillo. The output of Pla de Bages, a new DO to the northeast, follows in Conca de Barberà's footsteps.

Costers del Segre

This region in the northeast is virtually synonymous with the firm of Raimat, which makes good quality reds, whites, and sparkling wines, principally from classic French varieties – Cabernet, Merlot, Pinot Noir, and Chardonnay – but also Tempranillo.

Jumilla

There is still hefty, highly alcoholic red from Jumilla, but outside investment in this region inland from Alicante in eastern Spain has given rounder, fruitier reds and rosés that are often good value.

La Mancha

Spain's bleak central plateau (and largest DO) used to produce little that wasn't cheap, dull, and

(Above) In the north of Spain, to the north of Rioja, Navarra has made huge progress in the last decade: once renowned for its rosés, it now also has a deserved reputation for its juicy young reds – Spain's answer to Beaujolais – and for fuller, oak-aged alternatives to Rioja.

(Right) In Spain growers are traditionally growers only – with traditional modes of transport! Making wine is still mainly left to the large concerns – *bodegas* or, as here in Ribera del Duero, local cooperatives.

fruitless, whether it was white (the bulk of production) or red. Nowadays there is a growing volume of cheap but cheerful, full, juicy reds.

Málaga

A name from the past, Málaga, like so many other fortified wines, is crushingly unfashionable – and struggles more than most to survive. It comes from the Costa del Sol and is famously rich, sweet, raisiny, and wood-aged.

Montilla

The DO region, which lies northeast of Jerez, is called Montilla-Moriles and the wines are made in sherry styles, labelled dry, medium, and sweet, or *fino*, *oloroso* etc., according to the market.

Navarra

Just to the north of Rioja, grapes such as Cabernet, Merlot, Tempranillo, and Chardonnay have long since muscled in on what was once almost exclusively Garnacha territory. Both the young, fruity styles and the well-structured, oak-aged ones attract well-deserved attention. The rosés, for which Navarra was originally renowned, are among Spain's best.

Penedès

Miguel Torres is certainly not the only wine producer, or even the only good one, in Penedès, but he led the way in changing its image. The wines from Torres and other top producers are semi-international in style: the grape varieties are often familiar (Cabernet and Chardonnay among them), but they are frequently blended with varieties such as Tempranillo and Parellada which give the wines their own regional character.

Priorat

It took a handful of winemakers at the end of the 1980s less than a decade to transform Priorat from being a forgotten outpost of Tarragona's fortified wine industry to being recognized as a producer of magnificent, powerful red wines. These men were visionaries, but they knew they had the key ingredients in place already – very old, low-yielding, terraced vineyards on poor, stony soils. To the Garnacha and Carignan, they added a little Cabernet Sauvignon, Syrah, and Merlot.

In 2001, what used to be a subzone of Priorat called Falset was promoted to DO in its own right and renamed Montsant. The Garnachas offer an excellent poor man's Priorat.

Rías Baixas

This DO in Galicia, the cool, rainy northwest of Spain, produces exceptional, fragrant, apricoty dry whites from the Albariño grape, easily Spain's most fashionable (which, under the name of Alvarinho, appears in Vinho Verde just over the border in northern Portugal). The warmer, drier Ribeiro and Ribeira Sacra regions to the east make whites from various indigenous varieties, including Albariño and Godello, often at lower prices.

Ribera del Duero

It is not only in Portugal that the vineyards of the River Douro (in Spain called the Duero) produce fine wine. In northwest Spain, to the southwest of Rioja, the Ribera del Duero DO is notable for the fierceness of its temperatures (both hot and cold) and the quality – and price – of its red wines (including the legendary Vega Sicilia and its young arch-rival Pesquera). Tempranillo is the main grape and it makes, sometimes blended with a little Cabernet Sauvignon, powerful, aromatic, concentrated reds. All the wines need a few years' age and the best last twelve years or more – which gives them plenty of time to gather the sort of accolades that push up prices. It may be, however, that the Cigales DO region to the west will soon provide some competition. Renowned for its *rosados*, some of the region's producers have recently turned their attentions to serious reds.

Rioja

Spain's flagship red wine has gone through several phases in the last few decades. In the 1970s Rioja established itself as unmistakably oaky – the reds pale in colour with soft summer-pudding fruit and the whites fat and nutty. Then producers started

READING SPANISH LABELS

Spain still has its ultra-traditional labels, with extraneous details to wade through to find the essential details, but the trend is to crisper labels like this.

From top to bottom: **Rioja** is the region and it is a *denominación de origen calificada* (DOCa), Spain's top quality level; **Cirsion** is the name of the wine; **1999** is the vintage (year of harvest); *embotellado en la propriedad* means that it is an estate-produced and bottled wine; it confirms "estate bottled" at the bottom of the label; **Bodegas Roda** is the producer (*bodega* – the wine-producing cellar or winery); **14.5%** is the alcohol content, measured as a percentage of volume (high, so assume that it is a modern Rioja); **75cl** is the bottle size; the **"e"** means only that this is an official EU bottle size; in the right-hand corner is the official **Rioja** stamp of authenticity.

using less and less oak (also, barrels were getting old and flavourless after the rush of investment in oak in the seventies); whites became fresh, lemony, and anonymously international in style; and the reds, made from Tempranillo, Graciano, Garnacha, and Mazuelo, became less interesting. At the end of the 1980s a new generation began to make bigger, darker, fruitier wines, with more oak once again. But, as so often, the pendulum seemed to swing too far and now there is a move away from quite such dark and powerful red Riojas.

Rioja is in fact divided into three areas, Rioja Alta, Rioja Alavesa, and Rioja Baja, with the first being the coolest and the last the hottest, but most Riojas are a blend from all three because the majority of *bodegas* (producers) buy in their grapes from growers and do not own many vineyards themselves.

Rueda

In a country focused on reds, the Rueda region, northwest of Madrid, is understandably valued. Red Rueda is now permitted, but the dry whites are the stars. Made mostly from the herby, nutty Verdejo grape, and/or Sauvignon Blanc, they can be fresh and crisp, or barrel fermented for a richer flavour and longer life.

Sherry

Sherry comes only from a triangular area of chalky soil around the Andalucian town of Jerez de la Frontera near the coast in southwest Spain (anything else simply isn't sherry). It is made from the neutral, low acid Palomino grape and aged in *solera*, a system which produces highly complex wines which combine the freshness of youth with the depth of maturity (because the wines ageing in *solera* barrels are constantly "refreshed" with younger wine: twenty-five to thirty-three per cent of each cask is moved at a time, and at each stage the cask is topped-up with twenty-five to thirty-three per cent of sherry from a cask at the previous, younger, stage).

The *manzanilla* style, which is matured by the sea at Sanlúcar de Barrameda, is sherry's lightest style – searingly dry, delicate, and with an almost salty bite. *Fino* is similar but fractionally weightier. Both get their characteristic yeasty tang from the *flor* yeast which is left to grow as they mature in barrel*. They are the ultimate aperitif sherries, although some people prefer the fuller body of an *amontillado*, especially in winter.

Amontillado is *fino* on which the *flor* has lived, matured, and died and so it is an older, darker, and nuttier sherry, but one which should still have a certain tang. Sadly, short cuts are taken with the production of most commercial *amontillado* for export

* Flor is a natural yeast present in the Jerez region that grows in a porridge-like layer on the surface of young fino, protecting it from oxygen.

(Above) **The solera system of ageing sherry progressively through a series of barrels means that cooperage has always been a crucial craft industry in Jerez.**

markets and most of it is also sweetened which blurs its character.

Oloroso is sherry which did not grow *flor*. It is the fullest and richest – with nut, fig, and prune flavours – but it is still naturally dry. Again, commercial brands of *oloroso* are usually sweetened (and often called cream sherry), but when the finest *olorosos* are sweetened, as they are occasionally, they can make marvellous dessert wines. The rarely seen *palo cortado* style is a sort of half-way house between *amontillado* and *oloroso*.

(Below) **Sherry has been produced for centuries and has been beloved by the English since Elizabethan times when it was known as sherry sack; sadly, though, the late twentieth century has seen a steep slide in its popularity.**

(Left) **Sherry comes only from the demarcated Jerez region, an area of eye-catching, chalky white soil in the far south of Andalucia, centred on the town of Jerez from which sherry takes its name.**

Sherry is ready to drink when bottled and should be drunk as soon as it is bought. *Fino* and *manzanilla* are particularly fragile, so keep them in the fridge once opened, but preferably buy half bottles so that you can finish them in one go. And please, don't ever decant sherry.

Somontano

A rising star in the foothills of the Pyrénées. Both local and classic French grapes including Chardonnay, Merlot, and Pinot Noir are being grown in its coolish vineyards and a steady stream of fleshy, but elegant reds and whites is the result.

Toro

Only Spain could have a wine region called "Bull" – and, as if living up to the name, the Tempranillo-based wines of Toro are burly and powerful. They are also richly fruity and, though they are never as stylish and complex as the reds of Ribera del Duero to the east, they are considerably cheaper.

Valdepeñas

In the south of La Mancha, the drab white Airén grape still predominates in Valdepeñas vineyards, but there is also a tradition of soft, oak-matured red wines (Reservas and Gran Reservas). Made from Cencibel (a variant of Tempranillo) these can be remarkable bargains.

Valencia

Valencia in the east produces large quantities of modern, inexpensive whites, reds, and *rosados*, but it is known for its inexpensive, sweet, barley sugar-like Moscatel de Valencia. While nobody would make any claims for complexity in these wines, they are clean and fresh – and can be useful as a cheap alternative to Muscat de Beaumes-de-Venise. There is also a move to make light, dry Moscatels (Muscats).

To the west of the Valencia DO, the region of Utiel-Requena produces some surprisingly delicate, scented *rosados* and big strong reds, but a fair amount of production slips out under the Valencia name.

Vintages

Rioja

2002	7	▼
2001	9	▼
2000	8	▼
1999	8	★
1998	8	★
1997	6	★
1996	8	★
1995	8	★
1994	9	★
1993	6	▲

Ribera del Duero

2002	8	▼
2001	8	▼
2000	8	▼
1999	8	★
1998	5	★
1997	6	★
1996	8	★
1995	8	★
1994	9	★
1993	6	▲

Key

0–10 quality rating
(10 = top wine)

▲   should drink

★   can drink, but no hurry for the top wines

▼   must keep

(See also **When to drink**, pages 44–47)

PORTUGAL

Leaving aside its two most famous exports, port and lightly fizzy pink wines, Portugal's great strengths are its grapes and its ability to hang onto the baby while it throws out the bathwater. Entry into the EU gave the wine industry, especially the large cooperatives which dominated production, a much-needed boost, largely in the form of hefty subsidies. For years the co-ops only released their wines after they had first languished in worn-out wooden or cement vats – losing fruit and gaining astringency. The metamorphosis involved stainless steel, new oak barrels, earlier, more effective bottling, and, not least, skilled and motivated winemakers – some home-grown and some Australian.

READING PORTUGUESE LABELS

Like Spanish labels, Portuguese vary from traditional, like this, to the no-frills New World style.

From top to bottom: **Tinta da Anfora** is the name of the wine (*tinto* means red; *anfora* is the traditional winemaking vessel, the Ali Baba-type jar shown in the illustration); **A Vinho Regional** is a large region, equivalent in status to a French *vin de pays* (*see* Alentejo right); **1998** is the vintage (year of harvest); **J.P. Vinhos Ltd** is the producer; **75cl** is the bottle size; the **"e"** means only that this is an official EU bottle size; **13%** is the alcohol content, measured as a percentage of the volume.

The crucial point recognised by all the new winemakers, whether native or New World, was the value of the baby – in the form of Portugal's great wealth of interesting indigenous grape varieties. Instead of grasping every opportunity to show the world that Portugal, too, could make convincing Cabernet Sauvignon and Chardonnay (which it can), they have concentrated on developing the best and most characterful of Portugal's own grapes – like the white Fernão Pires, Loureiro, and Alvarinho, and the red Castelão (Periquita), Roriz (Aragonez), Trincadeira, Baga, and port varieties such as Touriga Naçional.

Portugal's appellation system, like so many, is based on that of France. The equivalent of France's ACs are the thirty-eight DOCs (*denominação de origem controlada*). On the next rung down is the small and diminishing group of IPRs (*indicações de proveniência regulamentada*), the equivalent of VDQS. Then come the far larger and more significant VRs (*vinho regional*, akin to *vin de pays*). Among them are Beiras, which covers the same territory as Bairrada and Dão and continues east and south, Trás-os-Montes, a promising region in the northeast which edges into the upper Douro and includes international grape varieties, and the Algarve, better known of course for its tourists. *Vinho de mesa* (table wine) is at the bottom of the pile.

Wines and regions

Alentejo

The Alentejo, which sprawls across the south of the country, is both DOC and, as Alentejano, a *vinho regional*. The DOC with its eight subzones (including Reguengos, Borba, and Evora) is dominated by efficient co-operatives. But it also has a handful of high-profile estates (both new and old) making rich, stylish red wines, mostly from Portuguese varieties.

Bairrada

Bairrada, to the west of the Dão region in the mid-north, began to come up in the world in the late 1980s. The Baga grape gives chunky, tannic, peppery, blackcurrant, and blackberry flavours, and the wines can be long-lived, although increasingly they are being made softer and less tannic. White Bairrada is crisp, herby, and well worth buying.

Dão

For years Dão was held back by the local cooperatives' stranglehold. Even after they were forced to let go, it took a while for growers to shake off the lazy, cooperative mentality and for individual estates to emerge. Now that they have, we are seeing the region starting to fulfil its potential for fruity, velvety reds and characterful dry whites.

Douro

Under half of each year's harvest in the northerly Douro Valley is generally authorised to be made into port. The rest remains as table wine and, until recently, with the exception of Barca Velha (Portugal's unofficial "first growth") and one or two others, no one put much effort into these. A tough port market has concentrated minds and several port houses and individual growers have started to make very impressive, powerful, but elegant, wines.

THE WINE REGIONS OF PORTUGAL

N

— Mair
— Alen

1:3,481,000

Km 0   40   80 Km
Miles 0   20   40 Miles

RIOS DO MINHO
VINHOS VERDES
Porto
PORTO E DOURO
TÁVORA-VAROSA
ENCOSTAS DA NAVE
BEIRA INTERIOR
LAFÕES
BAIRRADA
DÃO
BEIRA INTERIOR
CHAVES
TRÁS-OS-MONTES
VALPAÇOS
PLANALTO-MIRANDÊS
ENCOSTAS DE AIRE
ALCOBAÇA
LOURINHÃ
ÓBIDOS
ALMEIRIM
PORTALEGRE
TORRES VEDRAS
ALENQUER
RIBATEJO
ALENTEJO
ARRUDA
BUCELAS
COLARES
ESTREMADURA
LISBOA
PALMELA
CARCAVELOS
SETÚBAL
BORBA
ÉVORA
REDONDO
REGUENGOS
GRANJA AMARELIJA
VIDIGUEIRA
MOURA
ALGARVE
PORTIMÃO
LAGOA
TAVIRA
LAGOS
Faro

MADEIRA
Funchal

Estremadura

Once known only as Oeste, "the west", and home of the historic and idiosyncratic wines of Bucelas, Colares, and Carcavelos, the large Estremadura region to the west and north of Lisbon is known today for its large output of inexpensive, fruity,

(Left) **The port vineyards of the Douro are graded from A to F according to quality, but high up in the hills of the Upper Douro the vineyards are more suited to table wine, which is a growing sideline for port shippers.**

(Above) **Vines and bananas jostle for space on Madeira's terraced slopes and many of the vines are the inferior Tinta Negra Mole variety, but at least in future madeira will have to be made from the grape stated on the label.**

spicy reds. Most are cooperative-made and are sold under the *vinho regional* designation or the Arruda and Torres Vedras DOCs. The Alenquer DOC leads the quality wine charge from small estates.

Madeira

Madeira, one of the world's great fortified wines, has a distinctively tangy taste acquired through a long ageing process during which all but the very finest wines are heated in large tanks called *estufas*. The best wines are aged more gently and slowly in cask.

The famous styles of madeira are named after the island's four classic (white) grapes, though until an EU regulation came into force to ensure that the wines really do contain at least eighty-five per cent of the stated grape, most were based on Tinta Negra Mole, and lesser wines are still made from it. The driest is Sercial, followed by Verdelho, both of which are traditionally drunk chilled as aperitifs; Bual (sweet) and Malmsey (very sweet and dark) are pudding wines or postprandials. Most are labelled by age – five, ten, or fifteen years – and the older the more superior the quality. The Tinta Negra Mole madeiras may also be labelled by age and will usually also be described as either dry, medium dry, medium rich, or rich. Terms such as "finest" mean little, if anything. Vintage madeira, from a single year and a single variety, must have been aged at least twenty years and is rare and justifiably expensive. Harvest, or Colheita, is a new category indicating a younger, fruitier style from a single vintage but bottled after six years.

Port

This sweet, red fortified wine comes from the hot, dry Douro Valley where five grape varieties, led by Touriga Naçional, dominate (in terms of quality) the thin schistous soil and steep, sometimes precipitous, slopes and terraces. As seen already (page 81) the several styles

of port fall into two clear categories. Vintage port – long-lived and expensive – is made only in the best years and from the grapes of one vintage only. It is bottled two years after the harvest and then matured in bottle. Single Quinta, from a single property (the quinta), is a variation on the theme: vintage port from a lesser year – often excellent, but faster-maturing than traditional vintage wines.

Other ports are matured in wooden casks and are ready to drink when bottled. Of wood-aged ports, aged tawnies are usually high quality blends and give their average age on the label – ten, twenty, thirty, or forty years. Colheitas are those from a single (stated) year. All tawnies are lighter and nuttier than vintage wines.

Cheap tawny and ruby wines are of inferior quality. Late Bottled Vintage (from a single year) and Vintage Character wines are intended to have the style of vintage port at lower prices, but are mostly shadows of the real thing (the word Traditional on the label

should indicate a more authentic style). Crusted port, which throws a deposit in bottle and needs decanting like true vintage port and Single Quinta, is cheaper than both and can be a good buy.

White port ranges from sweet to dry and is not a drink of any great finesse. It is at its best drunk well-chilled while basking in the heat of the Douro.

Rosé

Portuguese rosés, led by the redoubtable Mateus, can come from anywhere, though most big brands come from the relatively cool north. They are semi-sweet and slightly sparkling.

Setúbal Peninsula

This peninsula south of Lisbon, particularly the newly promoted Palmela DOC, has been in the vanguard of new wave Portuguese winemaking, with forward-looking wineries making excellent New World-influenced wines: crisp, aromatic, and oaked whites, from grapes such as Muscat and Chardonnay, as well as native varieties; and alongside top quality, spicy, raspberry-scented red Periquita, there is rich, concentrated Cabernet and Merlot. Setúbal also has its own ultra-traditional wine, Moscatel de Setúbal: a sweet, fortified and sometimes very long-aged wine, with an orange-toffee-marmalade taste.

Vinho Verde

About a third of all Vinho Verde, from the Minho in the far north, is in fact lean, tart red wine, but the wine exported is white. The bone dry versions have a much more mouth-watering flavour than those sweetened for export, but whatever the style, drink it young (that is what "Verde" means in this context).

Vintages		
Dão & Bairrada		
2002	6	▼
2001	8	▼
2000	8	▼
1999	7	★
1998	7	★
1997	8	★
1996	8	★
1995	7	★
1994	8	★
1993	5	▲
Vintage port (including Single Quinta)		
2002	6	▼
2001	7	▼
2000	9	▼
1999	6	▼
1998	6	▼
1997	8	▼
1996	6	▼
1995	7	★
1994	9	▼
1993	3	▲
1992	8	★
1991	8	★

Key
0–10 quality rating
(10 = top wine)
▲ should drink
★ can drink, but no hurry for the top wines
▼ must keep

(*See also* **When to drink**, pages 44–47)

(Left) **Until the Douro was dammed during the 1960s and early 1970s, the distinctive** barcos rabelos **(moored left) were used to carry pipes of port (barrels containing about 600 litres) from the port farms high up in the Douro to the lodges (cellars) by the sea at Vila Nova de Gaia.**

USA AND CANADA

In theory the modern wine history of the USA dates from the ending of Prohibition in 1933, but in practice it took another three decades to get over post-Prohibition blues and it was not until the late 1960s that wine production began to spread rapidly and wine areas and growers multiplied. Today the USA ranks fourth in quantity among the world's producers. Only Italy, France, and Spain produce more, while Australia makes considerably less than half as much. And it is California that makes the majority of USA wine. Although most states now make *vinifera* wine of some sort, over ninety per cent comes from California – and it was California in the 1970s which first showed the world that great wines no longer came exclusively from Europe and predominantly from France.

(Below) **Old vines, meticulously trained younger vines and mustard on the Silverado Trail: mustard is often used by organic growers – it keeps weeds at bay and is ploughed in as "green" manure.**

In the intervening years, while California has had to face up to the challenge of better value varietal wines being offered by almost all other New World countries (most having the advantage of much cheaper land), it has taken its own top wines closer in style and quality to the great French classics. That they should come so near is slightly curious, because in many ways California viticulture is the

antithesis of French. In France, heavy emphasis is given to the soil; in California, though soil has gained credibility, especially in the Napa Valley, the accent is still on climate. Equally, each French wine has its framework laid down in the *appellation contrôlée* laws, so that an AC is a guide to style; California (and the rest of the USA) has a widespread appellation system of Approved Viticultural Areas, but the AVAs simply define regions. Growers can grow what they want, where they want, without bureaucratic stricture (and thus, on a label, the grape variety and the producer's name are the keys to style).

Despite the freedom, the range of grape varieties, at least for premium quality wines, is not extensive. Most Californian producers choose Cabernet Sauvignon, Chardonnay, and Merlot, although plantings of Pinot Noir and Syrah have grown exponentially in the last few years. The same, only from a much smaller base, applies to fashionable Rhône varieties such as Viognier and Roussanne, and to a lesser extent to Italian grapes such as Nebbiolo and Sangiovese, and they tend to be made by mavericks to impressive standards. Sauvignon Blanc and Riesling are abundant but seldom very interesting (sweet late-harvest Rieslings being an exception); and grapes such as Colombard, Chenin Blanc, and Grenache disappear into cheap blends, so-called "jug" wines. California does, however, have one world-class grape of its own, Zinfandel. Much of this is turned into vapid pink wine (known as "white" or "blush"), but, given the opportunity, it makes huge, ripe, spicy reds – sometimes made even bigger and darker by blending with a little of California's Petite Sirah.

In states such as Oregon, Washington, New York, Texas, and Virginia much the same applies (although with varying emphases), but for most other states the great standbys are North America's own indigenous (hardy, but generally low quality) *Vitis labrusca* and hybrids.

California

Mendocino

California's northernmost wine region boasts two distinct climates. The Pacific-cooled Anderson Valley produces first-class Chardonnay/Pinot Noir sparkling wines (the best so far from Roederer Champagne's USA offshoot) and some racy whites (especially Chardonnay, Riesling, and Gewürztraminer). The warmer, drier area to the east of the high Coastal Range produces soft, full-bodied reds, especially Cabernet, Merlot, and Zinfandel, and equally rounded fruity whites, especially Chardonnay. This region,

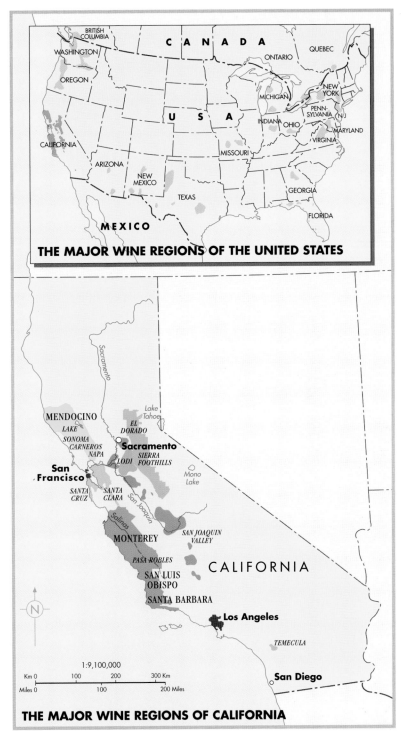

led by Fetzer, has also been at the forefront of organic viticulture.

Monterey

Cooled by sea breezes and fogs, and with the longest growing season of all the California wine regions, the Salinas Valley in Monterey, south of San Francisco Bay, was planted in the 1970s. A huge volume of wine is produced from cold, heavily irrigated vineyards and most is sold in bulk. High quality wines come from the AVAs of Arroyo Seco (whites), Chalone, Carmel Valley, and Mount Harlan.

Napa Valley

Napa Valley, to the north of San Francisco Bay, was the first area of California to make its mark and still has the highest profile. It makes barely one bottle in twenty of California's output and yet leads in terms of quality, great names, and important subregions. From AVAs such as Rutherford, Oakville, Stags' Leap, Howell Mountain, Spring Mountain, and Mount Veeder come California's greatest Cabernet Sauvignons and Cabernet Sauvignon/Merlot/Cabernet Franc blends – powerful, full-bodied wines with the potential to age ten years, but with a suppleness and fruitiness, too. Carneros, a cooler subregion at the south of the valley overlapping with the south of Sonoma, produces outstanding Pinot Noirs – indeed some of the best Pinot Noirs outside Burgundy. There are also some impressively crisp, elegant, yet richly buttery, complex Chardonnays from Carneros and its cool climate has attracted sparkling wine producers, including champagne houses. Napa's only problems are the threat of the deadly Pierce's disease, which has already hit the South, and wine prices too high relative to the rest of the world's.

San Francisco Bay

The Bay area, especially the Livermore Valley, was one of California's first wine regions. Cabernet, Chardonnay, Sauvignon, and Semillon are successful, if rarely thrilling, but pockets of exciting Cabernet and Zinfandel can be found in the high, rugged Santa Cruz mountains to the south of the Bay.

Santa Barbara and San Luis Obispo

Where these two coastal counties benefit from the cooling effect of the Pacific they can make outstanding Chardonnay, Pinot Noir, and, on a more limited scale, Syrah. Edna Valley is renowned for its Chardonnay, Arroyo Grande for Chardonnay and Pinot Noir, and Santa Maria Valley for all three. From the warmer areas, there is excellent rich, robust Paso Robles Zinfandel and Cabernet and good, fleshy Cabernet, Merlot, and Syrah from Santa Ynez Valley.

Sonoma

Less flashy than neighbouring Napa in its landscape, architecture, and wine, Sonoma, the other great wine district of California, has more vineyards and more varied climates. Being closer to the Pacific, it has more cool areas suited to Pinot Noir and fine Chardonnay, especially in the Russian River AVA and its subdivisions, but it also has warmer districts, such as the Alexander Valley and Dry Creek AVAs, where Cabernet and Zinfandel flourish. If Napa ultimately takes the Cabernet crown, Sonoma arguably takes the Chardonnay one, with wines that are marginally more structured and refined. Its Sauvignons, too, tend to have more vitality.

(Right) **The cooler coastal areas of Santa Barbara produce some excellent Pinot Noir, but here in the warmer Santa Ynez Valley varieties such as Merlot flourish and give rich, velvety reds.**

(Top right) **New vineyards in Dundee, Oregon, one of the hot spots of Pinot Noir – when the weather is kind.**

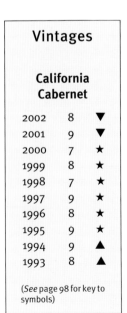

Vintages		
California Cabernet		
2002	8	▼
2001	9	▼
2000	7	★
1999	8	★
1998	7	★
1997	9	★
1996	8	★
1995	9	★
1994	9	▲
1993	8	▲

(*See* page 98 for key to symbols)

Other California regions

The hot, fertile Central Valley makes about seventy-five per cent of California's wine, the bulk of it cheap jug wine. More interesting wines, including old vineyards of red Rhône varieties and Zinfandel, come from the Delta (between Sacramento and Stockton) and even more venerable Zin hails from Amador County in the Sierra foothills.

Oregon

Quality winemaking having trickled slowly into the state from California, Oregon, with its cool, Pacific Northwest climate, was suddenly hyped in 1980 as the USA's best bet for Pinot Noir. There is potential, particularly in the Dundee Hills of the Willamette Valley (why else would the Burgundian producer Robert Drouhin being making wine there?), and it is being realized, but the climate is extraordinarily like Burgundy's, which means there will always be poor and mediocre vintages.

Other varieties that do well in these chilly conditions are the aromatic Pinot Gris and Chardonnay, with some of the latter being directed to very good sparkling wine.

Washington State

Oregon's larger, northern neighbour, Washington State, is not only more productive, but produces a wider range of high quality wines from irrigated semi desert. Intense fruit flavour and suppleness are their hallmarks, whether from Cabernet Sauvignon, Merlot, or, increasingly, Syrah. Chardonnay dominates the white wine vineyards, but there are other varieties and some late-harvest whites.

New York State

Anyone who has sampled a New York winter will have a fair idea of its climate – harsh, with a short growing season. Most of the vines are still hybrids or *Vitis labrusca*, but *vinifera* vines – varieties like Chardonnay, Rhine Riesling, and Merlot – are planted round the Finger Lakes, and on Long Island. And it is Chardonnay from Long Island that has been making waves and fooling people into thinking it is burgundy.

Canada

Canada may seem an unlikely source of good wine, but the Niagara Peninsula in Ontario, where most is made, is extraordinarily well sheltered by the lakes. And over in the west, the climate of British Columbia's Okanagan Valley is similar to that of its neighbour Washington State. *Labrusca* and hybrids used to dominate Ontario, but *vinifera* is now ahead for wine production (grape juice and jelly are still big business) and Chardonnay and Riesling are notably successful. Impressive as some of these are, Canada's unique selling point is its icewines – exceptionally sweet, concentrated wines made in winter from frozen grapes (*see* page 92).

SOUTH AMERICA

Vines arrived in Chile, Argentina, and Peru with the Spanish conquistadores in the sixteenth century and almost every South American country now makes wine, but there is gulf a between those, led by Chile, which are key players in the international arena, and those, like Brazil, which scarcely have to look beyond their own borders for sales.

READING CHILEAN LABELS

Like most New World producers, the Chileans take a simple, uncluttered approach to labels

From top to bottom: **La Palmeria is the name of the producer; 1999 is the vintage (year of harvest); Gran Reserva is an unregulated term, so can mean whatever the producer chooses; (It ought to indicate a superior quality wine aged in oak for longer than a Reserva, but Reserva is an equally unregulated term in Chile); Merlot is the grape variety; Rapel is the region – or, to be strictly accurate, the subregion, because Rapel is a subregion of the Central Valley; along the bottom are the alcohol content (14.5%), measured as a percentage of the volume; producer's address; and bottle size (75cl).**

Chile

Classic French varieties from Bordeaux – Cabernet Sauvignon, Cabernet Franc, Merlot, Malbec, Sémillon, and Sauvignon Blanc – so far as we know were all established in Chile in the 1850s and 1860s, and, when the rest of the world's vineyards were wiped out by phylloxera in the late nineteenth and early twentieth centuries, Chile's were not. Phylloxera simply never penetrated the country's natural barriers – desert in the north, polar extremes in the south, the Pacific to the west and the Andes, averaging 4,000 metres (13,120 feet), all along the east. Consequently Chile's vines do not need grafting onto phylloxera-resistant rootstock.

This is undoubtedly of historic and viticultural interest, but whether we should attribute too much to it in terms of quality and flavour of the wines is questionable. Indeed, if anything, Chile's reputation for being a grape-growing paradise – perfect light, ideal climate, protection against disease – has been something of a handicap. Until the 1990s most producers were so convinced their environment gave them perfect grapes they didn't check it was actually so. Instead they often took huge yields of over-irrigated, inevitably dilute fruit from all varieties. This was made worse in the case of Sauvignon Blanc by the fact that the variety so-named was often not Sauvignon Blanc but the blander, fast-fading Sauvignonasse (or Sauvignon Vert). Plantings since 1995 have been of the real thing, but that still leaves much in Chile that isn't, and most Sauvignon wines, with the exception of those from Casablanca, are a mix of both.

A similar case of mistaken identity occurred with red wines. In the mid-1990s it was discovered that much (between sixty and ninety per cent) of

what had always been called Merlot was an old Bordeaux variety called Carmenère. Fortunately, Carmenère turned out to be a distinctive, high quality variety in its own right – and thus a hero, because it gave Chile what it desperately needed – a unique selling point. By far the most important of Chile's wine regions is the fertile Central Valley, stretching south from Santiago for 250 miles (463 kilometres) parallel to the Andes. East-west valleys running from the Andes to the Pacific provide natural irrigation and the slopes, rather than plains, that produce the best wines.

From north to south, the four subregions of the Central Valley are Maipo, Rapel (with the two valleys of Cachapoal and Colchagua), Curicó (including the important subzone of Lontué), and Maule. Historic Maipo, closest to Santiago, is the warmest region and produces red wines, although its importance now is more as a base for wine companies than vineyards. Colchagua in Rapel is renowned for Merlot. Curicó, a long way south, makes some good whites as well as reds. Maule is still much occupied with the local País grape, but Merlot, Chardonnay, and Sauvignon Blanc plantings are growing promisingly.

The other important region is Aconcagua, which is divided into the Aconcagua Valley to the north of Santiago, known for its reds, and Casablanca to the west. Casablanca – new, cool, and fashionable – has made a name for its Chardonnay and Sauvignon Blanc and is now looking at Pinot Noir.

South of the Central Valley is the Sur (the "south"). It is still mainly planted with País and Moscatel, but the cool, wet climate has provided Chile with another much-needed haven for quality whites, particularly in the Bío-Bío subregion. Chardonnay, Sauvignon Blanc, Riesling, and Gewurztraminer all do well. Pinot Noir also shows potential.

Argentina

Argentina is the largest wine producer in South America and the fifth largest in the world, way ahead of Chile. And until the 1990s it seemed

happy to churn out huge volumes of low quality wine from vines that were pushed to their limits by irrigation. It was when tastes changed at home and sales went into freefall that the industry was forced to look overseas – and then radically to

(Above) **The Andes not only provide Chile's vineyards with a natural barrier against phylloxera – they supply natural irrigation too.**

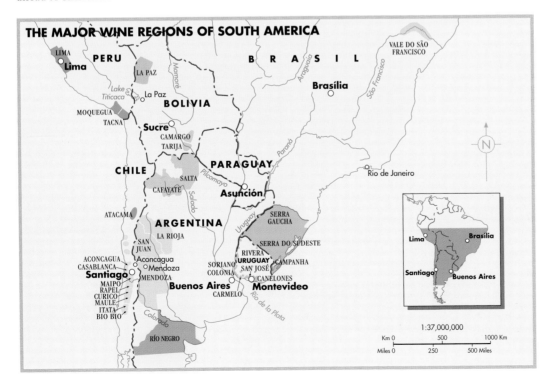

THE MAJOR WINE REGIONS OF SOUTH AMERICA

1:37,000,000

Km 0   500   1000 Km

Miles 0   250   500 Miles

overhaul itself. In a period of economic stability (since disrupted), vital investment was thankfully forthcoming: in came new buildings and equipment, new winemaking regimes and new vineyards, planted ever higher in the Andean foothills to reach cooler, less fertile terrain. The next stage, now underway, is to determine which varieties grow best where.

The Mendoza region accounts for three-quarters of output and is divided into five subregions and various appellations. Among them, the High River region in the north includes the appellations of Luján de Cuyo, famous for its Malbec, and Maipu, renowned for its Cabernet Sauvignon; the Uco Valley is home to trendy Tupungato, which is making a name for whites as well as reds; and the South (or San Rafael) produces good reds.

Argentina is fortunate in having Malbec as a calling card. Producing richer, more velvety wines than in its native Cahors in France, it's a style perfectly in tune with the times. The aromatic, Muscat-like Torrontes grape provides a comparable white wine speciality, except that it's not much in vogue at present. The finest Torrontes comes from the subregion of Cafayate in the Salta province in the north, although La Rioja, to the south, might dispute that. San Juan, between La

(Below) **The trend in Argentina is to plant vineyards at higher altitudes to benefit from the cooler climate.**

Rioja and Mendoza, is the other main region. The Río Negro Valley in Patagonia is making some good progress.

Brazil, Uruguay, and Peru

Brazil is the third largest wine producer in South America, but, with a large domestic demand for light, semi-sweet sparkling wine, it has had little need to cater for the tastes of export markets.

The Uruguayan wine industry has been equally well-served by its home market, but has a government keen to export and, just as important, suitable wines. Cabernet, Merlot, and Syrah, together with white grapes such as Sauvignon Blanc, Chardonnay, Semillon, and Ugni Blanc, are a good start, but Uruguay also has a useful point of difference in the Tannat grape. This is the variety behind the tannic reds of Madiran in South West France, but in Uruguay it gives softer, fleshier wines which blend well, when required to do so, with Merlot and Cabernet.

Peru's has a small output in comparison, but the proximity of its vineyards to the ocean mean that they are cooled and they are producing good Cabernet Sauvignon, Sauvignon Blanc, and sparkling wines.

(Left) **The vines' natural vigour has to be kept in check if Chilean vineyards are to yield good quality grapes.**

Mexico

With a mostly subtropical climate, it is not surprising that Mexico comes thirty-second in the world wine production league table and exports little. However, reds from Baja California are worth looking for – especially dark, chocolatey, peppery, bramble jelly-flavoured Petite Sirahs and Cabernet Sauvignons.

Established in the 1520s, the Mexican wine industry predates even those of South America, but today it is a long way behind its southern counterparts in quality and quantity. This is both a reflection of local taste, which favours brandy and cheap sweet wines, and a reflection of the largely subtropical climate, which is more suited to the production of table grapes, raisins, and the sort of low-grade grapes that can be used for brandy.

The outposts of modern, quality wine are in the highland areas north of Mexico City and, above all, in the north of Baja California. This is the long Pacific-cooled strip separated from the humid mainland by the Gulf of California. Red wines are far more successful than whites, especially Cabernet Sauvignon, Petite Sirah, and Nebbiolo.

AUSTRALIA

Australia has about half as much land under vine as Languedoc-Roussillon, and much, much less than California and Argentina, but what sets it apart – or rather ahead – is its sheer dynamism. Until the 1960s, three-quarters of its consumption and production was of fortified wines, and for a decade or so after that the red table wines which dominated were largely the sort of brawny heavyweights that you didn't know whether to drink, eat, or stir with a spoon. The first commercial Chardonnay was released only thirty years ago (by Tyrrell's in the Hunter Valley), when the white wine boom was just beginning. Yet now Australian Chardonnay is drunk in capitals around the world and it is Australian winemakers who have taught many of the world's new Chardonnay producers – in the south of France, Hungary, Chile – how to make their wines.

It is not only, or even most importantly, Chardonnay, of course. The global swing to red wines in the late 1990s is seen no more clearly than in Australia, where there is now substantially more of both Shiraz and Cabernet Sauvignon than there is of Chardonnay. Nor is it just these three. Although Australia's vineyards are confined almost entirely to the cooler points, furthest from the equator – to the southeast and to a lesser extent to the southwest (with all due respect to Chateau Hornsby of Alice Springs and the Granite Belt in Queensland) – there is sufficient climatic variation to suit more or less any grape variety. Alongside lesser varieties such as Colombard, Chenin Blanc, Trebbiano, and Ruby Cabernet, which are largely consigned to basic blends or

(Right) **For variety of style and quality levels, there is still no beating the Barossa – one of Australia's first wine regions and still the single most important.**

bag-in-box (or "cask"), Riesling, Semillon, Sauvignon, Verdelho, Grenache, Merlot, Pinot Noir, and Mourvèdre all flourish widely, although giving a naturally riper, fuller style than in Europe. Pinot Noir and Sauvignon Blanc have been typically much harder to please, but determined winemakers are increasingly finding cool, often high-altitude microclimates that favour Pinot Noir in particular. Similarly energetic winemakers are trying such varieties as Viognier, Pinot Gris, Petit Verdot, Nebbiolo, and Tempranillo.

It is also the cooler areas that are making Chardonnays, sparkling wines, and Cabernet Sauvignons of greater subtlety, complexity, and, it is hoped by their makers, longevity. But we should not let the appeal of the fashionable new regions, invariably Geographical Indications (GIs – *i.e.* appellations), with their inevitably more expensive, hand-crafted wines, overshadow what is still Australia's winning formula: uncomplicated, reliably fruity varietals and blends – wines made on a Brobdignagian scale, from heavily irrigated vineyards under blue skies and bright sunshine in giant high-tech wineries, by skilfully blending grapes trucked in hundreds, even thousands, of miles from any regions that come up with the right quality at the right price at harvest time.

Wines and regions

Fortified wines

Australia's most traditional style, these have steadily declined in favour of table wines, but are well worth trying. There are good port types, mostly from Shiraz and Grenache, and "sherries", but the flagships are the rich, intensely sweet, wood-matured "Liqueur" Muscat and Tokay from Victoria (*see* Rutherglen, page 147).

Sparkling wines

Australian sparkling wines deserve an entry of their own, not because the traditional method ones from cool climates can be excellent and the inexpensive ones good value, but because Australia has a unique style in its red sparkling wines. These are full-bodied, usually not quite dry and made from Shiraz, but sometimes from varieties such as Cabernet Sauvignon and Malbec.

(Left) **Even Grange itself has been blended at Penfolds' ultra-modern Nuriootpa winery in the Barossa, although production is now being moved back to the original Magill Estate cellars.**

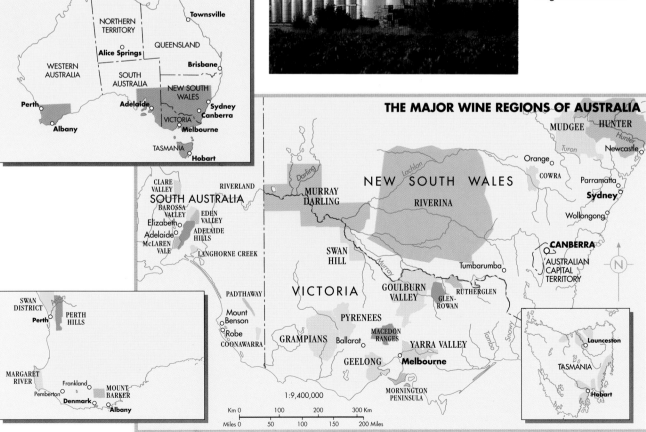

THE MAJOR WINE REGIONS OF AUSTRALIA

1:9,400,000

They can simply be robustly fruity, but the best, matured in wood for several years, are rich and complex with flavours of ripe berries, chocolate, spice, and mocha.

Adelaide Hills

East of Adelaide, the key feature of the Adelaide Hills, with the Piccadilly and Lenswood subdistricts, is the high altitudes, giving cool enough climates to produce concentrated, elegant wines in a variety of styles. The several strong suits are vivacious Sauvignon Blanc and Riesling, complex and age-worthy Chardonnay, and some of Australia's best Pinot Noir and sparkling wines.

Barossa and Eden Valleys

Colonized by German-speaking Silesians in the 1840s, the Barossa, northeast of Adelaide, is one of Australia's oldest wine regions, with many of the largest, oldest wineries still there. As well as making wines from grapes trucked in from all over South Australia, it produces its own styles, ranging from soft, fruity Rhine Rieslings to rich, oaky Semillons and Chardonnays, dense, ripe Cabernet Sauvignons and, above all, the monumental, long-lived, chocolatey, spicy Shiraz-based reds epitomized by Grange.

To the east of the Barossa Valley, the land rises up to the plateau-like Eden Valley. As it does so, the temperature drops, giving ideal conditions for producing elegant, cool-climate wines. These include fine, age-worthy Riesling, with the hallmark floral, mineral, and lime aromas, Australia's best Viogniers (pioneered by Yalumba), some exceptional, old-vine Shiraz, and some sophisticated Chardonnay and Pinot Noir.

Bendigo

Wine production in this former gold mining town in central Victoria was revived with great flair by Balgownie Estate in 1970. Since then, with other quality oriented producers, Bendigo has built a reputation for excellent, frank, and fearless Shiraz and Cabernet.

Clare Valley

Smaller than the Barossa and further north from Adelaide, the peaceful Clare Valley has a name for producing some of Australia's finest, most long-lived and intensely lime-flavoured Rieslings. The reds, from Cabernet and Shiraz, are also impressive.

Coonawarra

In southeast South Australia on the border with Victoria, lies Coonawarra, with its distinctive Terra Rossa (crumbly red soil over limestone) and cool climate. Its reputation was built on its superb Cabernet Sauvignons, with their seductively vivid mint and blackcurrant flavours, but Shiraz is also outstanding. There are also outposts of very good Chardonnay, Riesling, and Sauvignon.

READING AUSTRALIAN LABELS

The labels on the back of New World bottles can be rather wordy, but the main front labels are usually clear and to the point, like this one.

From top to bottom: 2000 is the vintage (year of harvest); Brokenwood is the name of the producer; Semillon is the grape variety; Hunter Valley is the region; 750ml is the bottle size; 11% is the alcohol content, measured as a per centage of the volume (the low figure of 11% will indicate to those in the know that this is a traditional Hunter Semillon intended to be aged – *see* Hunter Valley page 45).

Vintages

Margaret River Cabernet

2002	8	▼
2001	9	▼
2000	9	★
1999	9	★
1998	7	▲
1997	8	★
1996	9	★
1995	9	★
1994	8	▲

Key
0–10 quality rating (10 = top wine)

▲   should drink

★   can drink, but no hurry for the top wines

▼   must keep

(See also **When to drink**, pages 44–47)

(Right) **With several high-profile individuals based there, the pretty and peaceful-looking Hunter Valley has a reputation for producing five per cent of Australia's wine and fifty per cent of the noise.**

Grampians

For long known as Great Western, and famous for Seppelt's brand of sparkling wine of the same name, the Grampians region in Victoria continues to produce consistently good fizz in large quantities and great sparkling Shiraz in limited volumes. Benchmark peppery still Shiraz, polished Rieslings, and good Cabernet and Chardonnay demonstrate that this is not a one-style wine region.

Great Southern

Some of the subregions of the huge Great Southern region have made a name for themselves – notably Mount Barker and Frankland River – but Great Southern as a whole is still very much a developing region. With climates varying from mild, damp maritime to drier and more continental, established strengths so far include Riesling and Shiraz in Mount Barker, Riesling and Bordeaux blends in Frankland River, and Pinot Noir and Chardonnay in Denmark. In Pemberton the jury is still out as to whether growers should pursue Pinot Noir and Chardonnay, or forget ideas of Burgundy and go for other reds.

Hunter Valley

Hunter Valley Semillon, from north of Sydney in New South Wales, is one of Australia's unique wines. The original unoaked style can be drunk when it is young, crisp, and citrusy, or left about eight years to acquire a toasted, dry, honey-and-straw character; but increasingly Semillon is being made more in the Chardonnay mould, oak fermented and to be drunk young. Chardonnay itself is now more important and tends to be ebullient and oaky. Reds are dominated by broad, spicy, sometimes leathery Shirazes (which used to have the famous "sweaty saddle" character – *see* page 16). Surprisingly, for so warm a climate, there is also some reasonable Pinot Noir.

Limestone Coast

The Limestone Coast zone links regions near Coonawarra that have similar outcrops of Terra Rossa (*see* Coonawarra). Thus Coonawarra and Padthaway are technically part of the Limestone Coast, but have their own well-established identities. The other three regions (all GIs) are Wrattonbully (between Coonawarra and Padthaway) and the adjoining coastal regions of Mount Benson and Robe. Wrattonbully, with a climate warmer than Coonawarra's but cooler than Padthaway's, is gaining a name as a red wine alternative to Coonawarra, with Cabernet Sauvignon, Merlot, and Shiraz. Mount Benson and Robe are in the early stages, but, being cooler, are likely to prove more suitable for white wines.

(Above) **From tanks such as these in the Barossa Valley come vast quantities of cheap but sound wine – much of it destined for what Australians call "bladder packs" (alias bag-in-box).**

Vintages		
South Australia Shiraz		
2002	9	▼
2001	9	▼
2000	8	★
1999	8	★
1998	9	★
1997	8	★
1996	9	★
1995	7	★
1994	8	★
(*See* page 144 for key to symbols)		

Margaret River

The output of Western Australia's most prominent region is a mere drop in the Australian vinous ocean, but what it lacks in volume it makes up for in quality – and ability to attract media attention, much to the frustration of some other regions. From the beginnings in the 1970s, Margaret River Cabernet Sauvignons and Chardonnays have won plaudits for their purity, richness, and, in the case of the Chardonnays, longevity. Since then, vivid Semillon/Sauvignon Blanc blends and velvet-textured Merlot and Shiraz have been added to the portfolio.

McLaren Vale

Originally a producer of the kind of strapping, heavy reds that used to be prescribed as tonics by doctors (at least in Britain), McLaren Vale, south of Adelaide, is now renowned for its particularly voluptuous style of Shiraz, Cabernet Sauvignon, and Merlot. There is also some convincing Sangiovese and Zinfandel produced in this warm, but not bakingly hot, region.

Mudgee

Mudgee's high altitudes give it cool nights, warm days, and a longer growing season than the Hunter Valley further east in New South Wales. The result is intense, full-bodied Cabernet Sauvignon and Chardonnay.

Murray Darling, Riverland, and Riverina

Stretching across New South Wales and into Victoria, and linked by the Murray and Murrumbidgee rivers, these vast, inland, irrigated regions are not names you often see on labels, but together they produce about two-thirds of Australia's annual harvest. Most of it is destined for bag-in-box, mass-market brands and other price-fighting labels. The notable exception is the outstanding botrytis-affected Semillon produced by De Bortoli in the Riverina.

Orange

Southwest of Mudgee, the high altitude Orange region on the slopes of Mount Canobolas is New

(Below) **The cool Tasmanian climate doesn't make life easy for growers, but it does produce some excellent sparkling wines.**

South Wales' newest and most fashionable cool (or cooler) region. Cabernet Sauvignon, Shiraz, Chardonnay, Verdelho, and Semillon have all been successful on the volcanic soils of the now extinct Mount Canobolasand there is potential for other varieties such as Sauvignon and Pinot Noir.

Padthaway

North of the red wine region of Coonawarra in South Australia, Padthaway has some similar soils, but a warmer climate. Its reputation is for premium white wines – especially Chardonnay – but it also produces some good, concentrated reds, especially Shiraz.

Rutherglen

Rutherglen in northeast Victoria no longer has its gold mining, but it still has a claim on fame as the heartland of Australia's legendary liqueur Muscats and Tokays (Tokay is the local name for Muscadene). These are not, of course, liqueurs but immensely sweet brown wines, cask-matured using a *solera*-type process (*see* page 128). The result is layer upon layer of flavour – raisin and fig, toffee and coffee, chocolate, spice, and marmalade.

Tasmania

Tasmania is so cool it's positively cold, and high winds can be a problem for growers, but the potential is there for great cool-climate wines in favoured vintages. Pinot Noir, Riesling, and sparkling wines are the stars so far.

Yarra Valley

The Yarra in Victoria is one of Australia's most historic regions and now, once again, one of its high fliers. Apart from proximity to Melbourne, producers are attracted by the way its cool climate divides into several specialized microclimates giving scope for top Pinot Noirs, Chardonnays, Cabernets, Bordeaux-style blends, Shiraz, and outstanding sparkling wines. (Since the latter are made by Domaine Chandon – Moët & Chandon's Australian offshoot – the Champenois don't know whether to laugh or cry.)

Other regions

In Victoria: Goulburn Valley for full, flavoursome reds from Cabernet and Shiraz, and equally full and flavoursome dry white Marsanne; Geelong for concentrated Shiraz, Chardonnay, and classic Pinot Noir; Glenrowan, like nearby Rutherglen, for muscular Shiraz, liqueur Muscats, and Tokays; Mornington Peninsula for elegant Pinot Noir, Chardonnay, and Pinot Gris; Pyrenees for substantial, fleshy reds. In South Australia, Langhorne Creek provides good value, full, soft, often minty reds. In New South Wales, Cowra is the source of ripe extrovert Chardonnays. In Western Australia the hot Swan Valley produces good-value, full, soft yet sometimes surprsly ageworthy whites.

(Above) **One of the attractions of the Yarra Valley is the suitability of its varied mesoclimates to a range of different grape varieties.**

NEW ZEALAND

(Right) **Gleaming tanks at the Montana winery – familiarity with stainless steel through New Zealand's advanced dairy industry turned out to be a help to the early 1980s Sauvignon pioneers.**

READING NEW ZEALAND LABELS (label, page 149)

A model of consumer-friendly clarity.

From top to bottom: **Villa Maria is the name of producer; reserve can mean whatever the producer chooses; ideally, as in this case, it should indicate quality superior to the producer's basic wine or range; Clifford Bay is the name the producer has chosen for this particular Sauvignon Blanc (as distinct from other Villa Maria Sauvignons); 2000 is the vintage (year of harvest); Marlborough is the region from which the wine comes; the wine was bottled by the producer; 75cl is the bottle size; the "e" means only that this is an official EU bottle size; 13% is the alcohol content, measured as a percentage of the volume.**

New Zealand did not so much emerge as shoot onto the international wine scene in the late 1980s. Having dispensed with fortified wines during the 1960s and 1970s and then in the early 1980s with much of the Müller-Thurgau that had fuelled the transition from fortified to table wines, it produced its trump card, Sauvignon Blanc – and it was Sauvignon Blanc that reminded the world what the grape should really taste like.

Climate is the key. New Zealand is the cool-climate capital of the New World. Although it is a long country, covering the equivalent of the latitude between Germany's Rheingau and Algeria, the differences in climate are not so dramatic. The vineyards are largely concentrated in three areas on the drier eastern side of both North and South Islands where the long, cool growing season (provided it is not too long and cool) produces white wines of exceptional fruit intensity, varietal character, and nerve-tingling acidity – not only from Sauvignon Blanc, but barrel-fermented Chardonnay, Riesling (dry and sweet), Semillon, Pinot Gris, and Gewurztraminer. At the other end of the ripeness scale, lean Chardonnays and Pinot Noirs are used to make some very impressive sparkling wines.

It is still relatively early days for red wines, for which the climate seemed too cool at first, but they are catching up in quality now that grape varieties are being matched to soils and climates. The most promising results are coming from Merlot and Cabernet Sauvignon blends (sometimes with Malbec and Cabernet Franc) in the warmer North Island and, more recently, from Pinot Noir, which has been planted extensively on both North and South Islands.

New Zealand has no appellation system as such, but there are ten recognized regions, together with the designation East Coast, which is a catch-all (like Southeast Australia) to allow cross-regional blends.

Wines and regions

Gisborne

Gisborne, on the North Island, has been overshadowed by Marlborough and Hawkes Bay in recent years and rather demeaned by its own reputation for making New Zealand's cheap everyday wines. In fact its Chardonnay, which tends to be richer than Marlborough's, is especially successful, and there are other good whites, including Gewurztraminer and vibrant, fruity Chenin Blanc.

Hawke's Bay

Third in size of New Zealand's major regions, this is proving to be the most exciting for Bordeaux-style red wines. It lies south of Gisborne on the North Island and is hotter than both Bordeaux and Coonawarra. From poor, gravelly alluvial soils, above all those in the Gimblett Gravels zone, come some impressive claret-like Cabernet/Merlot blends and pure Merlot. There are good Chardonnays and Sauvignons too – the latter a little fuller than Marlborough's – and some Syrah, in its infancy but showing promise.

Marlborough

At the northern end of the South Island, Marlborough's reputation is based on its Sauvignon Blanc. Styles vary from the riper, more tropical fruit flavours to herbaceous gooseberry and occasionally mineral flavours, but always with the penetrating fruit and acidity.

Despite its Sauvignon fame, there is nearly as much Chardonnay and much of it is exceptionally good. Chardonnay is also often used with Pinot Noir in sophisticated sparkling wines, and Pinot Noir is increasingly being grown for still red wines. Cabernet Sauvignon, with or without Merlot, tends to have a grassy, blackcurrant freshness, rather than weight or richness.

Other regions

Martinborough, a subdistrict of Wairarapa in the south of the North Island, was the first to produce truly successful, burgundian Pinot Noir, along with some fine, buttery Chardonnay. But Martinborough is now being challenged by the South Island and not least by Central Otago, in the far south. Here, the continental climate can make viticulture nerve-racking, but it brings its rewards with Pinot Noir – and Pinot Gris and Riesling. Waiheke, an island in Auckland harbour, has some notable Cabernet Sauvignon/Merlot blends and Chardonnay. Auckland itself, more a centre of vinification than viticulture these days, still produces some interesting home-grown wines, especially burgundy-style Chardonnay from the Kumeu subdistrict. The small wineries of Nelson (in the north of the South Island) make full-flavoured Chardonnay, classic Sauvignon Blanc, late-harvest Riesling, and Pinot Noir. Good Chardonnay, Riesling, and Pinot Noir in are found in Canterbury.

READING NEW ZEALAND LABELS (*see* page 148)

SOUTH AFRICA

South Africa claims to have the oldest wine tradition in the New World (though South America would dispute that), but because of the years of international isolation, the industry developed along different lines from the anything-goes experimentation of, say, Australia and California.

Both qualitatively and stylistically, the wines presented to the world outside in the immediate post-apartheid years lagged well behind those of other key New World players. The bulk of the wines were simple, bland whites based on Chenin Blanc, the variety which at the time accounted for a third of the vineyards, but which has now dropped to a fifth. The more serious whites, the Chardonnays, were frequently clumsily over-oaked. And all too often, the signature of the reds was harsh tannin and acid with a combination of unripe and burnt, tarry flavours.

Lack of exposure to the tastes of other markets and to competition from the likes of Australia, New Zealand, and Chile was one obvious reason for the idiosyncratic, and often unattractive, wines. But there were others. The structure of the industry was extraordinarily restrictive. It was designed for a system where thousands of growers sold their grapes to giant cooperatives, principally for distillation or grape concentrate (wine and quality were secondary). Quotas and quarantine rules effectively prevented ambitious growers from exploring new regions and made it extremely difficult for anyone even to get hold of new vines to plant. Since the KWV, the giant cooperative that policed the industry, has been divested of its powers, quotas, and quarantine have been relaxed.

Another problem was endemic leafroll virus, which prevents the grapes, reds especially, from ripening fully – hence the tell-tale harsh and unripe flavours in the wines. The viral problem hasn't gone away, but it is handled with greater expertise, as is almost every aspect of vine growing and winemaking in the Cape today.

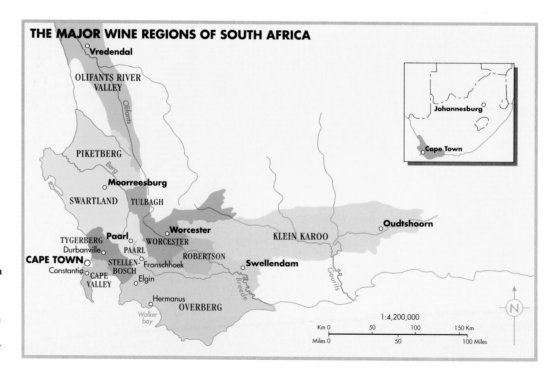

(Far right) **The years of isolation over, South Africa is now beginning to make the most of its enviable natural resources – not least in the Mediterranean climate and varied soils of Paarl's mountain foothills.**

THE MAJOR WINE REGIONS OF SOUTH AFRICA

Vredendal
OLIFANTS RIVER VALLEY
Olifants
Johannesburg
Cape Town
PIKETBERG
Berg
Moorreesburg
SWARTLAND
TULBAGH
Worcester
TYGERBERG
Paarl
WORCESTER
KLEIN KAROO
Oudtshoorn
Durbanville
PAARL
ROBERTSON
CAPE TOWN
STELLEN-
BOSCH
Franschhoek
Swellendam
Constantia
Elgin
Breede
Gourits
CAPE VALLEY
Hermanus
Walker bay
OVERBERG

1:4,200,000
Km 0   50   100   150 Km
Miles 0   50   100 Miles
N

The progress made this century has been phenomenal. In response to the global shift to red wines, red grapes, especially Shiraz, Cabernet Sauvignon, and Merlot, have been planted with great energy and the wines are much plumper and more velvety than in the past. Oaked Chardonnays now have real polish; Sauvignon Blanc has established a style that falls between the exuberance of New Zealand and the steeliness of the Loire; the inexpensive whites and reds are fresher than they were; and old vines of Chenin Blanc in favoured sites are being treated with the respect they deserve.

This is as it should be, since South Africa, or at least the eastern Cape, is well-endowed with natural resources. The vineyards stretch north, east, and south east of Cape Town which has an ideal Mediterranean climate and a patchwork of varied micro-climates, especially in the mountain foothills of Paarl and Stellenbosch. Such conditions obviously suit mainstream European grape varieties, but South Africa does have one variety of its own, the red Pinotage. A cross between Pinot Noir and workaday red Cinsaut, it gives anything from light, jammy wines to robust, dark, oaky reds that can be aged.

South Africa's Wine of Origin system divides the wine growing areas into regions, districts, wards, and estates, in decreasing order of size, and every bottle of wine exported carries a small paper seal on the capsule as a guarantee of authenticity.

Wines and regions

Constantia

The Constantia ward, south of Cape Town, gave its name to one of the most renowned wines of the nineteenth century – a dessert Muscat, made by leaving the grapes on the vines to dry. Under the name Vin de Constance, production was revived in 1986. Good Sauvignon and Chardonnay is also made.

Paarl

Thirty miles (48.3 kilometres) from Cape Town, Paarl has wet winters, long, warm, dry summers, and a variety of soils. Some fine wines come from the historic Franschhoek ward. Wellington is also important.

Robertson

Together with some of the better cooperatives, there are some excellent estates in Robertson, they all rely on irrigation in the hot, dry climate of this central region. White wines, including Chardonnay and Sauvignon, dominate, but there are some good reds.

Stellenbosch

Several of South Africa's top red wines come from the mountain foothills of the Stellenbosch district, where many of the country's foremost estates are found. Most varieties do well here, including whites, but Cabernet Sauvignon, especially when blended with Merlot and Cabernet Franc, can be impressive and long-lived.

Walker Bay and Elgin

Within Overberg, a large, relatively new district east of Cape Town, Walker Bay produces excellent burgundy-style Pinot Noir and Chardonnay, and Elgin yields racy Sauvignon Blanc and Chardonnay and elegant Pinot Noir.

READING SOUTH AFRICAN LABELS

A typically straightforward South African label. In addition to the label, all South African wines bear a paper seal guaranteeing any claims made on the label.

From top to bottom, left to right Steenberg is the name of the producer and the year it was founded is underneath; select can mean whatever the producer chooses; there are no rules governing its use; 2000 is the vintage (year of harvest); 13.5% is the alcohol content measured as a percentage of the volume; Sauvignon Blanc is the grape variety; Wine of Origin means a wine from a specified area, in this case the ward of Constantia (see Constantia below left); 750ml is the bottle size; the "e" means only that this is an official EU bottle size.

AUSTRIA AND SWITZERLAND

(Right) **Austria's vineyards lie in the east – on latitudes approximately corresponding with Burgundy in the south and Champagne in the north, but the main grape is Austria's own, its peppery white Grüner Veltliner.**

READING AUSTRIAN WINE LABELS

Austria has among the strictest wine laws in the world.

From top to bottom: **Brundlmayer is the name of the producer (one of Austria's foremost).** *weingut* means estate; **Zöbinger Heiligenstein indicates the village and specific vineyard;** *alte reben* means old vines; **1999 is the vintage (year of harvest); Qualitätswein is the quality category, the number is the official test number of this batch (all quality wine has one); 14.5% is the alcohol content, measured as a percentage of the volume (this wine is high in alcohol);** *trocken* means dry (*i.e.* the style of the wine); **Kamptal is the region; Osterreich: Austria; 75cl: the bottle size.**

Austria emerged in the 1990s as a small but outstanding producer of predominantly white wines, and yet outside its own borders its wines are too little known. The lack of recognition is partly because it keeps most of its best wines to itself, partly because Austrian wines, at least in Britain, are mistakenly thought of as little more than an extension of Germany's, and partly because of the enduring legacy of a wine scandal in 1985.

There are parallels with German wines: the classification based on ripeness is similar, with *Tafelwein*, *Qualitätswein*, *Kabinett*, and *Prädikatswein* – the latter covering *Spätlese*, *Auslese*, *Beerenauslese*, *Strohwein* (made from grapes dried on straw mats), *Eiswein*, *Ausbruch* (sweet wines from botrytized grapes), and *Trockenbeerenauslese*; and the two countries share several grape varieties, most notably Riesling.

But Austria has significant varieties of its own, including the crisp, peppery white Grüner Veltliner (a third of the country's vines), Bouvier (used for sweet wines), the white Neuburger, the

perfumed red Sankt-Laurent, and the cherry-flavoured red Zweigelt. Austria also does well with Chardonnay and Blauburgunder (Pinot Noir), which are often fermented in oak in the Burgundian manner, and with Cabernet Sauvignon and Blaufränkisch.

In fact, Austria's southerly wine areas lie on the same latitude as Burgundy (its northerly ones being closer to Champagne), but they have a more continental climate, with cold winters and warm summers. The results are mostly white wines: aromatic, with steely crispness but more ripeness, body, and alcohol than Germany's. Reds used to be light- to medium-bodied, but tastes have changed and there are now many more full-bodied, oaky wines in the weighty modern idiom.

Virtually all the vineyards lie in the east. Lower Austria (Niederösterreich) produces lively, spicy Grüner Veltliner, some superb, ageworthy Riesling, and Grüner Veltliner, especially from Wachau, Kremstal, and Kamptal, and light, clean whites from Vienna (Wien).

Burgenland is a mecca for sweet wine: noble rot arrives every year around the Neusiedlersee in the north and produces stunningly opulent wines from a range of grape varieties; away from the lake there are good dry whites, including Chardonnay, and most of Austria's important reds. Styria (Steiermark) produces impressive, bone dry Sauvignon Blanc, Chardonnay, Welschriesling, and Traminer.

Switzerland

Swiss wines scale the heights of excellence less often than those of Austria, but the best are admirably individual. Wine is made in all cantons, but most of the vineyards are concentrated in Valais on the River Rhône, Vaud around the north of Lake Geneva, the canton of Geneva itself, and Ticino. Chasselas (alias Fendant), is still the main grape, producing refreshing, modestly fruity whites, but reds are on the increase, in particular, in the Valais. The main red grapes are Pinot Noir, (Dôle from Valais) and Gamay. Bündner Herrschaft is also renowned for its Blauburgunder (Pinot Noir). Ticino concentrates on Merlot with results that vary from weak to excellent. Among the fascinating white rarities in Valais are Arvine, Humagne (red and white), Amigne, and Heida.

READING SWISS LABELS

The Swiss appellation system is based, like so many, on the French.

From top to bottom: 1999 is the vintage (year of harvest); Neuchatel is the *appellation contrôlée* region; Caves du Château d'Auvernier is the producer; the French word caves almost invariably means cooperative and Auvernier is an important wine-producing village in Neuchâtel; 375ml is the bottle size (this is a half-bottle); 13% is the alcohol content, measured as a percentage of the volume.

(Left) The main wine growing areas of Switzerland are in the cantons of Vaud and Valais in the west – of the two, Valais (left) produces the greatest variety.

EASTERN EUROPE

Gathering half a continent under "Eastern Europe" might seem cavalier, or naive, but the former Eastern Bloc countries, adjusting to capitalism, share many of the same problems, the same winemaking practices, and attitudes. When their wine industries were nationalized, prices were controlled, quantity was more important than quality, and most of the wine exported went to other Eastern Bloc countries. Bulgaria was the exception. Slowly, wineries, vineyards, and state cellars have been dismantled and handed over to private owners who need to sell to the West because Eastern export markets have dried up. Investment from Europe, the USA, Japanese, and Australia has brought with it essential expertise.

THE WINE REGIONS OF CENTRAL AND SOUTHEAST EUROPE

CZECH REPUBLIC

UKRAINE

SLOVAKIA

AUSTRIA

HUNGARY

MOLDOVA

SLOVENIA

CROATIA

ROMANIA

BOSNIA-HERZEGOVINA

YUGOSLAVIA

BULGARIA

ALBANIA

MACEDONIA

GREECE

TURKEY

N

1:13,500,000

Km 0   200   400 Km

Miles 0   100   200   300 Miles

For the winemakers and their backers these have been at the same time the most exciting and the most frustrating countries to make wine for. The raw material is there, in the form of classic French and German and worthwhile indigenous grape varieties, all growing in favourable climates, but winemaking attitudes are still sometimes primeval. Picking grapes at the right time and rejecting those in bad condition was rarely a priority under the earlier regimes; the need to protect wine from oxidation and bacteria was seldom understood; and there was a widespread conviction that older wine was better, no matter how dilapidated the barrels and the concrete tanks were.

But the reformation is well under way, progress is gathering its own momentum and there is a slowly rising tide of good wines from these countries. Providing more attention is now given to vineyards, there is no reason why it should not continue.

Bulgaria

For most of the Communist era Bulgarian Cabernet Sauvignon had no competition from its neighbours' wines – and none from Australia, Chile, South Africa, or the south of France either. That has all changed and, though some good is now beginning to come out of it for Bulgaria, it has sometimes been a painful learning curve for the wine industry.

White wines, never Bulgaria's strong suit, are much improved – both Chardonnay and the cheaper blends of varieties such as Rkatsiteli, Dimiat, Muscat Ottonel, and Aligoté. With red wines there has been a move to bottle some wines earlier, to preserve the fruit of Cabernet Sauvignon and Merlot, and to age others in newer oak barrels. Oak chips have also put in an appearance – though not always sufficiently subtly.

Bulgaria also has its own red grapes. The best are the burly, spicy Mavrud and the perfumed Melnik, but both are losing ground to the French varieties and to Gamza (Kadarka) and the workhorse Pamid.

The country's strict appellation system defines over twenty Controliran (equivalent to *appellation contrôlée*). Haskovo in the southwest has a reputation for Merlot and Assenovgrad in the central south for Mavrud, but, while wine quality depends so much on the amount of investment there has been in both equipment and expertise at any one winery, regional differences are not very pronounced. The word Reserve on the label denotes a wine that has been aged in oak and should signal superior quality.

Hungary

Hungary has the oldest wine tradition of any in Eastern Europe, based on its sweet Tokáji (Tokay), which comes from vineyards adjoining Slovakia in the northeast and is made according to a unique production process established in the seventeenth century (predating any comparable sweet wine tradition in France or Germany). Tokáji Aszú is the most significant wine and is classed according to its sweetness, measured in *puttonyos* or putts (the hods the pickers use) – three putts being the least sweet, aged for up to five years before bottling, and six putts the sweetest, aged up to eight years. Above these are Aszú Eszencia (seven putts) and then the almost mystical, nectar-like Eszencia. For years Tokáji coasted along on its reputation, but privatization and foreign investment have returned it to its former glory.

On the dry wine side, too, Hungary has made huge strides. White wines predominate, with racy, aromatic fruit characterizing the likes of Chardonnay, Sauvignon, Traminer, Muscats, and new crossings such as Irsai Oliver. What is exciting, though, is the revival of interest in Hungary's distinctive indigenous white varieties – Furmint and Hárslevelu leading many others. Note has also been taken of the world's new passion for reds and we are likely to see more Cabernet Franc, Merlot, Cabernet Sauvignon, Kadarka, and Kékfrankos (Blaufränkisch).

Moldova

Hundreds of thousands of hectares of vines, mostly Cabernet Sauvignon and Merlot growing in ideal climatic conditions, made Moldova a target for Western importers and their winemakers in the early 1990s, but they have now largely retreated. Potential wine quality was not an issue: the problem was, and is, lack of infrastructure and economic uncertainty.

Romania

Romania has far more land under vine than any other country in the former Eastern Bloc, yet wines that are little known outside for the simple reason that they are mostly consumed within its own borders. The trouble with this appreciative local audience is that it tends to be uncritical and, as a result, quality is not what it could be in such favourable growing conditions.

Most of the wines are white, from two strains of the local Feteasca, Welschriesling, Aligoté, and a little Chardonnay, but there is also Cabernet Sauvignon, Merlot and, a little Pinot Noir. The reds from Dealul Mare in the south east are particularly supple and fruity. There is also a tradition of botrytized sweet wines, notably in Cotnari and Murfatlar, which is being revived.

READING HUNGARIAN LABELS

From top to bottom: **1996** is the vintage (year of harvest); **Hétszolo** is the name of a leading producer (and a noted vineyard); **Tokáji** is wine from the Tokájhegyalja region; **aszú** indicates that this is a sweet wine; **6 Puttonyos** is the sweetest level; **10.5%** is the alcohol content, measured as a percentage of the volume; the bottle size (**500ml**); producer's address

(Below) **The post-communist return of vineyards, wineries and cellars to private hands in Bulgaria – and neighbouring countries – is now beginning to reap rewards in terms of new, especially younger, fresher, wine styles.**

THE REST OF THE
WORLD

The ancient world, centred on the Eastern Mediterranean, is where winemaking probably began, but an illustrious history is no guarantee of present-day quality. The climate in these countries is seldom less than hot and arid (but then so is Australia's), and old-fashioned winemaking for a captive local market predominates (which is where the comparisons with Australia end). And yet there are patches of excellence, above all in Greece.

Cyprus

Although it is hard to enthuse about Cyprus wines: most Commandaria falls short of its ancient reputation and the table wines have been sound at best, there has been, with government support, some progress. The four companies that dominate production have invested, small estates have emerged, the worst vineyards are disappearing, and Cabernet Sauvignon and Grenache are among the international set to join the native Mavro.

Greece

Greek wine are no longer Retsina or dull and oxidized. Over the last fifteen years, the large companies have been radically modernized and individual estates have blossomed. International varieties, such as Cabernet Sauvignon, Syrah, and Chardonnay are successful, but winemakers are rightly proud of their indigenous grapes. The dry red wine appellations of Naoussa and Nemea are well known, their wines are made

(Right) **Picturesque as they are, these old wine jars are far from ideal containers for satisfying the modern taste for fresh-tasting unoxidised wines.**

from Xynomavro and Aghiorghitiko (aka St George) respectively, but whites are more important. Cephalonia, Mantinia, Samos (for its sweet Muscats), and Santorini are notable regions. Assyrtiko, Athiri, Malagousia, Moschofilero, Robola, Roditis, and Savatiano are notable white grapes.

Greece

The advent, in the mid-1980s, of irreproachable kosher Chardonnay, Sauvignon Blanc, Cabernet Sauvignon, and Merlot from the cool, high-altitude Golan Heights region galvanized the whole of the Israeli wine industry into improvement, but the Golan Heights and Upper Galilee vineyards will always deliver the finest wines.

Lebanon

There is a handful of other producers high up in the Beka'a Valley east of Beirut, but to the outside world Lebanese wine is Château Musar. Musar is based on Cabernet Sauvignon and Cinsaut; other producers use Syrah and Mourvèdre as well. There is also some dessert wine and a little rosé and Chardonnay.

The UK

For a country still regarded by many as a non-producer – though not now by the Brussels bureaucracy – England has a remarkable number of vineyards. Out of 440 in England and Wales (all but a handful in England and mostly in the south) 250 make wine on a commercial scale – even if not all of them have their own wineries. With nearly 900 hectares under vine, Britain produced over 3.5 million bottles in 1992, in a surprising array of styles – dry, medium, and sweet; still, and sparkling; white, red, and rosé; unoaked and oak-matured.

Despite this apparent breadth, there is a characteristic style: white, dry or medium dry, crisp, and aromatic. Germanic grapes dominate, especially crossings (led by Müller-Thurgau and Reichensteiner) which were designed to beat the cold German climate.

Among the more characterful white varieties, Bacchus is England's answer to Sancerre; Schönburger has a Muscat-like flavour; Huxelrebe can be reminiscent of elderflowers; Faber and Ortega are good for rich sweet wines, as well as dry; and Seyval Blanc, although it is ill-regarded in the EU because it is not pure *vinifera*, can produce a Loire-like style. It also takes well to oak, and makes a good base for sparkling wine.

In fact, top quality, traditional method sparkling wines, some of them made purely from the Champagne grape varieties, emerged in the 1990s as England's ace. Reds will always be small fry, but quality has improved significantly. The most successful grapes are Rondo, Dornfelder, and, in warm years, Pinot Noir.

China

China has been making grape wine for millennia, and, in recent times, modern wine with Western investment and expertise. However, most is drunk locally.

India

In the hills east of Bombay, Champagne technology and Indian investment have been used, initially to good effect, to produce traditional method sparkling wine, from Ugni Blanc and, increasingly, Chardonnay. Still wines are also produced in India.

Japan

Much Japanese wine is blended with imported wine, but there are small plantings of Cabernets Sauvignon and Franc, Merlot, and Chardonnay producing creditable wines.

Luxembourg

Light, dry whites and sparkling wines (*crémants*) are produced along the Upper Moselle from Rivaner (alias Müller-Thurgau), Elbling, and, in smaller quantities, aromatic Alsace varieties.

North Africa

For years the vineyard area in North Africa was in decline, but now Morocco and Algeria have replanting programmes and Tunisia is also working to raise quality levels. Morocco is the most promising of the three countries and is already producing Cabernet Sauvignon, Syrah, and Merlot that can compete in the international arena.

Turkey

Barely three per cent of the grapes from Turkey's 600,000 hectares of vineyards and numerous grape varieties go to make wine (the rest remain as table grapes). The quality, whether from indigenous grapes or French imports and whether red or white, varies from pleasant to rustic.

READING ISRAELI LABELS

From top to bottom:
1999 is the vintage (year of harvest); Yarden is the name of the wine; Galilee is the region; Chardonnay is the grape variety; Golan Heights Winery is the producer; 13.5% is the alcohol content, measured as a percentage of the volume; the bottle size (75cl).

Index

Page numbers in **bold** refer to main reference.

PICTURE ACKNOWLEDGEMENTS

Cephas Picture Library: 93, 139 top; Jerry Alexander 83 bottom right; Nigel Blythe 73, 114; R & K Muschenetz 134; Alain Proust 151; Mick Rock 42 left, 51 top, 55 bottom, 56 bottom, 71, 75, 77, 83 main picture, 84, 85, 91 top left, bottom left, bottom centre and bottom right, 92, 120–1, 127, 130–1, 132–3, 136, 137, 143, 145, 153, 155; Ted Stefanski 53 top; Helen Stylianou 156. **Robert Dieth**: 112–3. **Patrick Eagar**: 106, 109, 110, 142, 148. **Explorer**: S Cordier 52 centre; P D Forestier 89 bottom left; Hug 54 top; Francis Jalain 87 right, 108; P Lorne 96; Philippe Maille 104; Michael Plassart 83 top; J P Nacivet 102; D Reperant 63, 68–9, 98, 99, 101; Philippe Roy 41 bottom right, 89 top right and bottom right, 91 top right, 139 bottom; P Thomas 79; H Veiller 132; Patrick Weisbecker 152. **Robert Harding Picture Library**: 115, 122–3; Robert Frerck 125; Adam Woolfitt 128 top. **Impact Photos**: Steve Benbow 89 top left. **Adrian Lander**: 146, 147. **Janet Price**: 144. **Octopus Publishing Group Ltd**: Alan Williams 31, 32, 33, 38, 42, 126, 128–9; Nicki Dowey 34; Jason Lowe 35, 39, 140, 141 **Scope**: Jean-Luc Barde 89 top centre, 116, 118–9, 128 bottom; Jacques Guillard 66–7, 81, 82–3, 103, 107; Michel Guillard 41 top, 91 top centre; Jean-Daniel Sudres 86–7, 89 bottom centre, 105. **John Ferro Sims**: 118. **Spiral Cellars Ltd**: 42 centre, 43 bottom.

James Johnson – cut-out photography (except 26), and 14 (bottom)   **Hugh Johnson Collection** – props for 18–9, 22–3, 25, 27, 28–9
Anita Corbin/John O'Grady – portraits of author   **Michael Johnson** (Ceramics) Ltd – suppliers of all glasses, all by Riedel
Russell Sadur – author portrait 7   **Simon Wheeler** – section openers (8–9, 48–9, 94–5)
Cosmographics – updated cartography - part three (original cartography by **Lovell Johns**)   **Radius** (locator map artwork - part two)